Sturgis
Standard Code of Parliamentary Procedure

ADVISORY BOARD

A book valued as a parliamentary authority is unique in that its use by individuals and its adoption by organizations continues over a long and indefinite time. To maintain its standard of excellence, two factors are vital: it must conform strictly to ever-changing law, and it must reflect accurately the current practices of outstanding organizations.

From its beginnings, this book has been founded on the experience and wisdom of leaders and scholars in diverse fields of interest. Necessary revisions can best be achieved by majority decision of such a group.

The author has arranged, by agreement with the publisher, that the determination and control of future editions of this book be vested in a permanent, self-perpetuating Advisory Board of specialists in the field and leaders of notable organizations. This Board has accepted responsibility for determining the need and nature of future revisions to keep this code current, complete, and legally correct.

In the following listing, titles cited reflect qualifying experience valuable to the Board. Titles are not all-inclusive and may not be current.

PERMANENT BOARD OF ADVISORS

HARRY BITNER, Professor of Law and Associate Director of Library, Cornell University

WALTER BORNEMEIER, M.D., Speaker, House of Delegates, President-elect, American Medical Association

ADVISORY BOARD

HOWARD R. BOWEN, President, University of Iowa

ERWIN D. CANHAM, Editor in Chief, *The Christian Science Monitor*

VERNON W. CLAPP, President, Council on Library Resources

ALVIN C. EURICH, President, Aspen Institute for Humanitarian Studies

JAMES A. FARLEY, Chairman of the Board, Coca-Cola Export Corporation

WILBUR E. GILMAN, President, Speech Association of America

HAROLD HILLENBRAND, D.D.S., Secretary, American Dental Association

PAUL G. HOFFMAN, Managing Director, United Nations Special Fund

FRANK W. JORDON, D.D.S., Vice President, American Dental Association; President, Kentucky Dental Association

ALLEN LAUTERBACK, General Counsel, The American Farm Bureau Federation

HAROLD MCGRAW, JR., President, McGraw-Hill Book Company
Hill Book Company

ROSS MALONE, President, American Bar Association

PAUL MASON, Parliamentary Consultant to State Legislatures

DAVID F. MAXWELL, Chairman, House of Delegates and President, American Bar Association

CARL B. MUNCK, President, National School Boards Association

JUDGE MARY BURT NASH, Chairman, National Panhellenic Conference

ROBERT C. POOLEY, Chairman, Department of Integrated Liberal Studies, University of Wisconsin; Parliamentarian, National Council of Teachers of English

THOMAS REED, Consultant in Municipal Government

FLOYD M. RIDDICK, Parliamentarian, United States Senate

ADVISORY BOARD

COLONEL WILLIAM A. ROBERTS, President, Federal Bar Association

MILTON A. SMITH, General Counsel, Chamber of Commerce of the United States

JAMES SQUIRE, Secretary, National Council of Teachers of English

JOSEPH D. STECHER, Legal Counsel, American Bar Association

J. E. WALLACE STERLING, President, Stanford University

WAYNE N. THOMPSON, Professor of Speech, University of Texas

RALPH W. TYLER, Director, Center for Advanced Study of Behavioral Sciences, Stanford University

ROY E. WILLY, Chairman, House of Delegates, American Bar Association

DAEL WOLFLE, Executive Officer, American Association for Advancement of Science

C. GILBERT WRENN, Professor of Educational Psychology, University of Arizona

EDWARD L. WRIGHT, Chairman, House of Delegates, American Bar Association

Sturgis Standard Code of Parliamentary Procedure

SECOND EDITION

by Alice Sturgis

McGraw-Hill Book Company
New York   Toronto   London   Sydney

STURGIS STANDARD CODE
OF PARLIAMENTARY PROCEDURE
Copyright, 1950, by Alice Sturgis
Copyright © 1966 by Alice Sturgis
All Rights Reserved.

Printed in the United States of America.
This book, or parts thereof, may not be
reproduced in any form without written
permission of the publishers,
except in the case of brief quotations embodied
in critical articles and reviews.

Library of Congress Catalog Card Number: 65-24530
Fifth Printing
62272

ACKNOWLEDGMENTS

This book draws its strength and completeness from the experience and judgment of outstanding persons in many fields. Some have contributed special knowledge on a particular question; others have supplied fundamental concepts based on a broad background; all have enriched the book immeasurably. These, together with the members of the Advisory Board, deserve special mention for their contributions either to the first or second edition, or to both.

ROBERT T. ANDERSON, City Attorney, Berkeley, California

ROBERT ASH, Executive Secretary-Treasurer, Central Labor Council of Alameda County, AFL-CIO

JACQUELINE BARTELLS, Assistant Law Librarian, University of California

JAMES E. BRENNER, Professor of Law, Stanford University

HAROLD H. BURTON, Associate Justice of the Supreme Court of the United States

CLARENCE CANNON, Parliamentarian of the United States House of Representatives

MARTHA LEE CARTER, Parliamentarian, Senior Congress Club

RUSSELL R. CROWELL, President, AFL-CIO Laundry and Dry Cleaning International Union

ARTHUR W. ECKMAN, General Counsel, First Church of Christ, Scientist

ROGER FLEMING, Secretary-Treasurer, The American Farm Bureau Federation

FELIX FRANKFURTER, Associate Justice of the Supreme Court of the United States

DAN F. HENKE, Professor of Law; Law Librarian, University of California

ALBERT J. HARNO, Dean of the College of Law, University of Illinois

S. I. HAYAKAWA, Semanticist; President, San Francisco State College

PAUL A. HEIST, Research Psychologist, Center for the Study of Higher Education, University of California

ROBERT H. HOLLAND, Director Office of Labor, Management, and Welfare-Pension Reports

MARIE KOUTECKY KING, Research Librarian

JOHN F. MALLEY, Chairman and Counsel, Board of Trustees, Elks National Foundation

T. V. MCDAVITT, Counsel, Bureau of Industrial and Personnel Relations, American Medical Association

HOWARD L. OLECK, Associate Dean, Cleveland-Marshall Law School

WILLIAM ROCHE, Attorney, National Labor Relations Board

FRITZ ROETHLISBERGER, Associate Professor of Industrial Research, Harvard Graduate School of Business Administration

ARTHUR SCHLESINGER, Professor of History, Harvard University

KEITH SEEGMILLER, General Counsel of the National Association of County Officials

REGINALD HEBER SMITH, Commission for the Survey of the Legal Profession, American Bar Association

MRS. W. GLENN SUTHERS, Parliamentarian

MARK STARR, Educational Director, International Ladies Garment Workers Union

EUGENE K. STURGIS, Attorney at Law

KENWOOD STURGIS, Park Supervisor

ARTHUR T. VANDERBILT, Chief Justice of the Supreme Court of New Jersey

CHARLES WATKINS, Former Parliamentarian, United States Senate

GEORGE H. WILSON, Board of Directors, The American Farm Bureau Federation

CONSTANCE M. WINCHELL, Chief Reference Librarian, Columbia University

B. E. WITKIN, Legal Author

J. ALBERT WOLL, Attorney AFL-CIO

NAOMI WRAGE, Department of Speech and Drama, Stanford University

CONTENTS

ADVISORY BOARD	*page* i
ACKNOWLEDGMENTS	vii
FOREWORD BY ERWIN N. GRISWOLD	xxvii
INTRODUCTION BY OWEN J. ROBERTS	xxix

Chapter 1
THE SIGNIFICANCE OF PARLIAMENTARY LAW

Parliamentary Law Safeguards Rights	1
What Is Parliamentary Law?	3
What Organizations Must Observe Parliamentary Law?	4
When Must Organizations Observe Parliamentary Law?	4
Where Parliamentary Rules Are Found	5
Requirements for a Parliamentary Authority	6

Chapter 2
FUNDAMENTAL PRINCIPLES OF PARLIAMENTARY LAW

The Purpose of Parliamentary Law	8
Equality of Rights	8
Majority Decision	9
Minority Rights	9
The Right of Discussion	9
The Right to Information	10
Fairness and Good Faith	10

Chapter 3
PRESENTATION OF MOTIONS

Steps in Presenting a Motion	11
Addressing the Presiding Officer	11
Recognition by the Presiding Officer	12
Proposal of a Motion by a Member	12
Seconding a Motion	13
Statement of a Motion by the Presiding Officer	13
Example of the Presentation of a Motion	14

Chapter 4
CLASSIFICATION OF MOTIONS

Classes of Motions	15
Main Motions	15
Subsidiary Motions	16
Privileged Motions	16
Incidental Motions	16
Classification of Unlisted Motions	17
Changes in Classification of Motions	18
Chart: *The Chief Purposes of Motions*	20

Chapter 5
PRECEDENCE OF MOTIONS

Order of Precedence	21
Basic Rules of Precedence	22
Example of Precedence	23

Chapter 6
RULES GOVERNING MOTIONS

The Basic Rules of Motions	24
What Is the Precedence of the Motion?	25
Can the Motion Interrupt a Speaker?	25

CONTENTS

Does the Motion Require a Second?	26
Is the Motion Debatable?	26
Can the Motion Be Amended?	27
What Vote Does the Motion Require?	28
To What Other Motions Can the Motion Apply?	28
What Other Motions Can Be Applied to the Motion?	29
Chart: *Principal Rules Governing Motions*	30
When Can a Motion Be Renewed or Substituted?	32
Changing Main Motions Already Voted On	32
Chart: *Changing Main Motions Already Voted On*	34

Chapter 7
MAIN MOTIONS

THE MAIN MOTION

Purpose	35
Form	35
The Main Motion Defined	36
Phrasing the Main Motion	36
The Main Motion in Resolution Form	37
Discussion on the Main Motion	37
Disposal of the Main Motion	38
Effect of the Main Motion	38
Rules Governing the Main Motion	38

MOTION TO RECONSIDER

Purpose	39
Form	39
What Votes Can Be Reconsidered?	39
Proposal of the Motion to Reconsider	40
Who Can Move to Reconsider?	41
Debate on the Motion to Reconsider	42
Effect of the Motion to Reconsider	42
Rules Governing the Motion to Reconsider	42

MOTION TO RESCIND

Purpose	43
Form	43
What Motions May Be Rescinded?	43
Vote Required to Rescind	43
Rescind and Expunge	44
Effect of the Motion to Rescind	44
Rules Governing the Motion to Rescind	44

MOTION TO RESUME CONSIDERATION

Purpose	45
Form	45
Limitations on the Motion to Resume Consideration	45
Precedence over Other Main Motions	46
Adhering Motions and Resuming Consideration	46
Effect of the Motion to Resume Consideration	46
Rules Governing the Motion to Resume Consideration	47

Chapter 8
SUBSIDIARY MOTIONS

MOTION TO POSTPONE INDEFINITELY

Purpose	47
Form	47
Suppression by Indefinite Postponement	48
Opening the Main Motion to Debate	48
Effect of the Motion to Postpone Indefinitely	48
Rules Governing the Motion to Postpone Indefinitely	48

MOTION TO AMEND

Purpose	49
Form	49
What Motions May Be Amended?	51
Amendments Must Be Germane	51
Amendments May Be Hostile	52
Limitations on Pending Amendments	52
Debate on Amendments	53

CONTENTS

Amending by Substitution of a New Motion	54
Filling Blanks	54
Withdrawing and Accepting Amendments	54
Adhering Amendments	55
Voting on Amendments	55
Vote Required on Amendments	56
Amending Actions Already Taken	56
Effect of the Motion to Amend	57
Rules Governing the Motion to Amend	57

MOTION TO REFER TO COMMITTEE

Purpose	57
Form	58
Provisions Included in the Motion to Refer	58
Instructions to a Committee	59
Effect of the Motion to Refer	60
Rules Governing the Motion to Refer	60

MOTION TO POSTPONE DEFINITELY

Purpose	60
Form	61
Differences in Motions to Postpone	61
Limitations on the Motion to Postpone Definitely	62
Postponing as a General or Special Order	62
Types of Postponement	63
Consideration of Postponed Motions	63
Effect of the Motion to Postpone Definitely	64
Rules Governing the Motion to Postpone Definitely	64

MOTION TO LIMIT OR EXTEND DEBATE

Purpose	64
Form	64
Types of Limitations on Debate	65
How Limiting Debate Affects Pending Motions	65
Termination of the Motion to Limit Debate	66
Effect of the Motion to Limit Debate	66
Rules Governing the Motion to Limit Debate	66

MOTION TO VOTE IMMEDIATELY
(Previous Question)

Purpose	67
Form	67
Confusion Caused by Former Name	67
Proposal of the Motion to Vote Immediately	68
How Voting Immediately Affects Pending Motions	68
Termination of the Motion to Vote Immediately	69
Two-thirds Vote Required	69
Question! Question!	69
Effect of the Motion to Vote Immediately	70
Rules Governing the Motion to Vote Immediately	70

MOTION TO POSTPONE TEMPORARILY
(Lay on the Table)

Purpose	70
Form	70
Reasons for Postponing Temporarily	71
Time Limits on the Motion to Postpone Temporarily	71
Adhering Motions also Postponed	72
Effect of the Motion to Postpone Temporarily	72
Rules Governing the Motion to Postpone Temporarily	72

Chapter 9
PRIVILEGED MOTIONS

QUESTION OF PRIVILEGE
(Request)

Purpose	73
Form	73
Member's Right to Request Privilege	74
Interruption by a Question of Privilege	75
Privileges of the Assembly	75
Personal Privileges	75

CONTENTS

Motions as Questions of Privilege	76
Effect of a Question of Privilege	76
Rules Governing a Question of Privilege	76

MOTION TO RECESS

Purpose	77
Form	77
Difference Between Recess and Adjourn	77
Limitations and Restrictions on the Motion to Recess	78
Effect of the Motion to Recess	78
Rules Governing the Motion to Recess	78

MOTION TO ADJOURN

Purpose	79
Form	79
Qualified and Unqualified Motions to Adjourn	80
Completion of Business Before Adjournment	80
Adjournment to an Adjourned Meeting	81
Adjournment and Dissolution	81
Voting on Adjournment	82
Adjournment at Previously Fixed Time	82
Business Interrupted by Adjournment	83
Effect of the Motion to Adjourn	83
Rules Governing the Motion to Adjourn	83

Chapter 10
INCIDENTAL MOTIONS

MOTION TO APPEAL

Purpose	84
Form	84
When an Appeal May Be Taken	84
Statement of the Question on Appeal	85
Statement of the Reasons for Appeal	85
Vote on an Appeal	85
Effect of the Motion to Appeal	86
Rules Governing the Motion to Appeal	86

MOTION TO SUSPEND RULES

Purpose	86
Form	87
Which Rules Can Be Suspended?	87
Which Rules Cannot Be Suspended?	87
Restrictions and Time Limits on Suspension of Rules	88
Effect of the Motion to Suspend Rules	88
Rules Governing the Motion to Suspend Rules	88

MOTION TO OBJECT TO CONSIDERATION

Purpose	89
Form	89
When Objection to Consideration May Be Raised	89
Objection Limited to Main Motions	90
Voting on Objection to Consideration	90
Presiding Officer May Rule Out Motions	91
Effect of the Motion to Object to Consideration	91
Rules Governing the Motion to Object to Consideration	91

REQUEST FOR POINT OF ORDER

Purpose	92
Form	92
How Points of Order Arise	92
When a Point of Order May Be Raised	93
Ruling on Points of Order	93
Effect of Request for Point of Order	94
Rules Governing Request for Point of Order	94

REQUEST FOR PARLIAMENTARY INQUIRY

Purpose	95
Form	95
Right of Members to Inquire	96
When an Inquiry Interrupts	96
Inquiry Addressed to the Presiding Officer	97
Effect of Request for Parliamentary Inquiry	97
Rules Governing Request for Parliamentary Inquiry	98

REQUEST TO WITHDRAW A MOTION

Purpose	98
Form	98
Right of the Proposer to Withdraw His Motion	99
Permission to Withdraw a Motion	99
Recording Withdrawn Motions	100
Effect of Request to Withdraw a Motion	100
Rules Governing Request to Withdraw a Motion	100

REQUEST FOR DIVISION OF QUESTION

Purpose	100
Form	101
Motions That the Presiding Officer Can Divide	101
Motions That the Presiding Officer Cannot Divide	102
When Division of Question May Be Proposed	102
Alternative Proposals for Dividing a Question	103
Effect of Request for Division of Question	103
Rules Governing Request For Division of Question	103

REQUEST FOR DIVISION OF ASSEMBLY

Purpose	103
Form	104
When Division May Be Requested	104
Verification of a Vote by the Presiding Officer	104
Effect of Request for Division of Assembly	105
Rules Governing Request for Division of Assembly	105

Chapter 11
NOTICE OF MEETINGS AND PROPOSALS

Importance of Notice	105
Notice Protects Members	106
Notice of Meetings	106
Notice of Proposed Actions	108
Waiver of Notice	109

Chapter 12
MEETINGS

Meetings and Conventions Defined	109
Regular Meetings	110
Special Meetings	110
Adjourned Meetings	111
Failure to Call Meetings	112

Chapter 13
QUORUM

Necessity for a Quorum	113
Quorum Requirements	113
Computing a Quorum	114
Raising a Question on Quorum	114
Presumption of a Quorum	115

Chapter 14
ORDER OF BUSINESS

Usual Order of Business	115
Flexibility in the Order of Business	116
Agenda	117
Call to Order	117
Reading of Minutes	118
Reports of Officers	119
Reports of Committees	119
Unfinished Business	119
New Business	120
Announcements	120
Adjournment	120

Chapter 15
DEBATE

The Right of Debate	121
Extent of Debate on Motions	121

CONTENTS

Obtaining the Floor for Debate	122
Recognition of Members During Debate	122
Speaking More Than Once	123
What Is Not Debate?	123
Relevancy in Debate	124
Dilatory Tactics	124
Members' Conduct During Debate	125
Presiding Officer's Duties During Debate	126
Time Limits on Debate	126
Cutting Off Debate	127
Bringing a Question to Vote	127
Informal Consideration	128

Chapter 16
VOTES REQUIRED FOR VALID ACTIONS

Significance of a Majority Vote	129
Requiring More Than a Majority Vote	130
Requiring Less Than a Majority Vote	131
Importance of Defining the Vote Required	131
Different Meanings of Majority Vote	132
Majority of the Legal Votes Cast	133
Plurality Vote	134
Unanimous Vote	135
Tie Vote	136
Vote of the Presiding Officer	136
Computing a Majority for Separate Questions	137
Computing a Majority When Electing a Group	137
Voting Separately for Equal Positions	139
When Members Cannot Vote	139

Chapter 17
METHODS OF VOTING

Voting Is a Fundamental Right	140
Voting in Meetings	140

CONTENTS

Voice Vote	141
Rising Vote	141
Roll Call Vote	142
Ballot Vote	142
Voting by Unanimous Consent	143
Voting by Mail	143
Voting by Proxy	145
Changing a Vote	145
Announcing the Result of a Vote	146
All Votes Binding During a Meeting	146

Chapter 18
NOMINATIONS AND ELECTIONS

Choosing Organization Leaders	147
Bylaw Provisions on Nominations and Elections	147
Nominations from the Floor	148
Voting for Candidates Not Nominated	149
Selecting a Nominating Committee	149
Duties of a Nominating Committee	150
Qualifications of Nominees	151
Nomination to More Than One Office	152
Nominating-Committee Members as Candidates	152
Single and Multiple Slate	153
Election Committee	154
Counting Ballots	154
Determining Legality of Ballots	155
Report of Election Committee or Tellers	156
Vote Necessary to Elect	157
Casting of Ballot by the Secretary	157
Motion to Make a Vote Unanimous	158
When Elections Become Effective	159
Challenging a Vote	159
Challenging an Election	159

Chapter 19
OFFICERS

The President as Leader	160
The President as Administrator	161
The President as Presiding Officer	162
When the President Presides	164
The President-elect	164
The Vice President	165
The Secretary	165
The Corresponding Secretary	167
The Treasurer	167
The Member Parliamentarian	168
The Sergeant at Arms	168
Honorary Officers	169
Powers and Liabilities of Officers	169
Delegation of Authority by Officers	169
Term of Office	171
Vacancies	172
Removal of Officers	173

Chapter 20
COMMITTEES AND BOARDS

Importance of Committees	175
Advantages of Committees	175
Standing Committees	176
Special Committees	176
Committees for Deliberation	177
Committees for Action	177
Selection of the Committee Chairman	177
Selection of the Committee Members	178
Ex Officio Members of Committees	178
Powers, Rights, and Duties of Committees	179

xxii   CONTENTS

Working Materials for Committees	180
Committee Meetings Limited to Members	181
Procedure in Committee Meetings	181
Committee Hearings	182
The Board of Directors	182
The Executive Committee of the Board	184
The Committee of the Whole	184

Chapter 21
COMMITTEE REPORTS AND RECOMMENDATIONS

Form of Committee Reports and Recommendations	185
Agreement on Committee Reports	186
Presentation of Committee Reports	187
Consideration of Committee Reports	187
Record of Committee Reports	189
Minority Reports	189
Presentation of Committee Recommendations	190

Chapter 22
CONVENTIONS AND THEIR COMMITTEES

General Structure of Conventions	191
Instruction of Delegates	192
Convention Committees	192
Use of Reference Committees	194
Duties of Reference Committees	195
Hearings of Reference Committees	196
Reports of Reference Committees	197

Chapter 23
MINUTES

Importance of Minutes	197
Responsibility for Minutes	198
Preparing Minutes	198
Reading and Correction of Minutes	199

Approval of Minutes	200
What Minutes Should Contain	200
What Minutes Should Not Contain	201
The Minute Book	202

Chapter 24
CHARTERS, BYLAWS, AND RULES

Types of Charters	202
Constitution and Bylaws	203
Drafting Bylaws	204
Adoption of the Original Bylaws	204
When Bylaws Go into Effect	205
Provisions for Amending Bylaws	205
Proposing Amendments to Bylaws	206
Form for Proposed Amendments to Bylaws	206
Considering Amendments to Bylaws	207
Vote Required on Amendments to Bylaws	209
Revision of Bylaws	209
Interpreting Bylaws and Rules	210
Special and Standing Rules	210
Parliamentary Authority	210
Detailed Procedures	211
Supplementing Procedural Rules by Motions	211
Adopted Policies	212

Chapter 25
FINANCES

Setting Up Financial Records	214
Report of the Treasurer	214
Report of the Auditor	215
Financial Safeguards	216

Chapter 26
LEGAL CLASSIFICATIONS OF ORGANIZATIONS

Meeting to Form an Organization	217

Temporary and Permanent Organizations 218
Incorporated and Unincorporated Organizations 219
Nonprofit Organizations 220

Chapter 27
RIGHTS OF MEMBERS AND OF ORGANIZATIONS

Relationship Between Member and Organization 221
Rights of Members 222
Rights of Organizations 223
Relationship of Individual and Organizational Rights 224
Discipline and Expulsion of Members 225
Resignations 226

Chapter 28
STAFF AND CONSULTANTS

The Executive Secretary 228
The Accountant 229
The Consultant to Nonprofit Organizations 229
The Attorney 230
The Parliamentarian 230

APPENDIX

GOVERNMENTAL BOARDS, COUNCILS, COMMISSIONS, AND COMMITTEES 235

Governmental Bodies and Parliamentary Law 235
Organization of Governmental Bodies 236
Notice Requirements 236
Quorum 237
Minutes 238
Presiding Officer 239
Powers and Duties of Members 239
No Seconds Required 240

Voting	240
Vacancies	241
Removal of Members	241
Parliamentary Authority	242
Rights of Citizens Attending Meetings	242
LABOR ORGANIZATIONS	243
Unions Have Additional Parliamentary Rules	243
Bylaws Should Include Statutory Provisions	243
Provisions to Include in Union Bylaws	245
Bill of Rights	245
Membership	247
Officers, Agents, and Other Representatives	247
The Executive Board	247
Eligibility for Nomination and Election	248
Time of Elections	248
Term of Office	248
Campaign Requirements	248
Voting in Elections	248
Challenging an Election	249
Removal of Officers	249
Voting Requirements	249
Discipline and Expulsion of Members	250
SUGGESTED BYLAW PROVISIONS FOR A LOCAL ORGANIZATION	251
MODEL MINUTES	253
REFERENCES	256
DEFINITIONS OF PARLIAMENTARY TERMS	263
INDEX	269

FOREWORD

The process of reaching group decisions is more difficult than we sometimes realize. Of course it can be done by fighting it out, and this has been done in primitive societies. But if we want to reach a rational decision, we must have procedures which will lead to a fully organized and fairly stated consensus. Indeed, as has been observed by Justice Frankfurter, "The history of liberty has largely been the history of observance of procedural safeguards." Whether the group is a club, a labor union, a college faculty, or a legislative body, the problem is essentially the same. The heart of the task is a procedure which will focus consideration on the right issues and lead to a resolution of these issues according to the views of the majority of the group.

For this purpose we have parliamentary law, more accurately called parliamentary procedure. By following proper procedures, the deliberative process can be kept orderly, the issues can be sharply stated, conclusions can be reached, and finality can be achieved. We take such procedures for granted in Congress or in a state legislative body. Of course the rules find their origin in the Parliament of Westminster, but, with proper adaptations, they can be made applicable to the process of reaching decisions in any group.

In this volume, the author has presented in clear terms an exposition of standard parliamentary procedures. Instead of a skeleton in the form of a mere "code" or "rules," she has put flesh on the bones, with clear explanations, illustrations, and illuminating comments. A presiding officer who uses this book can conduct a fair and effective meeting, can make sound rulings, and will be in a position to maintain the rulings if they are challenged. Many books on parliamentary law have been published in the past. Some of them are classics of their period, such as *Jefferson's Manual, Cushing's Manual,* and *Robert's Rules of Order.* But these are often technical, cryptic and really intelligible only to specialists. Moreover, they are dated, and do not reflect current practices with full accuracy. This book has the great merit of combining clarity and readability with sound and well-conceived procedures fully appropriate to the present time.

When people meet or work together to reach decisions, whether in private or in public groups, they represent democracy in action. Knowing how to proceed to a conclusion in any such group is an essential part of the training of a citizen. This book provides clear guidance to a wise understanding of that process. With its help, meetings can be run better, sounder conclusions can be reached, and all citizens can better learn the ways in which democracy can be made to work effectively.

Erwin N. Griswold
*Dean of the Law School,
Harvard University*

May, 1966

INTRODUCTION

This volume will supply a real need. It is not a mere manual of procedure, a mere catalogue of rules and their precedence. On the contrary, it is a complete exposition of the fundamental concepts which underlie the rules. One who wishes to become a parliamentarian will find it unique, both in its statement of the philosophy on which the system is founded, and in its integration of specific rules under the principles which have evoked them.

The reader who masters the book will find himself a skilled parliamentarian, who knows not merely the appropriate rule, and its place in the hierarchy, but the reasons for the rule and for its order of precedence.

The style is clear and terse and the order of treatment logical. The material is presented in an interesting way, tending to attract and hold the attention of the reader, but there is no unnecessarily long explanation or discussion. A pioneer feature is the citation in notes of about one hundred and fifty court decisions supporting the principles stated in the text. It is surprising that so often parliamentary rulings have been the subject of adjudication by the courts. There is also a useful glossary and a table showing the precedence of the various appropriate motions.

No such complete book on parliamentary procedure has been produced. The work should take a commanding place in the field.

Owen J. Roberts
*Former Associate Justice of the
Supreme Court of the United States*

Sturgis
Standard Code of
Parliamentary
Procedure

Chapter 1

THE SIGNIFICANCE OF PARLIAMENTARY LAW

"Procedure is more than formality. Procedure is, indeed, the great mainstay of substantive rights.... Without procedural safeguards—liberty would rest on precarious ground and substantive rights would be imperiled." [1]

"The history of liberty has largely been the history of observance of procedural safeguards." [2]

Thus two justices of the Supreme Court of the United States voice this vital fact—both our freedom and our rights can exist only if they are safeguarded by sound procedures, rigidly enforced.

Parliamentary Law Safeguards Rights

When Winston Churchill, during the abdication crisis in 1936, rose before a shocked House of Commons to discuss the constitutional question before a final decision was made, the House was in a hostile temper. A burst of disapproval greeted the great statesman. Churchill set his pugnacious jaw and, as the uproar subsided, declared:

"If the House resists my claim [to speak] it will only add more importance to any words that I may use."

Here in the mother of parliaments, which has lent its name

to the system of rules by which assemblies are conducted, we see at work procedural safeguards and the fundamental principles of democratic discussion. Here is the right of free and fair debate, the right of the majority to decide, and the right of the minority to protest and be protected. Here also is a demonstration that the violation of rights in assemblies lends weight to the cause of the suppressed.

Here is the essence of the democratic procedure of a free assembly, whether a professional organization, a labor union, or a high school debating society—a procedure based on what Thomas Jefferson called "equal and exact justice to all men."

Any great principle or right is only as strong as the procedures that support and enforce it. To vote by secret ballot is a fundamental right, but it is meaningless unless supported by procedures that insure equal opportunity to vote, freedom of choice, absolute secrecy, and honesty in counting. Even though this right to vote has procedural safeguards, it still is meaningless if they are not observed.

Parliamentary law is the procedural safeguard that protects the individual and the group in their exercise of the rights of free speech, free assembly, and the freedom to unite in organizations for the achievement of common aims. These rights, too, are meaningless, and the timeless freedoms they define can be lost, if parliamentary procedure is not observed.

One of the basic concepts of freedom is the right of people to join together to achieve their common purposes. This concept includes the right to assemble and to organize, to propose ideas, to speak without fear of reprisal, to vote on proposals, and to carry out the decisions of the group. Parliamentary law provides the procedures that give reality to these democratic concepts. Parliamentary procedure is not an end in itself. It is, rather, the guardian of the freedom to band together, to discuss, to decide, and to act.

What Is Parliamentary Law?

Parliamentary law is the code of rules and ethics for working together in groups. It has evolved through centuries out of the experience of individuals working together for a common purpose. It provides the means for translating beliefs and ideas into effective group action. It is logic and common sense crystallized into law, and is as much a part of the body of the law as is civil or criminal procedure. The rules of parliamentary procedure are found both in common law and in statutory law.

The common law of parliamentary procedure is the body of principles, rules, and usages that has developed from court decisions on parliamentary questions, and is based on reason and long observance. The common law of parliamentary procedure applies in all parliamentary situations except where a statutory law governs.

The statutory law of procedure consists of statutes, or laws, relating to procedures that have been enacted by federal, state, or local legislative bodies. These rules of parliamentary procedure apply only to the particular organizations covered by the law.

Parliamentary procedure is easy to learn. It is essentially common sense. It is simple to understand and easy to use. After a little practice one feels at home with parliamentary procedure. It works magic in meetings. It gives confidence and power to those who master it. It enables members and organizations to present, consider, and carry out their ideas with efficiency and harmony.

It is true that parliamentary law can be used to destroy as well as to construct. However, it can be used destructively only when a majority of the members are ignorant of their parliamentary rights.

What Organizations Must Observe Parliamentary Law?

All organizations, such as business, cultural, religious, social fraternal, professional, educational, labor, civic, scientific, medical, and governmental, are subject to the principles and rules of common parliamentary law. All profit and nonprofit corporations and associations, and the boards, councils, commissions, and committees of government, must observe its rules.

International and national parliaments, congresses, and state legislatures have developed complete sets of special rules to meet their own specialized needs, and most of these rules differ sharply from those of common parliamentary law. Therefore, these bodies are the only ones that are not subject to common parliamentary law.

Clarence Cannon, former member of Congress and parliamentarian of the House of Representatives, explains why the rules of Congress are not suitable for other bodies to use:

> "These rules of Parliament and Congress are designed for bicameral bodies, generally with paid memberships, meeting in continuous session, requiring a majority for a quorum, and delegating their duties largely to committees. Their special requirements ... have produced highly complex and remarkably efficient systems of rules peculiar to their respective bodies, but which are, as a whole, unsuited to the needs of the ordinary assembly." [3]

When Must Organizations Observe Parliamentary Law?

The courts hold that all groups, with the exception of state, national, and international governmental bodies, must follow general parliamentary law whenever they are meeting to transact business. If, however, a group meets solely for other

THE SIGNIFICANCE OF PARLIAMENTARY LAW

purposes—for example, social or educational—it is, of course, not subject to parliamentary rules.

Even a small group—for example, a finance committee or a board of education—must observe parliamentary law. However, the procedure in such groups is usually more informal than in a large convention.

When a group meets for the purpose of presenting proposals, discussing them, and arriving at decisions, parliamentary procedure is not only helpful, but indispensable. In all organizations the rules of procedure must be observed if the actions of the assembly are to be legal. When groups are making decisions, the time-tested processes of parliamentary procedure will always be necessary.

Where Parliamentary Rules Are Found

The four basic sources of the parliamentary rules governing a particular organization, arranged in the order of their rank, are:

1. **Law.** The law, consisting of the common law of parliamentary procedure and the statutes enacted by federal, state, or local governments, is the highest source of parliamentary rules for any organization.
2. **Charter.** The charter granted by government to an incorporated organization ranks second as a source.

    The charter granted by a parent organization to a constituent or component unit of the organization ranks next to its charter from government.
3. **Bylaws.** Any provisions of the bylaws of a parent organization that regulate the constituent or component units of the organization rank ahead of the bylaws adopted by the units. The bylaws, or the constitution and bylaws, and other adopted rules of an organization rank next.

4. **Adopted parliamentary authority.** The book adopted by an organization as its authority on all procedural questions *not* covered by the law or its charters, bylaws, or adopted rules completes the sources of the parliamentary rules governing an organization. A parliamentary authority is a compilation of the parliamentary rules from *all of these sources,* assembled and organized for convenient reference.

A parliamentary authority suited for adoption (*a*) explains the principles and procedures that are based on long-time parliamentary usages and accepted practices; (*b*) summarizes and interprets the common law of parliamentary procedure as determined by court decisions and the law contained in statutes applicable to particular organizations; and (*c*) presents practical ideas developed by leading organizations for efficient operation.

The rules of one source cannot conflict with the rules of the sources that rank above it. If there is a conflict between sources, the higher-ranking source prevails. For example, a charter must not conflict with the law; bylaws must not conflict with either the law or charter.

Organizations also have the right to adopt rules that supplement or change the less fundamental provisions of parliamentary procedure. None of these adopted rules may conflict with any rule of higher rank. For example, an organization cannot adopt a rule requiring six months' notice for a resignation, because the law gives a member the right to resign at any time he chooses.

Requirements for a Parliamentary Authority

Each organization adopts, as a parliamentary authority, a code that governs the procedures of the organization in all

THE SIGNIFICANCE OF PARLIAMENTARY LAW

situations not covered by rules from a higher source. Because of its importance to the organization, the parliamentary authority should be chosen with great care.

A parliamentary authority should be so clear and simple that anyone can understand it. It should be organized so that reference to the rules is quick and accurate, and it should be so complete that no other book or research will be needed. It should omit needless or outmoded procedures but must include all current, practical, businesslike procedures. It must present parliamentary law so accurately that the courts will uphold any action taken according to the rules it states. If the rules of the adopted parliamentary authority do not conform to the law, the organization that follows it may find itself in legal difficulties.

This book has been written to meet these standards, drawing its strength and completeness from the broad experience and sound judgment of leaders in many fields. It is truly a cooperative effort, for it embodies and reflects the experience and wisdom of hundreds of organizations and innumerable individuals. These leaders and organizations have contributed to this code because of their conviction that voluntary organizations are the highest fulfillment of democracy.

Chapter 2

FUNDAMENTAL PRINCIPLES OF PARLIAMENTARY LAW

A knowledge of the basic principles of parliamentary law enables one to reason out the answers to most parliamentary questions. A thorough understanding of these principles clarifies the entire subject of parliamentary procedure. When one understands the basic principles, it is easy to become familiar with the rules because most of them follow logically from the principles.

These basic principles are so simple and familiar that we may fail to recognize their importance. They are the same principles on which democracies are based and seem almost self-evident.

The most important principles of parliamentary procedure are the following:

1. The purpose of parliamentary procedure is to facilitate the transaction of business and to promote cooperation and harmony. The philosophy of parliamentary law is constructive—to make it easier for people to work together effectively and to help organizations and members accomplish their purposes.

Parliamentary procedure should not be used to awe, entangle, or confound the uninitiated. Technical rules should be used only to the extent necessary to observe the law, to expedite business, to avoid confusion, and to protect the rights of members.

Two basic procedural rules have developed to assure that the simplest and most direct procedure for accomplishing a purpose is observed. First, motions have a definite order of precedence, each motion having a fixed rank for its introduction and its consideration. Second, only one motion may be considered at a time.

2. All members have equal rights, privileges, and obligations. Every member has an equal right or privilege to propose motions, speak, ask questions, nominate, be a candidate for office, vote, or exercise any other right or privilege of a member. He necessarily has equal obligations.

The presiding officer should be strictly impartial and should use his authority to protect and preserve the equality of members in the exercise of their rights and privileges.

PRINCIPLES OF PARLIAMENTARY LAW

3. The majority vote decides. The ultimate authority of an organization is vested in a majority of its members. This is a fundamental concept of democracy.

A primary purpose of parliamentary procedure is to determine the will of the majority and see that it is carried out. By the act of joining a group, a member agrees to be governed by the vote of the majority. Until the vote on a question is announced, every member has an equal right to voice opposition or approval and to seek to persuade others to support his opinion. After the vote is announced, the decision of the majority becomes the decision of every member of the organization. It is the duty of every member to accept and to abide by this decision.

When the members of an organization select officers, boards, or sometimes committees, and delegate authority to them, this selection and delegation should be by the democratic process of majority vote.

4. The rights of the minority must be protected. Democratic organizations always protect certain basic rights belonging to all members. The right to present proposals, to be heard, and to oppose are valued rights of all members, although the ultimate authority of decision rests with a majority, except when a higher vote is required. The members who are in the minority on a question are entitled to the same consideration and respect as members who are in the majority.

The minority of today is frequently the majority of tomorrow. A member of the majority on one question may be in the minority on the next. The protection of the rights of all members, minority and majority alike, should be the concern of every member.

5. Full and free discussion of every proposition presented for decision is an established right of members. This is another democratic concept. Each member of the assembly has the right to express his opinion fully and freely without interruption or interference provided he remains within the rules. The right of every member to "have his say," "to have his day in court," or "to be heard" is as important as his right to vote.

6. Every member has the right to know the meaning of the question before the assembly and what its effect will be. The presiding officer should keep the pending motion clearly before the assembly at all times, and when necessary he should explain it or call on some member to do so. He should explain any procedural motion and its effect if there are members who do not understand it. A member always has the right to request information on any motion which he does not understand so that he may vote intelligently.

7. All meetings must be characterized by fairness and by good faith. Trickery, overemphasis on minor technicalities, dilatory tactics, indulgence in personalities, and railroading threaten the spirit and practice of fairness and good faith. If a meeting is characterized by fairness and good faith, a minor procedural error will not invalidate an action that has been taken by an organization. But fraud, unfairness, or absence of good faith may cause a court to hold any action invalid.

Parliamentary strategy is the art of using legitimately the parliamentary principles, rules, and motions to support or defeat a proposal. It includes, for example, such important factors as timing, wording of proposals, choice of supporters, selection of arguments, and manipulation of proposals by other motions. Strategy, ethically used, is constructive; however, if it involves deceit, fraud, misrepresentation, intimidation, railroading, or denial of the rights of members, it is destructive and actually illegal.

In 1776 John Hatsell, the famous British parliamentarian, wrote, "Motives ought to outweigh objections of form." The interpretations of the courts make it clear that the intent and over-all good faith of the group are of more importance than the particular detail of procedure used in a given instance. The

PRINCIPLES OF PARLIAMENTARY LAW 11

effectiveness and, in fact, often the existence of an organization are destroyed if its officers or members condone unfairness or lack of good faith.

Chapter 3

PRESENTATION OF MOTIONS

Steps in Presenting a Motion

A *motion* is the formal statement of a proposal or question to an assembly for consideration and action. An item of business is presented for decision in the form of a main motion, also referred to as a "question" or "proposition." Presenting a motion requires the following steps:

1. A member rises and addresses the presiding officer.
2. The member is recognized by the presiding officer.
3. The member proposes his motion.
4. Another member seconds the motion.
5. The presiding officer states the motion to the assembly.

Addressing the Presiding Officer

Any member has the right to present a motion. To do this, he rises and addresses the presiding officer by his official title, for example, "Mr. President," "Madam Chairman," or "Mr. Moderator." If the member does not know the official title of the presiding officer, it is always correct to address him as "Mr. Chairman" or, if a woman, as "Madam Chairman." Addressing the presiding officer indicates that the member wishes to *obtain the floor*, that is, to have the right to present a motion or to speak. After addressing the presiding officer, the member waits for recognition.

Recognition by the Presiding Officer

The presiding officer recognizes a member by calling the member's name, as "Mr. Andrews." If the presiding officer does not know the member's name, he may say, "Mr. Member," or "the delegate at the microphone in the center aisle," or nod to him, or designate him in some other way. In large organizations and in conventions, the member, when he is recognized, usually states his name and the organization, district, or nation he represents.

Having received formal recognition from the presiding officer, a member is said to *have the floor*, that is, he is entitled to present a motion or to speak. Other members who were also seeking recognition should be seated as soon as one member is recognized.

Proposal of a Motion by a Member

A motion must be stated in the form "I move that ...," which means "I propose that ...," followed by a statement of the proposal which the member wishes to bring before the assembly, for example: "I move that this organization purchase a site for a new headquarters building."

The enacting clause "I move ..." is the only correct wording for introducing a motion. It gives notice to the presiding officer and to the assembly that the speaker is submitting a proposal for decision. Awkward forms such as "I move you" or "I so move" are incorrect. Statements beginning "I propose" or "I suggest" should not be recognized as motions. The presiding officer should inquire of the member making such a statement, "Do you wish to state your proposal as a motion?" Aside from an occasional brief explanatory remark, no discussion is permissible until the presiding officer states the motion to the assembly.

PRESENTATION OF MOTIONS

The proposer of a lengthy, complicated, or important motion should prepare written copies of it and give them to the presiding officer and to the secretary.[1] The presiding officer may request the maker of such a motion to submit it in writing.

Seconding a Motion

After a member has stated his motion, he sits down. Another member may, without waiting for recognition, say, "I second the motion" or "Second the motion." In a large assembly or convention that records the names of seconders, the seconder rises and, after being recognized but before seconding the motion, states his name and the district or organization he represents. Seconding a motion indicates that the member wishes the motion to be considered by the assembly, but it is not necessarily an endorsement of the motion.

If, after stating a motion, the presiding officer does not hear a second, he inquires: "Is there a second to this motion?" A motion sometimes fails to receive a second because the meaning of the motion is not clear to the members. In such a case, the presiding officer should restate the motion more clearly and ask again if there is a second. If there is no response, after waiting a moment he may declare: "The motion is lost for want of a second," and proceed to other business.

Routine motions, such as approving the minutes, are frequently put to vote without waiting for a second. If any member objects to the lack of a second, the presiding officer must call for one.

Statement of a Motion by the Presiding Officer

When a motion has been properly moved and seconded, the presiding officer states it to the assembly. It is the duty of the presiding officer to state every motion as correctly and clearly as possible even though he may have to change the wording of the motion. He cannot change the meaning of any motion in any particular, however, without the consent of its proposer. If the presiding officer makes an error in stating a motion, or if there is a difference of opinion as to the exact wording of a motion, the motion as stated by the member is the legal motion.[2]

The presiding officer states the motion as follows: "It has been moved and seconded that this organization establish a summer camp for its members and their families" or "It has been moved and seconded that the following resolution be adopted: '*Resolved*, That this congregation commend the courageous action of our minister at the International Religious Council.'"

As soon as a motion has been stated to the assembly by the presiding officer, it is open for discussion if it is debatable. From the time a motion is stated by the presiding officer until it is disposed of, it is called a "pending question" or "pending motion."

Example of the Presentation of a Motion

MR. A (*rising and addressing the presiding officer*): "Mr. Chairman."

PRESIDING OFFICER: "Mr. A."

MR. A: "I move that this organization undertake a campaign to raise funds for the purchase of the property to the north of our clubhouse."

MR. B (*without rising*): "I second the motion."

PRESIDING OFFICER: "It has been moved and seconded that this organization undertake a campaign to raise funds for the purchase of the Beekman property. Is there any discussion? . . .

"Those in favor of the motion that this organization undertake a campaign to raise funds for the purchase of the

Beekman property say 'Aye.' ... Those opposed, 'No.' ... The motion is carried."

Chapter 4

CLASSIFICATION OF MOTIONS

Classes of Motions

Motions are classified, according to their purposes and characteristics, into four groups:
>Main motions
>Subsidiary motions
>Privileged motions
>Incidental motions

Main Motions

Main motions are the most important and most frequently used. The main motion is the foundation of the conduct of business. Its purpose is to bring substantive proposals before the assembly for consideration and action. After it is stated by the presiding officer, the main motion becomes the subject for deliberation and decision.

There are three main motions that have specific names and are governed by somewhat different rules. They are referred to as "*specific* main motions" to distinguish them from *the* main motion.

The most frequently used specific main motions are:
>Reconsider
>Rescind
>Resume consideration (take from the table)

Subsidiary Motions

Subsidiary motions are alternative aids for changing, considering, and disposing of the main motion. Consequently, they are subsidiary to it. Subsidiary motions are usually applied to the main motion but some of them may be applied to certain other motions.

The most frequently used subsidiary motions are:
>Postpone temporarily (lay on the table)
>Vote immediately (previous question)
>Limit debate
>Postpone definitely
>Refer to a committee
>Amend
>Postpone indefinitely

Privileged Motions

Privileged motions have no direct connection with the main motion before the assembly. They are emergency motions of such urgency that they are entitled to immediate consideration. They relate to the members and to the organization rather than to particular items of business. Privileged motions would be main motions but for their urgency. Because of their urgency, they are given the privilege of being considered ahead of other motions that are before the assembly.

The privileged motions are:
>Adjourn
>Recess
>Question of privilege

Incidental Motions

Incidental motions arise only incidentally out of the business before the assembly. They do not relate directly to the main motion but usually relate to matters that are incidental to the conduct of the meeting. Incidental motions may be offered at any time when they are needed. They have no order of precedence and it is only necessary that they be disposed of as soon as they arise and prior to the business out of which they arise.

Appeal, suspend rules, and object to consideration are motions and are therefore decided by vote of the assembly. Point of order, parliamentary inquiry, withdraw a motion, division of a question, and division of the assembly technically are classified as motions. Actually they are requests directed to the presiding officer and decided by him. Two of these requests, withdraw a motion and division of a question, if not granted by the presiding officer, may be presented as motions for decision by vote of the assembly. The most frequently used incidental motions are:

> Appeal
> Suspend rules
> Object to consideration
> Point of order
> Parliamentary inquiry
> Withdraw a motion
> Division of a question
> Division of the assembly

Classification of Unlisted Motions

The motions within each class—main, subsidiary, privileged, and incidental—differ somewhat but have similar purposes and characteristics. Only the more commonly used motions in each class are listed in charts and classifications. There are many other motions that may be proposed, and the presiding officer must know how to classify them in order to determine whether they are in order and what rules govern them. Therefore, it is essential to understand the purposes and characteristics of each class in order to classify the less used motions.

For example, while a main motion is being considered, a member might move "that the vote on the motion be taken by roll call." This might appear to be a main motion. It is, however, an incidental motion because it arises incidentally out of the business before the assembly. It would therefore be in order and would be decided immediately. Or a member might move "that the article in tonight's *Tribune* explaining the reason for the tax raise we are considering be procured and read to the assembly." This would be a privileged motion because of its urgency and would be considered immediately. Unless a presiding officer understands the classification of motions, he might mistakenly think that the examples just cited are main motions and rule them out of order on the ground that another main motion is pending.

The name given a motion by its proposer is not the determining factor in classifying the motion, because the proposer sometimes names his motion incorrectly. For example, someone might move "to postpone the motion temporarily until ten o'clock." This is a motion to *postpone definitely,* not to *postpone temporarily,* since a time is specified.

Changes in Classification of Motions

A motion that usually is listed in one classification may belong in another if it is proposed in a different situation. The classification of a motion usually is based on the relationship of that motion to the main motion. The main motion is the foundation motion that determines the classification of other motions.

Usually a main motion is already pending when a subsidiary, privileged, or incidental motion is proposed. But certain of the subsidiary, privileged, or incidental motions may be proposed when no main motion is pending. In this situation they are classified as main motions.

CLASSIFICATION OF MOTIONS

The following subsidiary, privileged, and incidental motions (with an example of a possible form in which each might be proposed), may be proposed as main motions when no main motion is pending:

Subsidiary motions

Limit Debate. "I move that debate on the proposed assessment, scheduled to come up at three o'clock this afternoon, be limited to one hour."

Postpone Definitely. "I move that all the reports of special committees be postponed until Friday evening."

Refer to Committee. "I move that we create a committee on insurance and refer to it the investigation of additional benefits."

Amend (if applied to an action already taken). "I move to amend the motion passed on January 3 'that the president appoint three members to act as a committee to arrange a seminar on foreign relations' by adding the words 'and that the membership elect two additional members.'"

Privileged motions

Adjourn. "I move we adjourn," or "I move we adjourn this evening promptly at nine o'clock so that we may attend the hearings of the reference committees."

Recess. "I move that we recess for five minutes," or "I move that we recess for lunch as soon as the finance report is presented."

Question of Privilege (presented as a motion). "I move that the author of the Survey on Fire Protection be asked to come this afternoon to answer questions on his report."

Incidental motions

Appeal. PRESIDING OFFICER: "Your request to make a brief presentation of your idea for increasing the membership is

THE CHIEF PURPOSES OF MOTIONS

PURPOSE	MOTION
Present an idea for consideration and action	Main motion Resolution Consider subject informally
Improve a pending motion	Amend Division of question
Regulate or cut off debate	Limit or extend debate Vote immediately
Delay a decision	Refer to committee Postpone definitely Postpone temporarily Recess
Suppress a proposal	Object to consideration Postpone indefinitely Withdraw a motion
Meet an emergency	Question of privilege Suspend rules
Gain information on a pending motion	Parliamentary inquiry Request for information Request to ask member a question Question of privilege
Question the decision of the presiding officer	Point of order Appeal from decision of chair
Enforce rights and privileges	Division of assembly Division of question Parliamentary inquiry Point of order Appeal from decision of chair

Consider a question again	Resume consideration
	Reconsider
	Rescind
	Renew a motion
Change an action already taken	Reconsider
	Rescind
	Amend by new motion
Terminate a meeting	Adjourn
	Recess

out of order since no motion is pending." MEMBER: "I appeal from the decision of the chair."

Suspend Rules. "I move that we suspend the rules prohibiting speeches by guests during business meetings so that when we meet tonight the mayor may speak on the plan for garbage disposal."

Chapter 5

PRECEDENCE OF MOTIONS

Order of Precedence

Precedence means the priority or order in which motions must be proposed, considered, and disposed of. The purpose of assigning a rank or order to each commonly used motion is to enable an assembly to propose, consider, and decide each motion without confusion. The order of precedence is:

Privileged Motions
1. Adjourn
2. Recess
3. Question of privilege

Subsidiary Motions
    4. Postpone temporarily
    5. Vote immediately
    6. Limit debate
    7. Postpone definitely
    8. Refer to committee
    9. Amend
   10. Postpone indefinitely

Main Motions
   11. The main motion and specific main motions

Incidental motions have no order of precedence. Since they arise incidentally out of the immediately pending business at any time and must be decided as soon as they arise, they present no problem of precedence.

Basic Rules of Precedence

There are two basic rules of precedence:

1. When a particular motion is being considered, any motion of higher precedence may be proposed, but no motion of lower precedence may be proposed. For example, when a main motion (11) is pending, a member may move to refer the motion to a committee (8). Another member may move to recess (2). There will then be three motions pending at the same time. Since the proper order of precedence was followed, there will be no confusion either in proposing these motions or in considering and disposing of them.

2. Motions are considered and voted on in reverse order to their proposal. The motion last proposed is considered and disposed of first. For example, if motions (11), (8) and (2) are proposed in that order and are pending, they are considered and decided in the reverse order, which is (2), (8) and (11).

Example of Precedence

Suppose that a member proposes a main motion (11) "that all members of the Chamber of Commerce be assessed five dollars for the Christmas Fund." While this motion is pending, another member moves to amend it by striking out the word "five" and inserting the word "ten" (9). While this amendment is being discussed, someone moves to "refer the main motion to a committee" (8). While reference to a committee is being considered, a member moves to postpone definitely the original motion to the next meeting (7).

Then another member moves to postpone the question indefinitely (10). Immediately, a member rises to a point of order (incidental motion) and calls attention to the fact that the motion "to postpone indefinitely" (10) is out of order because it is of lower precedence than the immediately pending question (7). The presiding officer rules the member's point "well taken" and declares the motion to postpone indefinitely out of order. He then states that the immediately pending question is the motion to postpone to the next meeting. A member then moves "to take a recess" (2).

All these motions, except the one ruled out of order, have followed correct precedence and are therefore in order. The following five motions are pending:

Motions Pending	*Order of Precedence*
Recess	2
Postpone definitely	7
Refer to a committee	8
Amend	9
The main motion	11

The presiding officer first takes a vote on the motion to recess. If it loses, he calls for restricted discussion on the motion to postpone definitely to the next meeting. If the motion to postpone definitely loses, he states the motion to refer the main motion to a committee and calls for restricted discussion on it. If the motion to refer loses, the presiding officer calls for discussion on the amendment. When the amendment has been voted on, he calls for discussion on the main motion.

While the assembly is considering one of the five motions in this chain of precedence, a member may present another motion, provided it has a higher precedence than the motion that is being considered. For example, while the motion to postpone definitely to the next meeting (7) is pending, a member may move to adjourn (7), because adjourn has higher rank.

Such complicated problems of precedence occur only rarely. However, quite frequently several motions are awaiting decision by the assembly. All motions that have been proposed and stated to the assembly but are not yet decided are called *pending questions* or *pending motions*.

The particular motion being considered by the assembly at any particular time is called the *immediately pending motion* (or *question*).

Chapter 6

RULES GOVERNING MOTIONS

The Basic Rules of Motions

Rules governing motions are definite and logical. If you understand the purpose of a motion, you can usually reason out the rules governing it.

The rules or facts that you need to know about each motion are:

RULES GOVERNING MOTIONS

1. What is the precedence of the motion?
2. Can the motion interrupt a speaker?
3. Does the motion require a second?
4. Is the motion debatable?
5. Can the motion be amended?
6. What vote does the motion require?
7. To what other motions can the motion apply?
8. What other motions can be applied to the motion?

What Is the Precedence of the Motion?

To avoid confusion, each motion is assigned a definite rank. This rank is based on the urgency of each motion. Motions are listed in the order of their precedence on pp. 30–31. When a motion is before the assembly, any motion is in order if it has a higher precedence or rank than the immediately pending motion, but no motion having a lower precedence is in order. Motions are considered and decided in reverse order to that of their proposal.

Can the Motion Interrupt?

Two types of motions, because of their urgency, can interrupt a speaker. The first are those motions that must be proposed and decided within a specific time limit: reconsider, object to consideration, appeal, and division of the assembly. Reconsider must be made during the same meeting or convention at which the vote to be reconsidered was taken. Object to consideration must be made before there has been progress in considering the main motion and before any other motion has been applied to it. An appeal and a call for division of the assembly must be made before other business intervenes.

The second are those motions that relate to the immediate rights and privileges of a member or of the assembly: question of privilege, point of order, and parliamentary inquiry. A question of privilege involving the immediate convenience, comfort, or rights of the organization or of its members is frequently so urgent that it justifies interrupting a speaker. A point of order involving a mistake, error, or failure to comply with the rules can interrupt a speaker if it relates to the speaker, to his speech, or to some error that cannot await the completion of the speech for its determination. To justify interrupting a speaker a parliamentary inquiry must relate to the speaker, his speech, or some other matter that cannot be delayed until the completion of the speech.

Does the Motion Require a Second?

All motions require seconds except in meetings of committees, boards, or governmental bodies. To justify the consideration of the assembly, a proposal should have the support of at least two members: one who makes the motion and another, the seconder, who indicates his desire to have the proposal considered.

A few motions do not require seconds because, although technically classified as motions, actually they are requests that are decided by the presiding officer. These are: point of order, parliamentary inquiry, withdraw a motion, division of a question, division of the assembly, and question of privilege. Questions of privilege and withdraw a motion are sometimes presented as motions instead of requests, in which case they require seconds.

Is the Motion Debatable?

Some motions are open to full debate, others to restricted debate, and some are undebatable. The only motions that are *fully debatable* are: main motions (including reconsider and rescind), amendments to fully debatable motions, postpone indefinitely, and appeal.

Main motions are debatable because they present substantive propositions requiring the consideration and decision of the organization. Amendments to debatable motions actually involve a part of the motion itself. The motion to postpone indefinitely is equivalent to a motion to reject the main motion.[1] An appeal from a decision of the chair is debatable because the presiding officer should give the reasons for his decision and the member appealing should present his reasons for the appeal. The motions to reconsider and rescind are debatable because they are main motions that also reopen the main motion to debate.

Four motions are open to *restricted debate:* recess, postpone definitely, refer to a committee and limit debate. Restricted debate means brief discussion confined to a few specific points. Debate on recess is restricted to brief discussion of the advisability and time of the recess. Debate on postpone definitely is restricted to the advisability of postponing and the time of postponement. Debate on the motion to refer a motion to a committee is restricted to the advisability of referral, the selection, membership, and duties of the committee, or instructions to it. Debate on limited debate is restricted to the type and time of limitations. None of the motions subject to restricted debate opens the main question to debate.

All other motions are *undebatable* because they deal with simple procedural questions which should not need discussion.

Can the Motion Be Amended?

A simple test determines whether a motion can be amended. If it can be stated in different words, it can be amended.

The motion "I move we recess for ten minutes" could as well be stated "I move we recess for fifteen minutes." Motions that can be varied in wording are necessarily amendable so that they can be changed to express the will of the majority.

On the other hand, a motion that cannot be stated in different words cannot be amended. The motion to postpone indefinitely, for example, can be stated in only one way and therefore cannot be amended.

Some motions can be amended freely, some can be amended with restrictions, and some cannot be amended. The only motions that can be amended freely are main motions and amendments. Four motions can be amended only within restrictions. Recess, limit debate, and postpone definitely can be amended only as to time. Refer to a committee can be amended only as to details such as the selection, membership, duties, or instructions to the committee. No other motions can be amended.

What Vote Does the Motion Require?

Basically, all motions require a majority vote. Four motions modify the right of members to propose, discuss, and decide proposals and therefore require a two-thirds vote. These motions are: vote immediately, limit debate, suspend rules, and object to consideration.

To What Other Motions Can the Motion Apply?

A motion is said to apply to another motion when it is used to alter or dispose of or affect the original motion in some way. For example, if a main motion is being considered, and a member moves "to postpone definitely the consideration of the motion until Friday at three o'clock," the motion to postpone definitely "applies to" the main motion.

Specific main motions apply only to the main motion. Subsidiary motions apply to main motions. The motions to vote immediately and to limit debate apply to all debatable motions. The motion to amend applies to any motion that may be stated in different words. Privileged motions relate to the organization and its members rather than to particular items of business and therefore do not apply to any other motion. Incidental motions do not apply to other motions, except that the motion to withdraw applies to any motion, and objection to consideration and division of a question apply to main motions.

What Other Motions Can Be Applied to the Motion?

When a motion is being considered, it is important to know what other motions can be applied to it.

1. Every motion can have the motion to withdraw applied to it.
2. All debatable motions can have the motions to vote immediately and limit debate applied to them.
3. All motions that may be worded in more than one way can have the motion to amend applied to them.
4. The main motion can have all the subsidiary and specific main motions applied to it, and also object to consideration. Specific main motions can have no other motions applied to them except that reconsider and rescind may have vote immediately and limit debate applied to them.
5. Privileged and incidental motions can have no other motion applied to them, except that recess may be amended, and an appeal may have vote immediately and limit debate applied to it.

In addition to the eight questions about each motion that have been summarized in this chapter and in the chart on pp. 30–31, there are two procedural questions that should be understood: "When can a motion be renewed?" and "What procedures apply to main motions already voted on?"

PRINCIPAL RULES

Order of precedence	Can interrupt?	Requires second?	Debatable?	Amendable?
PRIVILEGED MOTIONS				
1. Adjourn	no	yes	no	no
2. Recess	no	yes	yes [r]	yes [r]
3. Question of privilege	yes	no	no	no
SUBSIDIARY MOTIONS				
4. Postpone temporarily	no	yes	no	no
5. Vote immediately	no	yes	no	no
6. Limit debate	no	yes	yes [r]	yes [r]
7. Postpone definitely	no	yes	yes [r]	yes [r]
8. Refer to committee	no	yes	yes [r]	yes [r]
9. Amend	no	yes	yes	yes
10. Postpone indefinitely	no	yes	yes	no
MAIN MOTIONS				
11. a The main motion	no	yes	yes	yes
b Specific main motions				
Reconsider	yes	yes	yes	no
Rescind	no	yes	yes	no
Resume consideration	no	yes	no	no

No order of precedence	Can interrupt?	Requires second?	Debatable?	Amendable?
INCIDENTAL MOTIONS				
a Motions				
Appeal	yes	yes	yes	no
Suspend rules	no	yes	no	no
Object to consideration	yes	yes	no	no
b Requests				
Point of order	yes	no	no	no
Parliamentary inquiry	yes	no	no	no
Withdraw a motion	yes	no	no	no
Division of question	no	no	no	no
Division of assembly	yes	no	no	no

GOVERNING MOTIONS

Vote required?	Applies to what other motions?	Can have what other motions applied to it (in addition to withdraw)?
majority	none	none
majority	none	amend [r]
none	none	none
majority	main motion	none
⅔	debatable motions	none
⅔	debatable motions	amend [r]
majority	main motion	amend [r], vote imm., limit debate
majority	main motion	amend [r], vote imm., limit debate
majority	rewordable motions	vote imm., limit debate
majority	main motion	vote imm., limit debate
majority	none	specific main, subsid., obj. to cons.
majority	main motion	vote imm., limit debate
majority	main motion	vote imm., limit debate
majority	main motion	none

Vote required?	Applies to what other motions?	Can have what other motions applied to it (in addition to withdraw)?
majority	decision of chair	vote imm., limit debate
⅔	none	none
⅔ neg.	main motion	none
none	any error	none
none	none	none
none	all motions	none
none	main motion	none
none	indecisive vote	none

r = restricted

When Can a Motion Be Renewed or Substituted?

When a motion has been voted on and lost, the same, or substantially the same, motion cannot be proposed again at the same meeting or convention except under one condition.

Parliamentary law recognizes the right of members or assemblies to change their minds because of additional information, a change in the situation, or for any other reason. The presiding officer may permit a defeated main motion to be renewed at the same meeting or convention when, in his judgment, a new vote on the defeated motion might result differently. At a later meeting or convention, a defeated main motion may always be offered again.[2]

If a main motion has been defeated by an objection to its consideration or by indefinite postponement, it may be renewed under this same condition. All motions that are procedural rather than substantive may be renewed at the same meeting or convention unless they are proposed for obviously dilatory purposes.

One motion cannot be substituted for another kind of motion. For example, the motion to refer to a committee cannot be proposed as a substitute for the motion to postpone temporarily; nor can the motion to rescind be proposed as a substitute for the motion to reconsider, nor vice versa. Each is a different motion with a different purpose and each is subject to different rules.

Changing Main Motions Already Voted On

When an assembly decides a main motion by taking a vote on it, this decision is usually final. However, an assembly,

RULES GOVERNING MOTIONS

just as an individual, has a right to change its mind. Hence, there are motions and actions that may be used to affect a main motion that has already been voted on. The *motions* are reconsider, rescind, and amend by a new main motion. The *actions* are renewal of a motion and repeal by implication.

The motion to reconsider the vote on a main motion that was *either carried or lost* can be proposed during the same meeting or convention at which the main motion was voted on. Action to renew a main motion that was *lost* cannot be taken at the same meeting or convention but may be taken at a later meeting or convention. The motion to rescind and amend by a new main motion and the action of repeal by implication apply only to motions that have been *carried*. These three procedures just mentioned have no time limit and may be used at the same meeting or convention at which the main motion was decided, or at any future meeting or convention.

Repeal by implication automatically results from the adoption of a motion that conflicts in whole or in part with another motion or motions previously adopted. The first motion is repealed only to the extent that its provisions cannot be reconciled with those of the new motion.

Members may be unaware of related motions previously adopted or may have overlooked them. Before a member proposes a new motion, it is good procedure to search the records for adopted motions with which the new motion might conflict. Such motions should be repealed when a new motion is adopted. Repeal by implication is intended to correct inadvertent conflicts and not to be a blanket method for disposing of previously adopted motions without voting directly on their repeal.

Repeal by implication applies to any previously adopted motion, rule, or bylaw that is in conflict with a newly adopted motion, rule, or bylaw. If the new motion conflicts with a provision in a source of higher authority, for example a charter, it is out of order.

CHANGING MAIN MOTIONS ALREADY VOTED ON

	MAY BE USED:	APPLIES TO:
Motion to reconsider	Only at same meeting or convention	Any main motion carried or lost
Motion to rescind	At any meeting or convention	Any main motion carried
Amend by new main motion	At any meeting or convention	Any main motion carried
Renew by new main motion	At any meeting or convention	Any main motion lost
Repeal or amend by implication	At any meeting or convention	Any main motion previously carried which conflicts with later main motion

Chapter 7

MAIN MOTIONS

THE MAIN MOTION

Purpose

To bring a proposal before an assembly for discussion and decision.

Form

PROPOSER: "I move that we undertake a drive for new members."

or

"I move the adoption of the following resolution:
Whereas
the New Jersey Chamber of Commerce is rapidly outgrowing its present quarters, and
Whereas
the rental cost for suitable quarters is high and available buildings are inconveniently located, therefore, be it
Resolved
that we build our own state headquarters and appropriate $165,000 from our reserve fund to start a building fund for this purpose."

or

"I move that we hold our Annual Aviation Show on Friday, November 10."

PRESIDING OFFICER (*after hearing a second*): "It has been moved and seconded that we hold our Annual Aviation Show on Friday, November 10. Is there any discussion?"

The Main Motion Defined

The main motion is the presentation by a member to an assembly of any proposal that he wishes the group to consider and decide.[1] It is the basic motion for the transaction of business. Since only one subject can be considered at one time, the main motion can be proposed only when no other motion is before the assembly.

Phrasing the Main Motion

Since the main motion is a proposal of any action that a member wishes to recommend to the assembly, it is broad in scope and varies greatly in wording. It must be introduced by the words "I move." Otherwise, wide latitude in wording is permitted.

A motion should be concise and clear. If a member presents a motion that is confusing, unnecessarily long, or involved, the presiding officer should request the proposer to rephrase his motion and, if necessary, help him in doing so. The presiding officer can rephrase the motion only in wording that is approved by its proposer.

The proposer of the main motion may rephrase or withdraw his motion at any time before it is stated by the presiding officer to the assembly for consideration.

The main motion should be stated in the affirmative, since the negative form often confuses members in voting. If a motion is presented in the negative, the presiding officer may request the proposer to rephrase his motion, or he may himself rephrase it with the consent of the proposer. For example, the motion "I move that we do not permit any member to remain on the Survey Committee who has not been present at three consecutive meetings and has not been excused" is more clearly stated affirmatively as "I move that any member of the Survey Committee who is absent, without being excused, from three consecutive meetings be dropped from the committee."

The Main Motion in Resolution Form

Main motions that express sentiments or are a formal statement of the opinions of the assembly are sometimes stated in the form of resolutions. This form is also used when the proposal is highly important, or is long and involved. A resolution should be in writing and is usually introduced in such a form as:

"I move the adoption of the following resolution: 'Resolved, That this organization express its appreciation of the excellent service rendered by our retiring President during the past two years and, be it further

'Resolved, That we endorse him as a candidate for the National Executive Committee.'"

Often a resolution is prefaced by statements, each introduced by the word *whereas*, that state the reasons for the resolution. The statements contained in the whereases are of no legal effect and sometimes are the cause of disagreement. Members frequently attempt to debate and amend these prefacing statements, often to the neglect of the main resolution. The whereases are useful mainly when the organization plans to publish the resoultion and wishes the reasons for its adoption to be read with it.

Discussion on the Main Motion

As soon as the main motion has been formally stated to the assembly by the presiding officer, it is open for debate. It cannot be debated before this formal statement unless a motion has been passed to discuss it informally. (See *Informal Discussion,* p. 128.) Discussion on the main motion must conform to the rules governing debate.

Disposition of the Main Motion

Whenever the main motion has been stated to an assembly by the presiding officer, some action must be taken on it and recorded in the minutes. The main motion may be decided by a vote approving or defeating it, or it may be disposed of by some other motion such as refer to a committee. No main motion can be simply ignored; definite action must be taken on it.

No main motion can be substituted for another main motion except that a new motion on the same subject may be offered as a substitute amendment to the main motion. (See *Substitution of New Motion,* p. 54.) When a main motion has been acted on and lost, it cannot be renewed in the same or substantially the same words at the same meeting or convention but it may be reconsidered at the same meeting or convention or presented as a new motion at any later meeting or convention.

Effect of the Main Motion

To commit the organization to the proposal stated by the motion and approved by vote of the assembly.

Rules Governing the Main Motion

1. Cannot interrupt a speaker
2. Requires a second
3. Is debatable because it presents a substantive proposal for consideration
4. Can be amended

5. Requires a majority vote
6. Takes precedence over no other motions
7. Applies to no other motion
8. Can have applied to it all subsidiary motions, specific main motions, object to consideration, and withdraw

MOTION TO RECONSIDER

Purpose

To enable an assembly to set aside a vote on a main motion taken at the same meeting or convention and to consider the motion again as though no vote had been taken on it.

Form

PROPOSER: "I move to reconsider the vote by which the motion to enlarge our library was passed earlier this evening."

PRESIDING OFFICER (*after hearing a second*): "It has been moved and seconded to reconsider the vote by which the motion to enlarge our library was passed earlier this evening. Will the secretary please read this motion? ... Is there any discussion on the motion to reconsider this vote? ... Those in favor of reconsidering the vote say 'Aye.' ... Those opposed, 'No.' ... The motion to reconsider is carried. The motion to enlarge our library, as read by the secretary, is again open for discussion."

What Votes Can Be Reconsidered?

Main motions are occasionally approved or disapproved under a misapprehension or without adequate information, and sometimes later events cause an assembly to change its mind.

The vote on any main motion, whether carried or lost, can be reconsidered at the same meeting or convention, except when something that cannot be undone has been done as a result of the vote;[2] for example, when an affirmative vote has resulted in a contract, money has been paid, or when a time limit has passed.[3]

The motion to reconsider can be applied only to the main motion. The same result is accomplished for all other motions by more simple and direct means. Other motions that have *lost* can be proposed again or renewed as soon as, in the judgment of the presiding officer, the vote might result differently. (See *When Can a Motion Be Renewed?*, p. 32.) Other motions that have *carried* can be changed easily by procedural motions. For example, if a motion has been referred to a committee, it can be recalled; and if it has been postponed temporarily (laid on the table), it can be brought up again by a motion to resume consideration of it.

Proposal of the Motion to Reconsider

The motion to reconsider is a specific main motion and can be offered at any time during a meeting. It is unusual in that it may be proposed even though other business is under consideration, and, if necessary, it may interrupt a speaker. Proposal of the motion to reconsider suspends any action provided for in the motion that is proposed for reconsideration until the motion to reconsider is decided. When a motion to reconsider is proposed and seconded while other business is pending, the presiding officer directs the secretary to record its proposal; but the motion to reconsider is not considered until the pending business has been disposed of. It is then considered and decided immediately. If the motion to reconsider is offered when no other business is pending, it is considered immediately.

Who Can Move to Reconsider?

Luther Cushing, eminent lawyer and parliamentarian, pointed out in his manual of 1844 that the common law of parliamentary procedure provides that the motion to reconsider, just as any other motion, can be proposed by anyone.

Some authors later tried to establish the rule that only a member who had voted on the prevailing side could move to reconsider a vote. The purpose of this limitation, however, was defeated because under such a rule:

1. Any member could vote on the prevailing side, and alert members did, for the sole purpose of being eligible to move to reconsider.
2. If a member did not vote on the prevailing side, he could make himself eligible to move to reconsider by changing his vote at any time before the final announcement of the vote.
3. Except in votes by roll call, it was impossible to determine accurately how anyone had voted.
4. In a ballot vote, no one could be asked how he voted since the inquiry would violate the fundamental principle of the secret ballot.

All of these maneuverings have been set aside by court decisions that any member has the right to propose any motion, regardless of how he voted previously, unless the organization adopts a rule limiting this right. To deny any member the right to propose any motion because of his previous vote is discriminatory. The law validates Cushing's statement that "a motion to reconsider may be made at any time or by any member, precisely like any other motion." [4]

The motion to reconsider and have entered on the minutes was a device by which two members, one to make the motion and the other to second it, could tie up any motion that had already been approved, despite its urgency, until the next meeting, even though it be months away. It is not and never was a rule of parliamentary law. It exists only if the bylaws contain a specific provision that creates a motion to reconsider and have it entered on the minutes.

Debate on the Motion to Reconsider

The motion to reconsider is debatable and also opens the main motion to discussion. Even though a member has exhausted his right to debate the question to be reconsidered, he may debate it again under the motion to reconsider.

Since the proposal of the motion to reconsider suspends action on a motion that has already been voted on, the motion to reconsider should be decided immediately and cannot be postponed to a later time as older practice sometimes permitted.

Effect of the Motion to Reconsider

To cancel or wipe out a vote on a motion as completely as though it had never been taken [5] and to bring that motion before the assembly for consideration as though it had never been voted on.

Rules Governing the Motion to Reconsider

1. Can interrupt proceedings
2. Requires a second
3. Is debatable and opens the main motion to debate
4. Cannot be amended
5. Requires a majority vote
6. Takes precedence over no other motions
7. Applies to votes on main motions taken at same meeting
8. Can have applied to it vote immediately, limit debate, and withdraw

MOTION TO RESCIND

Purpose

To repeal (cancel, nullify, void) a main motion previously passed.

Form

PROPOSER: "I move to rescind the motion passed at the meeting on June 1 opposing new school bonds."

PRESIDING OFFICER (*after hearing a second*): "It has been moved and seconded to rescind the motion passed June 1 opposing new school bonds. The secretary will please read the motion referred to.... Is there any discussion?... Those in favor of rescinding the motion read by the secretary say 'Aye.'... Those opposed, 'No.'... The motion to rescind is carried. The motion that this organization go on record as opposed to the issuance of new school bonds is rescinded."

What Motions May Be Rescinded?

Any main motion that was passed, no matter how long before, may be rescinded unless as a result of the vote something has been done that the assembly cannot undo.[6]

The motion to rescind, if passed, affects the present and future only, since it is not retroactive. For example, if a motion to fine tardy members were rescinded, no more fines would be imposed; but fines already collected would be retained and fines imposed before the motion was rescinded would still be collectible.

Vote Required to Rescind

A motion to rescind requires a majority vote.[7] However, a motion that required more than a majority vote to pass can be rescinded only by the same vote that was required to approve it.[8] Similarly, if notice to members was required for the consideration of a motion, the same notice is required for the consideration of a motion to rescind that motion.

Rescind and Expunge

The motion to expunge is occasionally combined with the motion to rescind, as, for example "I move to rescind the motion passed January 5 relating to . . . and to expunge this motion from the minutes."

When a motion is expunged, the secretary does not erase the motion from the minutes, but draws a line around it, and marks it "expunged by order of this assembly," gives the date of the expunging, and signs the notation. The expunged motion is not included in any minutes published thereafter. This motion is used only rarely, when the assembly desires to remove the motion from its public record. The motion to expunge requires a majority vote, whether used alone or combined with the motion to rescind.

Effect of the Motion to Rescind

To repeal, cancel, nullify, or void the motion from the date of the adoption of the motion to rescind.

Rules Governing the Motion to Rescind

1. Cannot interrupt a speaker
2. Requires a second
3. Is debatable and opens to debate the motion it proposes to rescind
4. Cannot be amended
5. Requires a majority vote
6. Takes precedence over no other motions

7. Applies to main motions previously adopted
8. Can have applied to it limit debate, vote immediately, and withdraw

MOTION TO RESUME CONSIDERATION
(Take from the Table)

Purpose

To enable an assembly to take up and consider a motion that was postponed temporarily (laid on the table) during the same meeting or convention.

Form

PROPOSER: "I move to resume consideration of the motion concerning the campaign for new members that was postponed temporarily earlier in this meeting," *or* "I move that the motion to . . . be taken from the table."

PRESIDING OFFICER *(after hearing a second)*: "It has been moved and seconded that we resume consideration of the motion on the proposed campaign for new members. The secretary will please read this motion. . . . Those in favor of resuming consideration of the motion 'that this organization undertake a campaign for three hundred new members' say 'Aye.' . . . Opposed 'No.' . . . The motion to resume consideration is carried, and the motion 'that this organization undertake a campaign for three hundred new members' is now open for discussion."

Limitations on the Motion to Resume Consideration

The motion to resume consideration is a specific main motion that applies only to a main motion that has been postponed temporarily (laid on the table) at the current meeting or convention. Beyond the current meeting or convention, the temporarily postponed motion lapses and can be brought up only as a new main motion.

Precedence over Other Main Motions

The motion to resume consideration of a motion can be proposed only when no other motion is pending. However, it takes precedence over any other new main motion that another member may seek to present at the same time. If a member rises to move that consideration be resumed on a motion that has been postponed temporarily and the presiding officer recognizes someone else, the member should at once state that he has risen to move to resume consideration of a motion. The presiding officer will then give him priority over other members who wish to propose new main motions.

Adhering Motions and Resuming Consideration

If the main motion that was postponed temporarily had subsidiary motions attached to it—for example, a motion to amend—these motions still adhere to it when consideration is resumed and must be disposed of in the usual order. If the motion to limit debate or to vote immediately has been passed before the main motion was postponed temporarily, these motions are still in effect when consideration is resumed.

Effect of the Motion to Resume Consideration

To place the original main motion again before the assembly in the same state as it was when it was postponed temporarily.

Rules Governing the Motion to Resume Consideration

1. Cannot interrupt a speaker
2. Requires a second
3. Is not debatable
4. Cannot be amended
5. Requires a majority vote
6. Takes precedence over other new main motions only
7. Applies to any main motion that has been postponed temporarily
8. Can have applied to it no motion except withdraw

Chapter 8

SUBSIDIARY MOTIONS

MOTION TO POSTPONE INDEFINITELY

Purpose

To prevent discussion, or further discussion, and a vote on the main motion before the assembly; to suppress the motion without letting it come to a direct vote.

Form

PROPOSER: "I move to postpone the main motion indefinitely."

PRESIDING OFFICER (*after hearing a second*): "It has been moved and seconded to postpone the main motion indefinitely. Is there any discussion on indefinite postponement or on the main motion?"

Suppression by Indefinite Postponement

The motion to postpone indefinitely is not a motion to postpone, as its name indicates, but is a motion to suppress or kill the pending main motion. Postponing a motion indefinitely is equivalent to a negative vote on it.[1] At the same meeting or convention a postponed motion can be renewed if, in the judgment of the presiding officer, another vote might result differently. At a later meeting or convention, the motion postponed can come up again as a new main motion.

Opening the Main Motion to Debate

The motion to postpone indefinitely can be proposed at any time when the main motion is under consideration and no motion of higher precedence is pending. It is fully debatable because it makes final disposition of the main motion. It also opens the main question to debate. Members who have exhausted their right to debate on the main motion can speak again on a motion to postpone indefinitely, since technically this motion presents a different question.

Opponents of a main motion sometimes move to postpone it indefinitely in order to learn, without risk of adopting the motion, who favors and who opposes it.

Effect of the Motion to Postpone Indefinitely

To suppress the main motion to which the motion to postpone indefinitely is applied without the risk of adopting the main motion.[2]

Rules Governing the Motion to Postpone Indefinitely

1. Cannot interrupt a speaker
2. Requires a second

MOTION TO POSTPONE INDEFINITELY

3. Is debatable and opens the main motion to debate
4. Cannot be amended
5. Requires a majority vote
6. Takes precedence over the main motion only
7. Applies to main motions only
8. Can have applied to it vote immediately, limit debate, and withdraw

MOTION TO AMEND

Purpose

To modify or change a motion that is being considered by the assembly so that it will express more satisfactorily the will of the members.

Form

Assume that the following motion is under consideration: "I move that this organization send representatives to the Council and to the Planning Commission to present the need for a new park system."

1. Amendment by Addition (Insertion)

PROPOSER: "I move to amend the motion by inserting the word 'three' before the word 'representatives.'"

PRESIDING OFFICER (*after hearing a second*): "It has been moved and seconded to amend the motion by inserting the word 'three' before the word 'representatives.' The motion, *if amended*, would read, 'that this organization send *three* representatives to the Council and to the Planning Commission to present the need for a new park system. Is there any discussion on the amendment? . . . Those in favor of the amendment say 'Aye.' . . . Those opposed, 'No.' . . . The amendment is carried. Is there any discussion on the motion as amended?"

2. Amendment by Deletion (Striking Out)

PROPOSER: "I move to amend the motion by striking out the words 'and to the Planning Commission.' "

PRESIDING OFFICER (*after hearing a second*): "It has been moved and seconded to amend the motion by striking out the words 'and to the Planning Commission.' The motion, *if amended,* would read 'that this organization send representatives to the Council to present the need for a new park system.' "

3. Amendment by Substitution (Striking Out and Inserting)

a. Substituting words

PROPOSER: "I move to amend the motion by striking out the word 'representatives' and inserting in its place the words 'its executive committee.' "

PRESIDING OFFICER (*after hearing a second*): "It has been moved and seconded to amend the motion by striking out the word 'representatives' and inserting in its place the words 'its executive committee.' The motion, *if amended,* would read 'that this organization send its executive committee to the Council and to the Planning Commission to present the need for a new park system.' "

b. Substituting a new motion

PROPOSER: "I move to amend the motion by substituting for it the following motion: 'I move that our organization hold a conference with the City Manager to determine how we may cooperate in securing a new municipal park system.' "

PRESIDING OFFICER (*after hearing a second*): "It has been moved and seconded to amend the motion that this organization send representatives to the Council and the Planning Commission to present 'the need for a new park system' by substituting for it a new motion 'that our organization hold a conference with the City Manager to determine how we may cooperate in securing a new park system.' "

What Motions May Be Amended?

The test that determines whether a motion may be amended is whether it can be stated in different words. A motion that is variable in wording may be amended.

The only motions that may be amended without restriction are the main motion and the motion to amend.

Four motions are open to restricted amendment. The motions to postpone definitely, limit debate, and recess may be amended as to time. The motion to refer to a committee may be amended as to such details as name, number of members, method of selection of the committee, or instructions to it.

Amendments Must Be Germane

The most important principle concerning amendments is that they must be germane, that is, they must be relevant to, and have direct bearing on, the subject of the pending motion that the amendment seeks to change.[3] For example, a motion "that we hold our convention June 4 in Chicago" could be amended by adding the words "and pay the expenses of all delegates," because this amendment relates closely to the principal idea of the motion, which is to hold a convention.

If, however, an amendment is proposed to add the words "and that we raise the salary of the Executive Secretary," the amendment would not be germane to the subject of the motion. The presiding officer should immediately rule this amendment out of order, stating: "The amendment is out of order because it is not germane to the pending motion."

An amendment that would change one type of motion into another type of motion is never in order. For example, if a motion to postpone the pending main motion "until Friday at three o'clock" is before the assembly, and a member moves to amend this motion by striking out the words "until Friday at three o'clock" and inserting in their place the word "indefinitely," the amendment would change the motion to postpone definitely to a motion to postpone indefinitely and is therefore not in order.

Amendments May Be Hostile

An amendment may be hostile. That is, it may be opposed to the actual intent of the original motion. It may even nullify or change completely the effect of the motion. For example, the motion "that we condemn the action of the Committee on Labor in reopening hearings on the Wage Bill" might be amended by striking out the word "condemn" and inserting the word "endorse." Thus, the intent of the original motion would be reversed by a hostile amendment. But this amendment would be germane to the subject of the motion, which is to express the organization's attitude toward the action of the committee and therefore is in order.

An amendment that merely changes an affirmative statement of a motion to a negative statement of the same motion is not in order. For example, a motion "that we employ a caretaker" cannot be amended by inserting the words "do not" before the word "employ." Such an amendment only reverses the order of taking the affirmative and negative vote.

Limitations on Pending Amendments

Amendments are of two ranks. Those applied to the original motion are amendments of the first rank, and they must relate directly to the motion to be amended. Amendments to a pending amendment are amendments of the second rank; they must relate directly to the pending amendment.

Only one amendment of each rank can be pending at one time. When an amendment to a motion is pending, another amendment of the same rank is not in order, but an amendment of the second rank—an amendment to the amendment—is in order.

After an amendment of either rank is adopted or defeated, another amendment of the same rank is in order. Several amendments and amendments to amendments may be offered in succession, provided that only one amendment of each rank is pending at one time.

If the motion "that this organization entertain the veterans of Cleveland Hospital next Friday evening" is pending, and someone moves to amend it by adding the words "at a dinner party at the Wayside Inn," this is an amendment to the motion or an amendment of the first rank. If, during discussion on this amendment, someone proposes that the amendment be amended by adding the words "in a private dining room" after the word "Inn," this is an amendment of the second rank or an amendment to the amendment and is also in order. But if someone proposes an amendment to strike out the words "Cleveland Hospital" and insert the words "the veterans of all hospitals," this is not in order because it is an amendment to the original motion and therefore an amendment of the first rank; since one amendment of the first rank is pending, no other amendment of the same rank is in order until the pending amendment is disposed of.

A proposed amendment to the bylaws or to a motion already adopted is itself a main motion and is subject to amendments of both ranks.

Debate on Amendments

Amendments to debatable motions are debatable. Amendments to undebatable motions are not debatable. When an amendment to a motion is proposed, discussion is limited to that amendment until it is disposed of. When an amendment to the amendment is proposed, discussion is limited to it until it is disposed of.

Reference to the main motion is permissible only for the purpose of explaining the amendment or its effect. When opposing an amendment, it is in order to say that if the amendment is voted down, the speaker will propose another amendment, which he may state briefly.

Amendment by Substitution of a New Motion

When the wording or effect of a motion as proposed is not satisfactory, it is sometimes better, instead of proposing several amendments, to reword the motion and propose it as an amendment by substitution. Such an amendment must be germane to the subject of the original motion,[4] but it may differ completely from the original motion in wording, purpose and effect. The amendment by substitution of a new or reworded motion follows the usual rules governing amendments, and is subject only to an amendment to the substitute amendment. (See *When Can a Motion Be Renewed or Substituted,* p. 32)

Filling Blanks

Motions or resolutions are sometimes proposed with blank spaces for names, dates, or numbers to be filled by allowing members to propose suggestions. When no more suggestions are offered, the presiding officer takes a vote on each in the order of their proposal. Each member can vote for or against each suggestion. The name, date, or number receiving the highest affirmative vote is inserted in the blank. After the blanks have been filled, the motion as a whole is voted on.

Withdrawing and Accepting Amendments

The proposer of a motion or an amendment has the right to modify or withdraw his own motion or amendment at any time before the presiding officer has stated it to the assembly

MOTION TO AMEND

for consideration. As soon as it has been stated to the assembly by the presiding officer, it belongs to the body, and the proposer of the amendment can withdraw or change it only by unanimous consent or by vote of the assembly.

If another member proposes an amendment that the maker of the motion wishes to accept, he may save time by saying, "Mr. Chairman, I accept the amendment." The consent of the seconder is not necessary. The presiding officer then asks if there is objection to this acceptance. If no objection is made, he states that the motion is amended by unanimous consent. If anyone objects, the amendment must be voted on in the usual manner.

Adhering Amendments

When a main motion that has amendments pending is referred to a committee, postponed definitely, or postponed temporarily, all pending amendments adhere to it and go with it. When the main motion again comes before the assembly, the amendments still adhere and are also before the assembly for consideration.

Voting on Amendments

Amendments are voted on in the reverse order of their proposal. An amendment to an amendment is voted on first. The vote is then taken on the amendment to the motion and, finally, on the motion.[5]

If a debatable motion, an amendment to it, and an amendment to the amendment are pending, the procedure for disposing of them is as follows:

1. Discussion is called for on the amendment to the amendment and when discussion is complete or debate is closed, a vote is taken on it.
2. Discussion is called for on the amendment, either as

amended, if the amendment to the amendment carried, or as proposed if it lost. When discussion of the amendment is complete or debate is closed, a vote is taken on it.

3. Discussion is called for on the motion, either as amended, if the amendment carried, or as originally proposed if the amendment lost. When discussion on the motion is complete or debate is closed, a vote is taken on the motion. A vote adopting an amendment to a motion—even an amendment that substitutes an entirely new motion—does not adopt the motion, and a final vote on the adoption of the motion itself is required.

Vote Required on Amendments

An amendment to any pending motion or amendment requires only a majority vote, even though the motion requires a higher vote for adoption.

An amendment to the bylaws requires whatever vote the bylaws provide; but amendments to proposed bylaw amendments, or to a pending revision of the bylaws, require only a majority vote.

Amending Actions Already Taken

If a main motion has been passed previously, it may be amended by a new main motion providing for its change. Since this motion to amend an action previously taken is a main motion, it may have amendments and amendments to the amendments applied to it.

An amendment to bylaws or rules adopted previously is likewise a main motion, but it requires whatever notice or vote is provided for the adoption of bylaws or rules.

Effect of the Motion to Amend

To change the original motion as the amendment provides.

Rules Governing the Motion to Amend

1. Cannot interrupt a speaker
2. Requires a second
3. Is debatable, unless applied to an undebatable motion
4. Can be amended
5. Requires a majority vote, even though the motion to which it applies requires a higher vote
6. Takes precedence over main motions and postpone indefinitely
7. Applies to motions that may be stated in different words: the main motion, amend, refer to committee, postpone definitely, limit debate, and recess
8. Can have applied to it vote immediately, limit debate, and withdraw

MOTION TO REFER TO COMMITTEE

Purpose

To transfer a motion that is pending before the assembly to a committee:

1. To investigate or study the proposal, make recommendations on it, and return it to the assembly,

    or

2. To conserve the time of the assembly by delegating the duty of deciding the proposal, and sometimes of carrying out the decision, to a smaller group,

    or

3. To insure privacy in considering a delicate matter,

or
4. To provide a hearing on the proposal,
or
5. To defer a decision on the proposal until a more favorable time,
or
6. To delay or perhaps defeat the proposal by referring it to a hostile committee.

Form

PROPOSER: "I move to refer the motion to the standing Committee on Education (*or* 'to a special committee of three to be appointed by the president,' *or* 'to a committee consisting of Mr. A, Mrs. B, and Mr. C') with instructions to report at the next regular meeting."

PRESIDING OFFICER (*after hearing a second*): "It has been moved and seconded to refer the motion to the standing Committee on Education with instructions to report on it at the next regular meeting. Is there brief discussion?"

Provisions Included in the Motion to Refer

A member may propose the motion in the simple form, "I move to refer this motion to a committee," or he may include provisions in his motion such as: the type of committee, the number of members and how they are to be selected, its chairman, or instructions to it. If these provisions are not specified in the motion, the presiding officer may put the motion to refer to vote, and if it is adopted he may use his judgment in deciding on the membership of the committee, assigning its work, and giving instructions to it. If he does not wish to take this responsibility, he may request the assembly to determine the detailed provisions either before or after the motion to refer to committee is voted on. These provisions may be included in the motion to refer if the proposer of the motion accepts them. They may also be proposed as amendments to the motion to refer to a committee, or in a motion proposed after the motion to refer has passed.

If the pending motion is concerned with a subject that is within the scope of a particular standing or reference committee, the motion is ordinarily referred to this committee by unanimous consent.

When the assembly has voted that a committee be appointed, without further provisions, the presiding officer may appoint and announce the committee members at once or he may take a reasonable time to consider the appointments and announce them later.

Debate on the motion to refer or on amendments to it is restricted to brief discussion on the advisability of referring or to such details as the selection, membership, or duties of the committee or instructions to it. Similarly, amendment is restricted to these same details.

Instructions to a Committee

Instructions from the assembly or from the presiding officer may be given to a committee as a part of the motion to refer, or by a separate motion, or by oral directions from the presiding officer, or in a memorandum from the secretary. Additional instructions may be given to the committee at any time before its report is submitted. After the report is submitted, the motion or assignment may be re-referred to the committee with or without additional instructions.

An assembly that has referred a motion or a matter to a committee may vote at any time to withdraw it from the committee, refer it to another committee, or decide the question itself.

If no main motion is pending and a member moves to refer a subject, problem, or proposal to a committee, or moves to create a new committee or to give instructions to an existing committee, this motion is a main motion.

Effect of the Motion to Refer

To transfer the referred motion to the designated committee immediately with any pending amendments.

Rules Governing the Motion to Refer

1. Cannot interrupt a speaker
2. Requires a second
3. Debate restricted to brief discussion on the selection, membership, or duties of the committee, or instructions to it
4. Amendments restricted to such details as the selection, membership, or duties of the committee, or instructions to it
5. Requires a majority vote
6. Takes precedence over amend and postpone indefinitely
7. Applies to main motions only
8. Can have applied to it amend, vote immediately, limit debate, and withdraw

MOTION TO POSTPONE DEFINITELY

Purpose

To put off consideration, or further consideration, of a pending main motion and to fix a definite time for its consideration.

Form

PROPOSER: "I move to postpone definitely the motion until later in this meeting when we have finished the reading of the budget."

or

"I move to postpone definitely the motion until the next meeting [or convention]."

or

"I move to postpone definitely the motion and make it a general order for the September meeting."

or

"I move to postpone definitely the motion to the convention next year and make it a special order for two o'clock at the second business meeting."

PRESIDING OFFICER (*after hearing a second*): "It has been moved and seconded that the motion be postponed definitely to the convention next year and made a special order for two o'clock at the second business meeting."

Differences in Motions to Postpone

The motion to postpone definitely is one of three motions to postpone a pending main motion. Each differs in purpose, rules, and effect.

The motion to *postpone temporarily* (lay on the table) defers the pending main motion temporarily but specifies no time for its consideration and is not debatable. Its effect terminates at the end of the current meeting or convention.

The motion to *postpone indefinitely* kills the pending main motion. It is fully debatable and opens the main motion to debate. Its effect terminates at the end of the current meeting or convention.

The motion to postpone *definitely* defers consideration of a pending main motion to a later time but also fixes a definite date for its consideration, and may make it a general or special order for a particular time. Debate on this motion is restricted to brief discussion of the time or reason for postponement.

Limitations on the Motion to Postpone Definitely

A main motion cannot be postponed definitely:
1. To a meeting or convention that is not already scheduled; for example, to a special meeting that has not been called.
2. To any time that would be too late for the proposed motion to be effective, if adopted. For example, a motion "to prepare an exhibit for the Centennial Convention" cannot be postponed definitely to a meeting later than the Convention.

Postponing as a General or Special Order

Any main motion that is postponed definitely to a particular time becomes a *general order* for that time. When that time arrives, the presiding officer states the postponed motion to the assembly for consideration immediately unless another item of business is pending. If another item of business is pending, he states the general order to the assembly as soon as the pending item of business has been disposed of. A majority vote is required to postpone a main motion definitely and set it as a general order for a particular time.

Any main motion that is postponed definitely to a particular time and is set as a *special order* becomes a special order for that time. When that time arrives, the presiding officer states the special order to the assembly for its consideration. If another motion is pending at the specified time, the special

MOTION TO POSTPONE DEFINITELY

order interrupts and is stated immediately to the assembly for its consideration. Because a special order interrupts any pending business it requires a two-thirds vote to postpone a main motion definitely and make it a special order.

Types of Postponement

A main motion may be postponed definitely:
1. To a later time in the *same meeting or convention* as a general or special order.
2. To a *later meeting or convention* as a general or a special order or as an item of business to come up under unfinished business at the specified meeting or convention. If a motion is postponed definitely to a particular meeting or convention but not to a specified time, it comes up under unfinished business at the meeting to which it was postponed.

A main motion may be postponed definitely as a general or special order to a time that is not stated but that is dependent on some other item of business. For example, a main motion might be postponed definitely "until after the report of the treasurer."

Consideration of Postponed Motions

If a motion that was postponed definitely or set as a general or special order is not taken up at the meeting for which it was set, it comes up as unfinished business at the next meeting.

When a motion that has been postponed definitely is stated to the assembly for consideration, it may again be postponed definitely to a later time and day.

If no main motion is pending and a motion is proposed to postpone definitely a motion that is to come up later, the motion to postpone definitely is a main motion.

Effect of the Motion to Postpone Definitely

To postpone the pending main motion and to fix a definite date or date and time for its consideration.

Rules Governing the Motion to Postpone Definitely

1. Cannot interrupt a speaker
2. Requires a second
3. Debate restricted to brief discussion on reasons for, or time of, postponement
4. Amendments restricted to time of postponement
5. Requires a majority vote
6. Takes precedence over refer to a committee, amend, and postpone indefinitely
7. Applies to main motions only
8. Can have applied to it amend, vote immediately, limit debate, and withdraw

MOTION TO LIMIT OR EXTEND DEBATE

Purpose

To limit or determine the time that will be devoted to discussion of a pending motion or to modify or remove limitations already imposed on its discussion.

Form

PROPOSER: "I move to limit the time of each speaker on this question to three minutes."

or

"I move to limit debate on this question to a total time of two hours."

or

"I move that the time of the speaker be extended by twenty minutes."

PRESIDING OFFICER (*after hearing a second*): "It has been moved and seconded that the time of each speaker on this question be limited to three minutes. This motion is not debatable but may be amended with restrictions.... Those in favor of the motion, please rise.... Be seated. Those opposed, please rise.... Be seated. The vote is 208 to 61. Since there is a two-thirds affirmative vote, the motion is carried."

Types of Limitations on Debate

The motion to limit debate on a pending question or to modify limitations already set up usually relates to the number of speakers who may participate, the length of time allotted each speaker, the total time allotted for discussion of the motion, or some variation or combination of these limitations. The most common example of a motion extending limitations on debate is one that extends the time allowed a particular speaker.

If one form of the motion to limit or extend debate is pending before the assembly, another form that does not conflict with the first may be moved as an amendment; for example, if the motion "to limit each speaker to five minutes" is pending, an amendment may be proposed to add "and limit the number of speakers to three on each side."

How Limiting Debate Affects Pending Motions

A motion to limit or extend debate may be applied to all pending debatable motions, to some of them, or only to the immediately pending motion. To illustrate, if a main motion, an amendment, and an amendment to the amendment are pending and the proposer of the motion to limit debate does not specify the motion or motions on which he desires to limit discussion, only the immediately pending question—in this case the amendment to the amendment—is affected.

Termination of the Motion to Limit Debate

A motion limiting or extending debate is in force only during the meeting or convention at which it was adopted. If the main motion is postponed until another meeting, the motion limiting or extending debate is no longer effective.

If no main motion is pending and a motion is made to limit or extend debate on a motion that is to come up later, this is a main motion.

Effect of the Motion to Limit Debate

To limit discussion on a pending question or to extend or remove limitations already adopted.

Rules Governing the Motion to Limit Debate

1. Cannot interrupt a speaker
2. Requires a second
3. Debate restricted to type and time of limitations
4. Amendments restricted to limitations, extensions, or removal of limitations on debate
5. Requires a two-thirds vote because it limits freedom of debate or sets aside already adopted limitations on debate
6. Takes precedence over postpone definitely, refer to committee, amend, and postpone indefinitely
7. Applies to debatable motions only
8. Can have applied to it amend and withdraw

MOTION TO VOTE IMMEDIATELY
(*Previous Question*)

Purpose

To prevent or to stop discussion on the pending question or questions, to prevent the proposal of other subsidiary motions except to postpone temporarily, and to bring the pending question or questions to vote immediately

Form

PROPOSER: "I move to vote immediately on the motion."

or

"I move to vote immediately on all pending motions."

or (the old form)

"I move the previous question."

PRESIDING OFFICER (*after hearing a second*): "It has been moved and seconded to vote immediately on the motion before the assembly. Those in favor of voting immediately, please rise.... Be seated. Those opposed, please rise.... Be seated. The vote is 251 to 33. Since there is a two-thirds affirmative vote, the motion to vote immediately is carried. We will now vote on the motion."

Confusion Caused by Former Name

The purpose of the motion "I move the previous question," first introduced in Parliament in 1604, was to suppress the pending motion. The modern purpose is to terminate or prevent debate on a motion. Its old English name and form are misleading and have been largely replaced by the name "vote immediately."

The motion to vote immediately is more than a motion to

close debate since, if adopted, it also prevents the proposal of any further subsidiary motions, except postpone temporarily, and brings the question or questions to which it is applied to an immediate vote. The term "vote immediately" is therefore accurate and descriptive.

Proposal of the Motion to Vote Immediately

The motion to vote immediately is a powerful tool for expediting business. It may be proposed at any time after the motion to which it applies has been stated to the assembly. It cannot be combined with the motion to which it applies; for example, the motion, "I move that we enlarge our assembly hall and that we vote immediately on this motion," is out of order.

If the motion to vote immediately is proposed as soon as a main motion has been stated to the assembly, its adoption prevents any debate.

How Voting Immediately Affects Pending Motions

If the motion to vote immediately is unqualified—"I move that we vote immediately" or "I move the previous question," for example—it applies to the immediately pending motion only.

If more than one motion is pending, the motion to vote immediately should specify the pending motions to which it applies. For example, suppose a main motion, an amendment, and an amendment to that amendment, are all pending; if the proposer of the motion to vote immediately wishes it to apply only to the amendment to the amendment and to the amendment, he must state this qualification. If he wishes it to apply to all pending motions, he must state this. If the motion to vote immediately on all pending motions is adopted, an immediate vote must be taken on the amendment to the amendment, then on the amendment, and then on the main motion. The motion to vote immediately may be applied only to successive pending motions and must include the immediately pending question.

Termination of the Motion to Vote Immediately

The effect of the motion to vote immediately terminates with the meeting or convention at which it is adopted. For example, if, after the motion to vote immediately is carried, the assembly postpones the main question temporarily but resumes consideration of it later at the same meeting or convention, the motion to vote immediately still applies. But if the assembly votes to postpone the main question until the next meeting, the motion to vote immediately is no longer in effect when the question again comes before the assembly.

Two-thirds Vote Required

The motion to vote immediately is the most drastic of the motions that seek to control debate. Common parliamentary practice requires a two-thirds vote to terminate debate.[6]

Question! Question!

The motion to vote immediately is the only legal method of securing an immediate vote. Members are out of order who call "Question!" to urge the presiding officer to put a pending motion to vote at once. A presiding officer should ignore these members or call them to order. The only situation where members may properly call "Question!" is in response to the query from the presiding officer, "Are you ready for the question?"

Effect of the Motion to Vote Immediately

To prevent or stop debate on the motion (or motions) to which it is applied and bring it to an immediate vote.

Rules Governing the Motion to Vote Immediately (Previous Question)

1. Cannot interrupt a speaker
2. Requires a second
3. Is not debatable
4. Cannot be amended
5. Requires a two-thirds vote because it prevents or cuts off debate
6. Takes precedence over all subsidiary motions except postpone temporarily
7. Applies to debatable motions only
8. Can have no motion applied to it except withdraw

MOTION TO POSTPONE TEMPORARILY
(*Lay on the Table*)

Purpose

To set aside temporarily a pending main motion in such a way that, if the assembly wishes, the postponed motion can be taken up again for consideration at any time during the current meeting or convention by a motion to resume its consideration.

Form

PROPOSER: "I move that the main motion be postponed temporarily."

MOTION TO POSTPONE TEMPORARILY

or (the old form)

"I move that the motion be laid on the table."

PRESIDING OFFICER *(after hearing a second)*: "It has been moved and seconded that the main motion be postponed temporarily. All those in favor say 'Aye.' . . . Opposed, 'No.' . . . The motion is postponed temporarily."

Reasons for Postponing Temporarily

The early name of the motion to postpone temporarily, "to lay on the table," grew out of the legislative custom of laying a bill on the clerk's table awaiting further consideration. Both forms of the motion are used, but the term "postpone temporarily" is clear and self-explanatory.

Frequently an assembly wishes to put a pending main motion aside temporarily without discussing it or to defer further discussion and decision until later in the same meeting or convention.[7] The usual reasons for postponing a motion temporarily are that some more urgent business has arisen or that some members want additional information or more time before voting on the motion. It is also used to sidetrack an unwelcome motion in the hope that it will not be taken up again.

The motion to postpone temporarily applies only to main motions and not to communications or committee reports.

Time Limits on the Motion to Postpone Temporarily

A motion to postpone temporarily sets aside the pending main motion for the current meeting or convention unless the assembly votes to resume its consideration. Its effect terminates with the current meeting or convention.

During the same meeting or convention, the assembly may resume consideration of the matter, which has been postponed temporarily, by a motion to "resume consideration of the motion."

The motion that has been postponed temporarily cannot be brought up again as a new motion during the same meeting or convention, but may be brought up at any future meeting or convention.

A motion that is postponed temporarily is postponed to an undetermined time. A motion specifying a definite time is a motion to postpone definitely.

Adhering Motions also Postponed

When a main motion is postponed temporarily, all pending amendments and other adhering motions are postponed with it. If it is again brought before the assembly, all adhering motions come with it and must be disposed of in regular order. If the motion to limit debate or vote immediately has been passed before the main motion was postponed temporarily, these motions remain in effect when consideration is resumed.

Effect of the Motion to Postpone Temporarily

To stop debate on the main motion and remove it, with any amendments and adhering motions, from the consideration of the assembly during the current meeting or convention unless the postponed motion is brought back before the assembly by a motion to resume its consideration.[8]

Rules Governing the Motion to Postpone Temporarily (Lay on the Table)

1. Cannot interrupt a speaker
2. Requires a second
3. Is not debatable
4. Cannot be amended

5. Requires a majority vote
6. Takes precedence over all other subsidiary motions
7. Applies to main motions only
8. Can have no motion applied to it except withdraw

Chapter 9

PRIVILEGED MOTIONS

QUESTION OF PRIVILEGE

Purpose

To enable a member to secure immediate decision and action by the presiding officer on a request that concerns the comfort, convenience, rights, or privileges of the assembly or of himself as a member, or permission to present a motion of an urgent nature, even though other business is pending.

Form

1. Question of Privilege of Assembly (Request)
PROPOSER (*without waiting for recognition*): "Mr. Chairman, I rise to a question of privilege of the assembly."
PRESIDING OFFICER (*without waiting for a second*): "State your question of privilege."
PROPOSER: "May we have the windows in the rear of the hall closed?"
PRESIDING OFFICER: "Your request is granted. Will the ushers please close the windows?"

2. Question of Personal Privilege (Request)

PROPOSER (*without waiting for recognition*): "I rise to a question of personal privilege."

PRESIDING OFFICER (*without waiting for a second*): "State your question of privilege."

PROPOSER: "May I be excused from further attendance at this convention because I have just been handed a subpoena to appear in court immediately?"

PRESIDING OFFICER: "Your privilege is granted."

3. Motion of Privilege

PROPOSER (*without waiting for recognition*): "I rise to a question of privilege to present a motion."

PRESIDING OFFICER: "State your motion."

PROPOSER: "As a motion of privilege, I move that the secretary be directed to have the office prepare enough copies of the proposed amendments to the bylaws so that every member may have one before the evening business meeting."

PRESIDING OFFICER (*after hearing a second*): "As a motion of privilege, it has been moved and seconded that the secretary be directed to have the office prepare enough copies of the proposed amendments to the bylaws so that every member may have one before the evening business meeting."

Member's Right to Request Privilege

A member has the right to request decision and action by the presiding officer or by the assembly on urgent questions involving the immediate convenience, comfort, rights, or privileges of the assembly, or of another member, or of himself. A question of privilege may be in the form of a request to the presiding officer which is decided by him or of a motion which is voted on by the assembly. The presiding officer may decide that a particular motion is not a proper question of privilege and rule it out of order.

Interruption by a Question of Privilege

The importance or emergency nature of a question of privilege allows its proposer to interrupt a speaker. When a speaker is interrupted by a question of privilege, he takes his seat. The presiding officer must rule immediately on the question of privilege by granting or denying it. Any member may appeal from this decision.

If the presiding officer decides that the request is a proper question of privilege and of sufficient urgency, he grants the privilege and carries out the request immediately. If he decides that it is a proper question of privilege but can wait, he states that the privilege will be granted when the speaker who was interrupted has finished. If he decides that the question of privilege is not a proper request, he denies it. As soon as the question of privilege has been disposed of, the speaker who was interrupted is again given the floor.

Privileges of the Assembly

Questions relating to a privilege of the assembly have to do with the rights, safety, integrity, comfort, or convenience of the whole assembly. They frequently are concerned with the heating, lighting, or ventilation of the hall, the seating of members, or the control of noise. A question of privilege relating to the assembly takes precedence over a question of privilege relating to a member.

Personal Privileges

Questions of personal privileges pertain to an individual member and usually relate to his rights, reputation, conduct, safety, or convenience as a member of the body.

Motions as Questions of Privilege

Sometimes when one main motion is pending it is necessary to propose another main motion to take care of an emergency. The emergency motion can interrupt only as a question of privilege. The presiding officer will usually grant the member the right to state his urgent motion. If the presiding officer, after hearing the motion, believes that it needs immediate decision, he states it to the assembly and opens it for debate, thus setting aside pending business. If he believes that the motion is not urgent or is not a question of privilege, he rules it out of order until the pending business is disposed of.

For example, if during a convention an embarrassing discussion arises which should not be made public, the presiding officer might allow a member, as a motion of privilege, to move "that nonmembers be required to leave the room."

When a question of privilege is presented as a motion, it is a main motion which is given special privilege. It follows all the rules of a main motion except that it may interrupt and has the precedence of a question of privilege.

Effect of a Question of Privilege

To secure appropriate action by the presiding officer on a request or by the assembly on a motion in order to meet an immediate need or emergency.

Rules Governing a Question of Privilege (Request)

1. Can interrupt a speaker if it requires immediate decision and action
2. Requires no second because it is a request
3. Is not debatable because it is decided by the presiding officer

4. Cannot be amended
5. Requires no vote
6. Takes precedence over all motions except adjourn and recess
7. Applies to no other motion
8. Can have no motion applied to it except withdraw

MOTION TO RECESS

Purpose

To permit an interlude in a meeting and to set a definite time for continuing the meeting.

Form

PROPOSER: "I move that we recess for five minutes
or (in a convention)
"until tomorrow morning at 9:00 A.M."

PRESIDING OFFICER (*after hearing a second*): "It has been moved and seconded that we recess for five minutes. Is there brief discussion? ... Those in favor say 'Aye.' ... Those opposed, 'No.' ... The motion is carried. The meeting is recessed for five minutes."

Difference Between Recess and Adjourn

A motion to recess *suspends* the current meeting until a later time; the unqualified motion to adjourn *terminates* the meeting. When an assembly reconvenes following a recess, it resumes the meeting at the point where it was interrupted by the motion to recess. When an assembly reconvenes following an adjournment, it begins an entirely new meeting, starting with the first step in the regular order of business. The only exception to this procedure is when an assembly adjourns to an adjourned meeting. (See *Adjourned Meetings,* p. 111.) This type of adjournment is really a recess.

Conventions often transact business for several days, and the series of periods for the transaction of business are actually one meeting. A convention, therefore, may move to recess to the next period for transacting business and then adjourn at the end of the convention.

Limitations and Restrictions on the Motion to Recess

The duration of a recess is usually brief, but there is no definite limitation on its length except that a recess cannot extend beyond the time set for the next regular or special meeting or, in a convention, beyond the time set for the next business meeting or for adjournment of the convention.

The motion to recess may be amended only as to the time or duration of the recess, and debate on it is restricted to the time, duration, or need of the recess.

As are all privileged motions, recess is privileged only if it is proposed when a main motion is pending. If it is proposed when no main motion is pending, it is a main motion.

Effect of the Motion to Recess

To suspend the meeting until the time stated for reconvening.

Rules Governing the Motion to Recess

1. Cannot interrupt a speaker
2. Requires a second
3. Debate restricted to brief discussion on the time, duration, or need of recess

4. Amendments restricted to the time or duration of recess
5. Requires a majority vote
6. Takes precedence over all motions except adjourn
7. Applies to no other motion
8. Can have applied to it amend and withdraw

MOTION TO ADJOURN

Purpose

To terminate a meeting or convention.

Form

1. Unqualified Form (Privileged Motion)
PROPOSER: "I move that we adjourn."

or

"I move that the Eighteenth Annual Convention of the National Association of Broadcasters now adjourn."

PRESIDING OFFICER (*after hearing a second*): "It has been moved and seconded that we adjourn. Those in favor say 'Aye.' ... Those opposed, 'No.' ... The motion is carried. The meeting is adjourned."

2. Qualified Forms (Main Motions)
   a. Adjourn to an adjourned meeting
   "I move that we adjourn to continue this meeting next Friday evening at eight o'clock in this room as an adjourned meeting."
   b. Making adjournment conditional
   "I move that, if the Committee on Finance does not report before ten o'clock, we adjourn at that time."
   c. Fixing time for future adjournment

"I move that we adjourn in ten minutes"

or

"at 6:00 P.M."

Qualified and Unqualified Motions to Adjourn

There are two forms of the motion to adjourn—the qualified and the unqualified. The simple unqualified form of the motion to adjourn is a privileged motion. It is privileged only when a main motion is pending, and if it is stated as a simple, unqualified motion that would take effect immediately if carried. The unqualified motion to adjourn may be proposed at any time except that it cannot interrupt a speaker or the taking of a vote. If the vote is by ballot, however, the assembly may adjourn while the ballots are being counted.

All qualified motions to adjourn are main motions. Even the unqualified motion to adjourn, if it is proposed when no main motion is pending, is a main motion.

Completion of Business Before Adjournment

When a motion to adjourn is made, it is the duty of the presiding officer to see that no important business is overlooked before putting the motion to a vote. If the presiding officer knows of any important matter that has not been considered but requires action before adjournment, he should call it to the attention of the assembly. If he fails to do this, any member may call attention to the oversight. For example, if delegates have not been selected for a convention that is to be held before the next meeting, it is important that this be done before adjournment.

When attention is called to some action required before adjournment, the presiding officer usually asks the proposer of the motion to adjourn to withdraw his motion until the essential business has been completed. If the member refuses to do so, and if the assembly chooses to disregard the warning of the presiding officer, it has the right to vote to adjourn.

Adjournment to an Adjourned Meeting

When an assembly cannot consider all its important business in the time available for a meeting, it is desirable to continue the meeting at a later time.[1] The motion to adjourn to an adjourned meeting is a qualified motion to adjourn and, therefore, a main motion. No exact form is required, but it must be clear that the meeting is to continue at a later date, and the time and place of the adjourned meeting must be specified. No additional notice of the adjourned meeting is required unless provided for in the bylaws.

The interval between the current meeting and the adjourned meeting is, in fact, a recess, and the adjourned meeting is actually a part of the original meeting. (See *Adjourned Meetings,* p. 111.)

Adjournment and Dissolution

The general rule is that an unqualified motion to adjourn is a privileged motion if made while a main motion is pending. There is one exception to this rule. If an unqualified motion to adjourn is made when there is no provision for a further meeting of the organization, the motion is, in fact, a motion to dissolve and is a main motion. The presiding officer should call the attention of the assembly to the fact that there is no provision for another meeting and that the assembly might, in effect, be dissolved by adaptation of the motion to adjourn. Actually dissolution is only a theoretical problem since another meeting could be called in the same manner as the first.

A final adjournment that has the effect of dissolving the

assembly or closing a convention is termed *adjournment sine die,* or adjournment without day.

Voting on Adjournment

The motion to adjourn must be voted on by the assembly.[2] The presiding officer does not have the authority to adjourn a meeting unless there is no quorum present,[3] but the meeting is not terminated until he announces the vote and the adjournment.

Frequently there is confusion in phrasing motions to adjourn. The presiding officer should find out which type of adjournment the proposer of the motion intends and then rephrase the motion, if necessary, to make it clear. For example, a member may say, "I move that we adjourn until next Friday at three o'clock." If the next regular meeting is scheduled for that date and hour, the member is merely calling attention to the time of the next regular meeting. The presiding officer should restate the motion as "It has been moved and seconded that we adjourn." In announcing the result, he may add, "We are now adjourning until our next regular meeting, which is at three o'clock on Friday, December third." It is good practice for the presiding officer, in declaring any meeting adjourned, to state the time and place of the next meeting.

If the motion to adjourn is qualified and is in order, the presiding officer should call attention to the fact that it is an adjournment to an adjourned meeting, makes adjournment conditional, or fixes the time for future adjournment, and that it therefore is a main motion.

Adjournment at Previously Fixed Time

When a definite hour for adjournment has been fixed by the adoption of a program, by rule, or by a previous motion, it is the duty of the presiding officer, when the hour of adjournment arrives, to interrupt a speaker or the consideration of business and to state that the time fixed to adjourn has arrived. A member should then move to adjourn, to suspend the rule requiring adjournment, or to set another time for adjournment.

Business Interrupted by Adjournment

Business that is interrupted by adjournment is affected as follows:

1. Business that was interrupted by adjournment of a *meeting* comes up as the first item under unfinished business at the next meeting.
2. Business that was interrupted by the final adjournment of a *convention* is dropped unless a motion or report is postponed definitely to a later convention or a committee is instructed to continue its work and report at the next convention.

Effect of the Motion to Adjourn

Terminates a meeting or convention with the announcement of adjournment by the presiding officer.

Rules Governing the Motion to Adjourn

1. Cannot interrupt a speaker
2. Requires a second
3. Is not debatable
4. Cannot be amended
5. Requires a majority vote
6. Takes precedence over all other motions
7. Applies to no other motion
8. Can have no motion applied to it except withdraw

Chapter 10

INCIDENTAL MOTIONS

MOTION TO APPEAL

Purpose

To enable a member who believes that the presiding officer is mistaken or unfair in his ruling to have the assembly decide by vote whether the presiding officer's decision should be upheld or overruled.

Form

PROPOSER (*immediately after the presiding officer has announced his decision, and without waiting for recognition*): "I appeal from the decision of the chair."

PRESIDING OFFICER (*after hearing a second*): "The decision of the chair has been appealed from."

The presiding officer then states the reasons for his decision, and the member may state the reasons for his appeal. After opportunity for discussion, the vote is taken, not on the appeal, but on sustaining or overruling the chair's decision. "Those in favor of sustaining the decision of the chair say 'Aye.' ... Those opposed, 'No.' ... The decision of the chair is sustained [or overruled]."

When an Appeal May Be Taken

An appeal is the motion by which an assembly may review a ruling or decision of its presiding officer.[1] Any decision of the presiding officer involving his judgment is subject to appeal. His statement of a fact such as a vote count is not.

An appeal is permissible only immediately after the presiding officer's decision has been rendered. If any other business has intervened, an appeal is not in order. However, if another member has secured the floor, he may be interrupted by an appeal if it is made promptly.

Statement of the Question on Appeal

The presiding officer must always state the question in the form "Those in favor of sustaining the decision of the chair...." He cannot state the question on the appeal in a biased form. For example, if the presiding officer has ruled that a motion is out of order because it is in conflict with the bylaws, he may state this fact and explain it in support of his ruling. However, he cannot state the question as "those in favor of sustaining the bylaws...."

Statement of the Reasons for Appeal

An appeal is debatable because it may involve questions of importance to the assembly. The presiding officer states the reasons for his ruling or decision without leaving the chair.

If the explanation of the decision by the presiding officer convinces the member who has appealed that the decision is correct, the member may withdraw his appeal. If the member's statement of his reasons for appeal proves to the presiding officer that his decision is incorrect, the presiding officer may himself change his decision; thereupon the appeal is automatically dropped.

Vote on an Appeal

The presiding officer's decision is sustained on an appeal by a majority vote or by a tie vote. A tie vote sustains the decision of the presiding officer because a majority vote is necessary to overrule his decision. The presiding officer votes to sustain his own decision.

If no main motion is pending, an appeal is a main motion.

Effect of the Motion to Appeal

If the decision of the presiding officer is sustained by an affirmative majority or by a tie vote, his decision becomes the decision of the assembly. If his decision fails to receive an affirmative majority or tie vote, it is overruled.

Rules Governing the Motion to Appeal

1. Can interrupt a speaker because it must be proposed immediately
2. Requires a second
3. Is debatable
4. Cannot be amended
5. Requires a majority vote in the negative to overrule the presiding officer's decision
6. Takes precedence as an incidental motion and must be decided immediately
7. Applies to rulings and decisions of the presiding officer
8. Can have applied to it vote immediately, limit debate, and withdraw

MOTION TO SUSPEND RULES

Purpose

To permit an assembly to take some action that otherwise would be prevented by a procedural rule or by a program already adopted.

Form

PROPOSER: "I move to suspend the rule requiring that the reports of standing committees be completed before the budget is considered so that we may consider the budget now."

PRESIDING OFFICER (*after hearing a second*): "It has been moved and seconded to suspend the rule that interferes with the consideration of the budget at this time. Those in favor, please rise.... Be seated. Those opposed, please rise.... Be seated. The vote is 'Yes' 92, 'No' 18. Since there is a two-thirds affirmative vote, the motion is carried, and the rule requiring that the reports of standing committees be completed before the budget is considered is suspended. We will proceed with the consideration of the budget."

Which Rules Can Be Suspended?

When an organization desires to accomplish a specific purpose or to take a specific action, and is prevented from doing so by some of its special rules of procedure or by an adopted program, it may vote to suspend the rules that interfere with the accomplishment of the particular action.[1]

Which Rules Cannot Be Suspended?

Suspension of the rules is limited strictly to procedural rules. The suspension cannot deprive members of any fundamental right. Most rules cannot be suspended. For example, an assembly cannot suspend:
1. A rule stated in a statute or a charter
2. A basic rule of common parliamentary law such as rules governing notice, quorum, vote requirements, and voting methods

3. A rule in the bylaws unless they contain a provision permitting the suspension of certain bylaws governing the method or order of considering business [2]

Restrictions and Time Limits on Suspension of Rules

The motion to suspend rules may be made when no motion is pending, or it may be made when a motion is pending if the suspension is for a purpose connected with that motion.

Rules may be suspended only for a specific purpose and for the limited time necessary to accomplish the proposed action. Any suspension for a longer period would be an amendment of the rules and not a suspension. For this reason the object of the suspension must be specified in the motion to suspend the rules, and only action that is specifically mentioned in the motion to suspend the rule can be taken under the suspension.

A suspended rule becomes effective again as soon as the purpose for which it was suspended has been accomplished. If no main motion is pending, a motion to suspend the rules on a motion that is to come up later is a main motion.

Effect of the Motion to Suspend Rules

Enables an assembly to take a specific action which is otherwise invalid under its procedural rules.

Rules Governing the Motion to Suspend Rules

1. Cannot interrupt a speaker
2. Requires a second
3. Is not debatable
4. Cannot be amended
5. Requires a two-thirds vote
6. Takes precedence as an incidental motion and must be decided immediately

7. Applies to no other motion
8. Can have no motion applied to it except withdraw

MOTION TO OBJECT TO CONSIDERATION

Purpose

To avoid entirely discussion and decision on a main motion that the assembly believes is embarrassing, unnecessarily contentious, unprofitable, or inopportune, or which, for good reason, it does not wish to consider at the time.

Form

PROPOSER (*immediately after the motion is stated by the presiding officer and without waiting for recognition*): "Mr. Chairman, I object to the consideration of this question."

PRESIDING OFFICER (*after hearing a second*): "Objection has been made to the consideration of this question. All in favor of considering the question, please rise. . . . Be seated. Opposed, please rise. . . . Be seated. The vote is 'Yes' 25, 'No' 78. Since there is a two-thirds negative vote, the objection is sustained, and the question will not be considered."

or

"The vote is 'Yes' 82, 'No' 19. Since the objection failed to receive a two-thirds negative vote, the objection is not sustained, and the question is now open for discussion."

When Objection to Consideration May Be Raised

A motion is sometimes proposed that is of such a nature that it is unworthy of consideration. It may be foolish or absurd, untimely, reveal confidential information, or reflect unjustly on the character or reputation of someone.

Objection to considering a motion must be made promptly after the motion has been stated by the presiding officer, and before debate has progressed or any subsidiary motion had been applied to it.

Recent decisions and practice establish objection to consideration as a motion, not a request, since it is decided by vote of the assembly and not by the presiding officer. As a motion, it requires a second. Since the main motion objected to has required a second, it is logical that an objection to that motion should also require a second. There is no reason for allowing one objector to forestall the two supporters, the maker and the seconder of the main motion.

Objection Limited to Main Motions

Objection to consideration applies only to main motions, including resolutions and recommendations, but does not apply to reports of officers or committees.

As an example of the use of object to consideration, suppose that some excitable member has offered the following motion: "I move that we reprimand the members of our Board of Directors for their scandalous conduct at our Christmas party." Objection to consideration might be appropriate in this instance.

Voting on Objection to Consideration

When an objection to consideration is made, the presiding officer immediately puts the question of consideration to a vote. A two-thirds vote against consideration is required to sustain the objection because it sets aside the right of any member to present a proposal and have it considered. Since a voice vote cannot be counted a rising vote should be taken.

When an objection is sustained, the motion objected to cannot be renewed at the same meeting or convention unless, in the opinion of the presiding officer, a new vote might result differently.

Presiding Officer May Rule Out Motions

If a motion is outrageously tactless, foolish, unnecessary, or completely unsuitable for consideration, or if it is proposed at an inopportune time, or for the purpose of heckling, delaying, or embarrassing, the presiding officer may rule the motion out of order on his own initiative.

Effect of the Motion to Object to Consideration

To remove the motion objected to from consideration at the current meeting or convention.

Rules Governing the Motion to Object to Consideration

1. Can interrupt proceedings because the objection must be raised before debate has progressed or another motion made
2. Requires a second
3. Is not debatable
4. Cannot be amended
5. Requires a two-thirds negative vote to prevent the consideration of the motion objected to
6. Takes precedence as an incidental motion and must be voted on immediately
7. Applies to main motions only
8. Can have no motion applied to it except withdraw

REQUEST FOR POINT OF ORDER

Purpose

To call the attention of the assembly and of the presiding officer to a violation of the rules, an omission, a mistake, or an error in procedure, and to secure a ruling from the presiding officer on the question raised.

Form

MEMBER (*without waiting for recognition*): "Mr. Chairman, I rise to a point of order."

or

"Point of order!"

PRESIDING OFFICER (*without a second*): "State your point of order."

MEMBER: "The motion just proposed is out of order because there is another main motion before the assembly."

PRESIDING OFFICER: "Your point of order is well taken. The last motion is out of order."

or

"Your point of order is not well taken. The assembly just referred the main motion to a committee; therefore, there is no other main motion pending. Will the member who was speaking please continue?"

How Points of Order Arise

Whenever a member violates a rule, whether intentionally or not, the presiding officer should call the member's attention to the violation and either require him to conform to the rule or rule him out of order. The presiding officer is, in effect, raising a point of order.

REQUEST FOR POINT OF ORDER

If the presiding officer fails to enforce a rule, of the assembly or of parliamentary procedure, or does not notice an error or omission or mistake made by him or by a member or by the assembly, it is the right of any member to call attention to the violation by rising to a point of order.

Rising to a point of order is a request that the presiding officer give a ruling or decision on the point raised by the member.

When a Point of Order May Be Raised

A point of order must be raised immediately after the mistake, error, or omission occurs. It cannot be brought up later unless the error involves a violation of law, or of the bylaws, or the accuracy of the minutes.

Since it is important that a mistake be corrected immediately, a point of order may be raised at any time, even though a speaker has the floor. The member making a point of order may interrupt a speaker by announcing that he rises to a point of order so that the presiding officer may know that he is entitled to recognition.

Ruling on Points of Order

As soon as the member has stated his point of order, the presiding officer must rule on it; that is, he must declare that the point is "well taken" or "not well taken." He may state the reasons for his decision if he desires.

If the presiding officer is in doubt as to the correct decision, he may defer his decision briefly. Meanwhile action on the matter affected by the point of order is deferred. When a point of order raises a complicated or important question and the presiding officer is uncertain of the matter, he may refer the matter to the assembly for decision: [3]

"Mr. A has raised the point of order that the amendment just proposed is not germane to the motion. I am referring it to the assembly for decision. The question is 'Is this amendment [stating it] germane to the motion?' Is there any discussion? ... Those who believe that the amendment is germane to the motion say 'Aye'. ... Those who believe that it is not say 'No'. ... The decision is in the affirmative; the amendment therefore is in order."

When the presiding officer refers a point of order to the assembly for decision, discussion is not in order unless he invites it. No appeal may be taken from a decision by the assembly on a point of order.

If a member wishes to challenge a decision of the presiding officer on a point of order, he must appeal from the decision of the chair.

Effect of Request for Point of Order

Interrupts business until the presiding officer either rules that the point of order is well taken and orders the mistake or omission corrected or rules that the point of order is not well taken and resumes business at the point where it was interrupted.

Rules Governing Request for Point of Order

1. Can interrupt a speaker because a mistake should be corrected immediately
2. Requires no second because it is a request
3. Is not debatable unless the presiding officer refers it to the assembly for discussion and decision
4. Cannot be amended
5. Requires no vote, because it is a request and is decided by the presiding officer

6. Takes precedence as an incidental motion and must be decided immediately
7. Applies to any mistake, violation, or omission
8. Can have no motion applied to it except withdraw

REQUEST FOR PARLIAMENTARY INQUIRY

Purpose

To enable a member to ask: (1) the presiding officer a question relating to procedure in connection with the pending motion or with a motion that he may wish to bring before the assembly immediately, or for information on the meaning or effect of the pending question; or (2) the speaker or the proposer of the motion a question about the pending motion.

Form

1. Parliamentary Inquiry

MEMBER (*without waiting for recognition*): "I rise to a parliamentary inquiry."

or

"Parliamentary inquiry."
PRESIDING OFFICER (*without a second*): "State your inquiry."
MEMBER: "Is an amendment in order at this time?"
PRESIDING OFFICER: "It is."

2. Request for Information

MEMBER (*without waiting for recognition*): "I rise to a parliamentary inquiry."
PRESIDING OFFICER (*without a second*): "State your inquiry."
MEMBER: "Has this proposed motion been approved by our National Board?"
PRESIDING OFFICER: "Yes, it has."

3. Permission to Ask a Question

MEMBER: (*without waiting for recognition*): "I rise to a parliamentary inquiry."

PRESIDING OFFICER (*without a second*): "State your inquiry."

MEMBER: "May I ask the speaker a question?"

PRESIDING OFFICER: "Is the speaker willing to answer a question?"

SPEAKER: "Yes."

or

"I will answer questions later."

or

"I am not willing to be interrupted."

Right of Members to Inquire

Any member has the right to inquire at any time about procedures directly connected with the pending motion, or with a motion that he may wish to bring before the assembly immediately, or about the meaning or effect of the pending motion. He may also seek permission from the presiding officer to ask a question of a speaker. These rights are exercised through a parliamentary inquiry, which is a request and not a true motion.

When an Inquiry Interrupts

A parliamentary inquiry, whether it is a parliamentary question or a request for information, or a request to ask a question of a speaker, may interrupt a speaker only if it requires an immediate answer. No member should interrupt a speaker with an inquiry if it can reasonably wait until the speaker has finished speaking. In order that the presiding officer may know that a member is rising to a parliamentary inquiry and has the right to the floor while he presents it, the member must state that he is rising to an inquiry instead of merely waiting for recognition.

Inquiry Addressed to the Presiding Officer

A parliamentary inquiry is always addressed to the presiding officer and is answered by him.

If a member wishes to ask a question of a speaker, he states his request to the presiding officer, who asks the speaker if he is willing to be interrupted by a question. If the speaker consents to be interrupted by a question, the member states the question to the presiding officer. The speaker, after hearing the question, may answer it, decline to answer until he has finished speaking, or decline to answer at all. An answer to a question is also addressed to the presiding officer.

If a speaker is interrupted by a parliamentary inquiry and the presiding officer decides that the question does not require an immediate answer, he replies that he will answer the inquiry as soon as the speaker has finished and directs the speaker to continue. The presiding officer should never allow a parliamentary inquiry to be used as a method of annoying a speaker who has the floor, and he should refuse recognition to any member who is using parliamentary inquiries to harass or delay.

The presiding officer should answer reasonable questions on parliamentary law that are pertinent to the pending business. It is not his duty, however, to answer general questions on parliamentary law that are not related directly to business before the assembly.

Effect of Request for Parliamentary Inquiry

Interrupts business until the presiding officer answers the inquiry or request for information, gives permission to ask the speaker a question, or rules that the inquiry is out of order.

Rules Governing Request for Parliamentary Inquiry

1. Can interrupt a speaker if it requires an immediate answer
2. Requires no second because it is a request
3. Is not debatable
4. Cannot be amended
5. Requires no vote because it is a request and is decided by the presiding officer
6. Takes precedence as an incidental motion and must be decided immediately
7. Applies to no other motion
8. Can have no motion applied to it except withdraw

REQUEST TO WITHDRAW A MOTION

Purpose

To enable a member who has proposed a motion to remove it from consideration by the assembly.

Form

1. *Before* the motion has been stated to the assembly by the presiding officer:

PROPOSER of the motion (*without waiting for recognition*): "I withdraw my motion."

PRESIDING OFFICER: "The motion is withdrawn."

2. *After* the motion has been stated to the assembly by the presiding officer:

PROPOSER of the motion (*without waiting for recognition*):

"I wish to withdraw my motion."

PRESIDING OFFICER: "Mr. B asks to withdraw his motion. Is there any objection? . . . Hearing no objection, I declare the motion withdrawn."

or (if *any member objects*)

"Those in favor of allowing Mr. B to withdraw his motion say, 'Aye.' . . . Opposed, 'No.' . . . The motion is carried and Mr. B's motion is withdrawn."

Right of the Proposer to Withdraw His Motion

Withdraw is a request and not a true motion and may be applied to every other motion. Before a motion has been stated by the presiding officer, its proposer may change it or withdraw it if he wishes, and any member or the presiding officer may request him to withdraw it. Usually this request is made because some more urgent business needs prior consideration. The proposer may decline to withdraw his motion.

Permission to Withdraw a Motion

After a motion has been stated to the assembly by the presiding officer, it becomes the property of that body, and the proposer may withdraw it only if no objection is raised. If a member objects, the proposer or some other member may move that the proposer "be allowed to withdraw his motion." This motion is undebatable, can have no other motions applied to it, and requires a majority vote.

The consent of the seconder is not necessary. A motion can be withdrawn if there is no objection, or with permission from the assembly, up to the moment the final vote on it is taken, even though other motions affecting it may be pending or debate has been limited or closed. When a motion is withdrawn, all motions adhering to it are also withdrawn.

Recording Withdrawn Motions

A motion that is withdrawn after it has been stated by the presiding officer is recorded in the minutes with a statement that it was withdrawn. No mention is made in the minutes of a motion that is withdrawn before it has been stated to the assembly by the presiding officer.

Effect of Request to Withdraw a Motion

To remove a motion that has been proposed from the consideration of the assembly.

Rules Governing Request to Withdraw a Motion

1. Can interrupt a speaker
2. Requires no second because it is a request
3. Is not debatable
4. Cannot be amended
5. Requires no vote because it is a request and is decided by the presiding officer
6. Takes precedence as an incidental motion and must be decided immediately
7. Applies to all motions
8. Can have no motion applied to it

REQUEST FOR DIVISION OF QUESTION

Purpose

To secure the division of a motion that is composed of two or more independent parts or ideas into individual motions that may be considered and voted on separately.

Form

Assume that the following motion has been introduced:

"I move that an educational foundation be established by this organization and that a library of technical books be created for the use of our members."

MEMBER: "I request that the motion be divided into two motions: (1) 'That an educational foundation be established by this organization, and (2) 'That a library of technical books be created for the use of our members.'"

PRESIDING OFFICER (*without a second, if in his opinion the motion contains more than one distinct and independent proposal*): "It is requested that the motion be divided into two separate motions. This will be done. The motion now before the assembly is 'that an educational foundation be established by this organization.' Is there any discussion?"

Motions That the Presiding Officer Can Divide

When a motion contains two or more separate and distinct propositions, any member has the right to request that it be divided into separate motions. If the presiding officer agrees that the motion contains more than one independent proposition, he must then divide it into separate motions since members may favor one part of the motion but be opposed to another. To be divisible on the request of a member, the motion must consist of two or more propositions, each of which is capable of standing alone as a reasonable motion that might have been offered independently, and each of which must be suitable for adoption even if the other motion, or motions, is rejected.

For example, a motion "that the salary of the executive director be raised by $2,500 per year and that new furnishings be bought for the national headquarters office" is clearly divisible.

On the other hand, a motion "that this organization erect a headquarters building and rent the two top floors to suitable tenants" cannot be divided because if the motion to erect a headquarters building were defeated, it would be ridiculous to vote on a motion to rent the two top floors. A request to divide such a motion must be ruled out of order. Resolutions or committee recommendations may be divided in the same way.

Motions That the Presiding Officer Cannot Divide

There are certain situations in which a presiding officer does not have the right to divide a question at the request of a member. In these circumstances a motion to divide may be presented. If there is any objection to division of the motion by unanimous consent, a formal vote must be taken on the proposed division. A motion to divide a question is an incidental main motion and follows the rules of a main motion, except that it may be proposed while the main motion that it seeks to divide is pending. Situations in which a vote is required to divide a question are:
1. When a motion contains only one idea, no matter how complicated
2. When a motion contains several propositions so worded that they cannot be divided without extensive rewriting. Such motions are sometimes referred to a committee to be rewritten.

When Division of Question May Be Proposed

A request to divide a question is most effective if it is proposed immediately after the introduction of the motion that it seeks to divide. However, since it is an incidental motion, it may be proposed at any time, even when a motion to postpone indefinitely or to vote immediately is pending.

Alternative Proposals for Dividing a Question

A motion to divide must state clearly how the question is to be divided, and any member may propose a different division. Such proposed divisions are alternative proposals, not amendments, and should be voted on in the order in which they are proposed. The proposal receiving the largest vote is chosen.

Effect of Request for Division of Question

To divide a motion containing two or more independent proposals and enable the assembly to vote on each proposal separately.

Rules Governing Request for Division of Question

1. Cannot interrupt a speaker
2. Requires no second because it is a request
3. Is not debatable
4. Cannot be amended
5. Requires no vote because it is a request and is decided by the presiding officer
6. Takes precedence as an incidental motion and must be decided immediately
7. Applies to main motions only
8. Can have no motion applied to it except withdraw

REQUEST FOR DIVISION OF ASSEMBLY

Purpose

To verify an indecisive voice or hand vote by requiring the voters to rise and, if necessary, to be counted.

Form

MEMBER (*immediately after the vote has been taken or announced and without waiting for recognition*): "Division!"

PRESIDING OFFICER: "Division has been called for. Those in favor of the motion that (*stating motion just voted on*) please rise. The secretary will please count.... Be seated. Opposed, please rise.... The vote is 'Yes,' 62, 'No,' 47. The motion is carried."

When Division May Be Requested

A call for division is a request that an indecisive vote which has been taken by voice or the raising of hands be verified by a rising vote and, if necessary to determine the result, that the vote be counted.

Any member, without waiting for recognition, may call for division as soon as a question has been put to a vote and even before the vote is announced. This right continues even after the vote has been announced and another speaker has claimed the floor, but the right must be exercised promptly.[4]

Any member has the right to insist on verification of a vote that he feels has not been correctly reported, but he cannot use this privilege to obstruct business by calling for division on an obviously decisive vote.

Verification of a Vote by the Presiding Officer

The responsibility of announcing a vote correctly rests on the presiding officer. If he is in doubt as to the result of the vote, he may verify it on his own initiative by taking a rising vote.

Effect of Request for Division of Assembly

To require the presiding officer to take a rising vote on the motion just voted on and to count the votes if there is any doubt as to which side prevails.

Rules Governing Request for Division of Assembly

1. Can interrupt proceedings because it requires immediate decision
2. Requires no second because it is a request
3. Is not debatable
4. Cannot be amended
5. Requires no vote because it is a request and is decided by the presiding officer
6. Takes precedence as an incidental motion and must be decided immediately
7. Applies to indecisive voice or hand votes
8. Can have no motion applied to it

Chapter 11

NOTICE OF MEETINGS AND PROPOSALS

Importance of Notice

All meetings and conventions and certain important proposals require notice to members. The courts will not uphold the decisions of a meeting if the notice requirements for the meeting, or for any action that requires notice, have not been complied with. If there is proof that notice is purposely or negligently withheld from any member, none of the actions at that meeting is valid.[1] The only variation from this rule is that a vote of *all* of the members may waive the lack of proper notice. (See *Waiver of Notice,* p. 109.)

Notice Protects Members

Common parliamentary law provides for the full protection of every member by rigid enforcement of notice requirements before a meeting. It does not protect absentees who have had notice but who fail to attend or members who come late or leave early. If a member has been sent notice of a meeting, or of an action that requires notice, and does not attend, he relinquishes his right of decision to those who are present. When proper notice has been given and a quorum is present, it cannot be contended that those members present are "not representative" or that the meeting is "not representative," since legally all members are equal.

Notice of Meetings

Notice of any meeting must state clearly the date, the time and place of the meeting and should be signed by the secretary. The time and place of a meeting cannot be changed after notice has been sent unless notice of the change is also sent. Notice of any meeting sent so late that a substantial percentage of the members cannot attend is not valid notice, even if all other requirements have been fulfilled.

When the quorum of an organization is small or consists of less than a majority of the members, it is wise to provide specifically in the bylaws for the time and place of meetings and to state explicitly the time and place in the notice of each

NOTICE OF MEETINGS AND PROPOSALS 107

meeting. This prevents more than one group of members from meeting and claiming to be the official meeting of the organization. The notice of a meeting should:

1. State the exact time of calling the meeting to order so specifically that two or more separate meetings could not be held at different times in conformity with the notice.
2. State the place of the meeting with such certainty that meetings could not be held in two separate places even in the same building.

Convention notices are often issued in the form of a call to the convention. The call must give notice of the time and place of the convention and usually includes the method of accrediting delegates, and directions for sending in resolutions, reports of officers and committees, and proposed amendments to the bylaws. The call is usually sent by letter or is printed in the organization's magazine. A call can be in the form of a notice, a greeting, or in any form that makes it clear when and where the convention will be held.

Annual meeting may refer either to the annual convention of an organization or to that meeting of a local organization which is held annually at the termination of the organizational year to elect or install officers and to hear reports. Annual meetings require notice to all members of the time and place of the meeting and of any special business to be transacted, such as election of officers.

Regular meetings require whatever notice is stated in the bylaws. Any regular meeting of an organization may transact any business not requiring special notice. If the officers responsible for giving notice know that a proposal of great importance, but which may not require special notice, will be brought up at a regular meeting, they should, as a matter of good faith, send out notice of the proposal.

Special meetings require notice of time and place of meetings and also notice of specific proposals to be considered and decided, and of subjects to be discussed. At the meeting the members may amend the proposals stated in the notice but cannot consider any business that is not stated or reasonably implied in the notice.[2] For example, the purpose stated in the notice, "to employ a new office manager," reasonably implies that the removal of the present office manager is imminent. Under this statement of purpose, however, the meeting could not consider the employment of a consultant. (See *Special Meetings*, p. 110.)

Adjourned meetings do not require special notice unless this requirement is in the bylaws. If either a regular or a special meeting that has been properly called, and has a quorum present, votes to adjourn to a later time, this is sufficient notice to those present. However, good organizational practice requires that notice of the adjourned meeting be sent to all members.

Board and *committee* meetings require that members be sent whatever notice is specified by the rules.

Notice of Proposed Actions

No proposal that according to the law, charter, or provision of the bylaws requires notice can be considered at any meeting unless proper notice of the proposed action has been sent to every member. Amendments to the bylaws or charter, sale of property, large and unusual expenditures, election of officers, and other items of similar importance require whatever notice is specified by the bylaws or rules of the organization. The proposals to be voted on must be stated specifically.

When an action that required special notice has been taken, any motion having the effect of voiding or changing the original action requires the same notice. For example, if a motion to lease property belonging to an organization originally required notice for its adoption, a motion to cancel the lease requires the same notice.

Waiver of Notice

If there was a mistake in a notice or a failure to send notice to every member and yet every member is present at the meeting, and no one protests a lack of notice, the members waive notice by the fact of their attendance and their participation in the meeting. Members may also waive notice by signing a written waiver of notice before, during, or after the meeting.

Chapter 12

MEETINGS

Meetings and Conventions Defined

A *meeting* is an official assembly of the members of an organization or board for any length of time during which the members do not separate except for a recess. It covers the period from the time the group convenes until the time it adjourns.

Convention usually refers to a series of adjourned or recessed meetings that follow in close succession. It is regarded as a single meeting with intervening recess periods.

The term "session" has two distinct meanings. It may refer to a single meeting, such as "a morning session," or it may refer to a series of meetings, such as "a session of Congress." Because of this confusion, the term "session" is not used in this book.

Regular Meetings

Most organizations have fixed times stated in their bylaws for holding meetings. Meetings held in accordance with these provisions are regular meetings. Since members are presumed to be familiar with the bylaws, no additional notice of regular meetings need be given unless the bylaws provide for further notice or unless notice of regular meetings is customary. The regular time and place for meetings that have been established by rule or custom cannot legally be changed without notice to all members.

At any regular meeting any business can be transacted that comes within the scope of the organization and does not require special notice.

No meeting may begin before the time stated in the notice or set by custom unless all members are present and consent.

Special Meetings

A special meeting is a meeting that is not regularly scheduled and is held to transact specified business only. Any special meeting of an organization or a board must be called in accordance with the bylaw provisions governing special meetings.

All members must be notified of a special meeting and the call or notice must state the items of business that will be considered and voted on. A copy of the call for the special meeting must be inserted in the minutes of the meeting. The order of business for a special meeting consists only of the proposals for consideration and decision and the subjects for discussion as stated in the call for the meeting.

The statement of business to be considered must be specific, and if action is to be taken at the meeting, this fact must be stated in the notice. If a notice states that one of the purposes of a special meeting is "to hear a report of the Refurnishing Committee," the report can be read, but no action can be taken on recommendations of the committee unless these are stated in the notice and it is clear that they are to be voted on at the meeting. Blanket statements describing business to be transacted, such as "any other proper business," do not give valid notice.[1]

Provisions in the bylaws for special meetings of the whole membership of a large state, national, or world organization are unnecessary and unrealistic. The governing board is empowered to handle emergencies.

Adjourned Meetings

When members wish to continue a regular or a special meeting at a later time, a motion to adjourn the meeting and to continue it as an adjourned meeting at a definite later time makes the second meeting an *adjourned meeting* of the first. The interval between the adjournment and the reconvening of the adjourned meeting is, in effect, a recess, and such meetings are referred to either as adjourned or recessed meetings. An adjourned meeting is legally a continuation of the same meeting.[2]

An organization can do any business at an adjourned meeting that might have been done had no adjournment been taken. Limitations at the original meeting remain in force at the adjourned meeting. An adjourned special meeting can transact only such business as could have been transacted at the original special meeting.

Instead of following the order of business for a regular meeting, the adjourned meeting is called to order and, after the presence of a quorum is recorded in the minutes, the meeting continues from the point at which it was adjourned. Any business pending at the time the original meeting adjourned is still pending when the adjourned meeting is called to order.[3]

Special notice is not required for an adjourned or recessed meeting, since it is legally a continuation of the original meeting, but it is good practice to notify all members of adjourned meetings.

Adjourned meetings may themselves be adjourned to later adjourned meetings. No adjourned meeting may be set for the same time as, or a time later than, the next regular meeting.

Failure to Call Meetings

If the officers or directors who are responsible for calling a *regular* meeting, such as a monthly or annual meeting of an organization or of a board of directors, fail to perform their duty and do not call it, a group of members or even one member may demand that the officers call the meeting. Such a demand is strengthened if an election or some important matter has been set for that meeting. If the officers or directors fail to call a meeting after a demand is made, statutes often provide that a group of members or a single member after a reasonable time may call the meeting and designate the time and the usual place. When a quorum is present, the meeting may proceed.

The bylaws of some organizations provide that a *special* meeting must be called when a petition from a specified percentage of the members is presented to the president.

Chapter 13

QUORUM

Necessity for a Quorum

A *quorum* is the number or proportion of the members of an organization that must be present at a meeting in order to transact business legally.[1] If there is any question as to whether a quorum is present at the time set for a meeting, the presiding officer should not call the meeting to order but should determine the presence or absence of a quorum by counting the members present. *Until a quorum is present, there can be no meeting.*

Quorum Requirements

The bylaws of an organization should state the number or proportion of members that constitutes the quorum. In the absence of such a provision, parliamentary law fixes the quorum at a majority of the members.[2] This quorum requirement is often too high, and most groups have a more realistic provision.[3] The number required for a quorum should be small enough to insure that a quorum will usually be present but large enough to protect the organization against decisions being made by a small minority of the members.

In organizations with a fluctuating membership it is wise to select a *proportion* of the membership as a quorum so the quorum will vary as the membership varies. Many organizations provide, for example, that one-eighth or one-tenth of the members constitutes a quorum. When a fixed number is required for a quorum, a reduction or increase in the number

113

of members of the organization does not alter the number constituting a quorum.[4]

In conventions where the business of the organization is transacted by delegates who are expected to be present at all business meetings, the required quorum should be higher—for example, a majority of the delegates registered at the convention.

A mass meeting or an organization without a definite membership counts the members present, no matter what their number, as a quorum.[5] A committee or board requires a majority of its members for a quorum.

Computing a Quorum

A quorum always refers to the number of members *present* and not to the number *voting*.[6] If a quorum is present, a vote is valid even though fewer than the quorum vote.[7]

In computing a quorum, only members in good standing are counted. The meaning of the phrase "in good standing" varies with different organizations according to their bylaws. However, a member in good standing may be disqualified from voting on a particular question because of personal interest or benefit in it. In such a case he could not be counted for the purpose of computing a quorum for a vote on that question.[8] The presiding officer is counted in computing a quorum.[9]

If a quorum is present, a majority of those voting, which is often a small proportion of the total membership, has the right to make decisions for the organization. Since this is true, rigid requirements for notifying all members of meetings should be observed so that all members will have an opportunity to attend and vote.

Raising a Question on Quorum

It is the duty of the presiding officer to declare the meeting adjourned at any time that he knows that a quorum is not present. If he does not do so, it becomes the duty of any member who doubts that a quorum is present at a particular time during a meeting to rise to a point of order and request that the members be counted. Or a member may ask, "Mr. Chairman, is there a quorum present?" This question is in order at any time.

The presence of a quorum is determined by counting the members present or by calling the roll. The presence or absence of a quorum at any particular time can be established by entering the number present in the minutes. When a quorum is obviously present, the question of the presence of a quorum cannot be raised repeatedly for the purpose of delay.

Presumption of a Quorum

The question as to the presence of a quorum at the time of voting on a particular motion must be raised at the time the vote is taken, if it is to be raised at all. It cannot be raised later. Unless the minutes show that a quorum was not present at the time of voting on a motion, the law presumes that since the minutes show that a quorum was present when the meeting began, a quorum continued to be present until recess or adjournment.[10] It is not permissible at some later time to question the validity of an action on the ground that there was not a quorum present at the time it was voted on.[11]

Chapter 14

ORDER OF BUSINESS

Usual Order of Business

An *order of business* is a blueprint for meetings. It lists the different divisions of business in the order in which each will be called for at business meetings. Its purpose is to provide a systematic plan for the orderly conduct of business.

If the bylaws do not include an order of business, parliamentary law has established the following pattern:

1. Call to order
2. Reading, correction, approval, or disposition of minutes of previous meetings
3. Reports of officers
4. Reports of boards and standing committees
5. Reports of special committees
6. Unfinished business
7. New business
8. Announcements
9. Adjournment

When there is a prayer or roll call, it should follow the call to order. Some organizations also include a period called "organization welfare" or "good and welfare." During this period, which comes just before adjournment, members may make suggestions or announcements but no motions may be proposed.

Flexibility in the Order of Business

The regular order of business should be followed, but should have reasonable flexibility. For example, if no standing committee is ready to report but a special committee is ready, the presiding officer might state, "The Committee on Membership is not ready to report until later in the meeting. Is there any objection to hearing at this time the report of the Special Committee on a New Bookkeeping System?" If there is objection, a vote must be taken to authorize the variation from the regular order of business.

The order of business for a special meeting consists only of the call to order, consideration of the items of business stated in the notice of the meeting, and adjournment.

The order of business of a convention should be prepared to fulfill the particular needs of the convention. When a program or schedule for a business meeting has been adopted by a convention and a time fixed for considering certain items of business, this schedule cannot be deviated from except by unanimous consent or by majority vote. If an item that has been set for a particular time is postponed to a later time in the same meeting, the motion to postpone is sufficient notice to all delegates present.

Agenda

An *agenda* is a list of the specific items under each division of the order of business that the officers or board plan to present to a meeting.

The list under "unfinished business," for example, would include any item of business that was interrupted by the adjournment of the previous meeting or any motion that was postponed definitely to the current meeting.

An agenda is usually prepared by the president and the secretary and is sometimes mailed to the members. Unless the organization has a rule to the contrary, the use or even the adoption of an agenda does not preclude other items of business from being proposed, considered, and decided during the meeting. An agenda is flexible, and items may be changed or omitted by the presiding officer, or by unanimous consent, or a majority vote.

Call to Order

The presiding officer calls the meeting to order promptly at the scheduled time by rapping with his gavel and announcing: "The meeting will please come to order," or "The Eighty-third Annual Meeting of the House of Delegates of the American Bar Association is now convened."

Reading of Minutes

Unless there is a prayer or roll call, the first business is the reading, correction, and approval of the minutes of the previous meeting. The presiding officer directs the secretary to read the minutes. When the minutes have been read, the presiding officer inquires, "Are there any corrections to the minutes?" If there are no corrections, he continues, "If not, the minutes are approved as read," or some member may move that the minutes be approved. When corrections are suggested and there is a difference of opinion on them, the presiding officer takes a vote on the corrections before the minutes are approved. After the corrections are settled, some member may move to approve the minutes as corrected, or the presiding officer may state, "If there is no objection, the minutes will be approved as corrected. Is there any objection?" If there is an objection, a vote must be taken on approving the minutes.

If minutes have been printed and sent to each member before the meeting, they are not usually read in the meeting or convention. The presiding officer must call for corrections, however, before the minutes may be approved.

The reading of the minutes may be postponed to a definite time or meeting by unanimous consent or by majority vote. If the reading of the minutes of several previous meetings has been postponed to the current meeting, the presiding officer directs the secretary to read all minutes that have not been corrected and approved.

If the organization has a standing committee on minutes, this committee usually corrects the minutes and reports at regular intervals. On the certification of the minutes committee that the minutes are correct, the body may, by unanimous consent or by majority vote, approve the minutes.

Reports of Officers

The presiding officer usually calls on the treasurer to give a brief report summarizing collections and expenditures since the last meeting and mentioning any unusual items. The presiding officer inquires whether there are any questions on the report. If questions are asked, the treasurer answers them. The presiding officer then states that the report of the treasurer will be filed. Some organizations also call for reports from the president, secretary, or other officers.

Reports of Committees

When there is a report of the board of directors or governing board, this report comes first. The presiding officer next calls on the chairman of each board or standing committee and then of each special committee to report. The reports of committees usually are filed but not voted on.

If an officer or committee also presents recommendations, these are considered and voted on either immediately after the report or under new business, as the organization chooses.

Unfinished Business

The presiding officer introduces this section of the order of business with the statement, "Unfinished business is now in order."

Unfinished business includes only two types of items:

1. Any motion or report that was being considered and was interrupted when the previous meeting adjourned
2. Any motion or report that was postponed definitely to the current meeting but not set as an order for a particular hour

The presiding officer presents an item of unfinished business to the assembly by stating, for example: "Discussion on the motion to send delegates to the International Conference at Antwerp was interrupted by adjournment at our last meeting. The secretary will please read this motion." After the motion is read, he continues: "Discussion is now in order on the motion as read by the secretary."

The fact that a subject has been discussed previously does not make it old or unfinished business. Items of business that were postponed temporarily or referred to a committee are not unfinished business.

New Business

The presiding officer opens new business by declaring, "New business is now in order."

New business includes any proposal that any member may wish to present to the assembly, except items of business that must be presented under other divisions of the order of business. The opportunity to present new proposals continues until the meeting is declared adjourned.

Announcements

A meeting is expedited by having a regular place in the order of business for announcements and requiring that they be made only at that time. The presiding officer usually calls first for announcements from members and then concludes with any that he wishes to make.

Adjournment

A meeting can be adjourned only after a motion to adjourn has been made, seconded, and carried. The announcement of adjournment by the presiding officer formally terminates the meeting. The presiding officer may ask if some member wishes to move to adjourn, but he cannot adjourn the meeting without a vote unless a quorum ceases to be present.

Chapter 15

DEBATE

The Right of Debate

The purpose of deliberative bodies is to secure the mature judgment of the group on proposals submitted to it for decision. This purpose is best served by free interchange of thought through discussion and debate.

The right of every member to participate in the discussion of any matter of business that comes before the assembly is one of the fundamental principles of parliamentary law.[1]

Debate is regulated by parliamentary rules in order to assure every member a reasonable and equal opportunity to present his viewpoint. A knowledge of the rules governing debate is essential to every member wishing to exercise his rights.[2]

Extent of Debate on Motions

Motions are classified into three groups according to the extent of debate that is permitted on them. These are:
1. Motions that are fully debatable
2. Motions that are debatable with restrictions
3. Motions that are not debatable

Motions that are *fully debatable* are those that may require unlimited discussion for their decision. These motions are:

main motions, including reconsider and rescind, amend (unless applied to an undebatable motion), appeal, and postpone indefinitely.

There are three motions that are *debatable with restrictions*: recess, postpone definitely, and refer to a committee. Debate on them is restricted to a brief time and to a few points.

All other motions are *not debatable* and must be put to vote immediately. To permit debate on the motion to postpone temporarily, limit debate, or vote immediately, for example, would defeat the purpose of the motion.

Obtaining the Floor for Debate

As soon as a debatable motion has been stated to the assembly by the presiding officer, any member has the right to discuss it after obtaining the floor. A member waits until no one has the floor, then rises, addresses the presiding officer, and waits for recognition. He obtains the floor in the same manner, whether he wishes to present a motion or to discuss one.

When a member is recognized, he is entitled to protection in his exclusive right to be heard so long as he conforms to the rules of debate.

Recognition of Members During Debate

Usually the first person who rises and asks for recognition when no member has the floor is entitled to recognition. When several members seek recognition at the same time, the following logical rules help the presiding officer to decide which member should be recognized first:

1. Preference is given to the proposer of a motion or to the committee chairman who has presented a report. He should be allowed the first opportunity to explain his motion or report and usually is also allowed to speak last on it.

2. A member who has not spoken has prior claim over one who has already discussed the question. Similarly, a member who seldom speaks should be given preference over one who claims the attention of the assembly frequently.
3. The presiding officer should alternate between proponents and opponents of a motion whenever possible. When there are opposing opinions, the presiding officer may inquire of a member seeking recognition which viewpoint he will present. Thus the presiding officer is able to divide the opportunity to speak more equitably.

Speaking More Than Once

No member or small group of members should be permitted to monopolize the discussion on a question. If a member has already spoken and other members wish to speak, they should be recognized in preference to the member who has already spoken on that question. However, if no other members seek recognition, a member who has already spoken may be recognized again.

Sometimes a few members who are interested in and informed on the subject being discussed will speak several times on that particular question. This is permissible provided members who have not already spoken are not seeking recognition.

What Is Not Debate?

A brief comment or remark by the proposer of a motion before he states it is sometimes permissible. Similarly, a brief explanatory remark or a question is sometimes permitted on an undebatable motion. An inquiry, or a brief suggestion, is not debate.

When debate has been limited, and a member speaks in answer to a question addressed to him through the presiding officer, his reply is not debate and the time is not subtracted from his allotted time.

Before voting on a question every member is entitled to know precisely what the question is and what its effects will be. He is also entitled to ask for a reasonable explanation or to raise a parliamentary inquiry. A member has the right to have a question restated before voting or at any time when there is uncertainty about its meaning or wording.

Relevancy in Debate

All discussion must be relevant to the motion before the assembly. A member is given the floor only for the purpose of discussing the pending question; if he departs from that subject, he is out of order. He may use illustrations or tell a story in discussing a point so long as these are pertinent to the motion under discussion.

If a speaker departs from the subject, the presiding officer should interrupt him and request that he confine his remarks to the question. If the presiding officer fails to interrupt a speaker whose discussion is irrelevant, any member may rise to a point of order and call the attention of the presiding officer to the speaker's digression. The presiding officer should then direct the speaker to confine his discussion to the question before the assembly.

Discussion is always restricted so far as possible to the immediately pending motion. When a motion is under discussion and a motion of higher precedence is made, unless the new motion opens the main motion to debate, discussion is confined to the motion of higher precedence until it is decided.

Dilatory Tactics

Dilatory tactics—that is, delaying the proposal or the vote on a subject by making unnecessary motions, asking pointless questions, or talking around and not on the question—are always out of order. As soon as it is evident that a member or group of members is using dilatory tactics, the presiding officer should point out that such conduct is out of order, and if members persist, he should refuse to recognize them.

Members' Conduct During Debate

Debate must be fundamentally impersonal. All discussion is addressed to the presiding officer and must never be directed to any individual.

A motion—its nature or consequences—may be attacked vigorously. But it is never permissible to attack the motives, character, or personality of a member either directly or by innuendo or implication. It is the duty of the presiding officer to stop any member instantly if he engages in personalities or attacks the motives of another member or is ungentlemanly in word or manner. It is the motion, not its proposer, that is the subject of debate. Meetings must discuss measures, not men.

Arguments and opinions should be stated as clearly and concisely as possible. The speaker should remember that he is talking, not for his own pleasure or for the entertainment of others, but to assist the assembly in arriving at a decision on the question under discussion.

A member enhances his effectiveness in debate by his courtesy toward the presiding officer and other members. If a member uses improper language or conducts himself in a disorderly manner, he should be promptly called to order by the presiding officer. When a point of order is raised concerning the conduct of a speaker, he must be seated until the point of order is decided by the presiding officer.

If a member fails or refuses to conduct his discussion in an orderly and courteous manner, he may be denied the right to the floor. If necessary, he may be ejected from the meeting by order of the presiding officer or by a vote of the assembly.

Presiding Officer's Duties During Debate

The presiding officer has the responsibility of controlling and expediting debate. When a member has been assigned the floor, he has the right to the quiet and undivided attention of the assembly so long as he conducts himself properly. It is the duty of the presiding officer to protect the speaker in this right by suppressing disorder, by eliminating whispering and walking about, and by preventing annoyance, heckling, or unnecessary interruption. The presiding officer should insist that every member be attentive to the business before the assembly. The assembly owes respectful attention to the presiding officer and to each speaker.

It is also the presiding officer's duty to keep the subject clearly before the members, to rule out any irrelevant discussion, and to restate the question whenever necessary.

If the presiding officer believes that there are important viewpoints on the question that are not being presented during the discussion, he should seek to bring out these aspects of the subject. If he feels that the members do not have a real understanding of the motion, or of its implications, or its consequences, he should seek to draw out all facts that will contribute to a clear understanding of the motion and its effects.

Time Limits on Debate

Parliamentary law fixes no limit on the length of speeches during debate. Each organization has the right to fix limits in its bylaws or rules if the members wish to do so. Debate can ordinarily be kept within reasonable time limits by the presiding officer's insistence that all discussion be confined strictly to the subject.

Cutting Off Debate

It is unwise to make a practice or habit of cutting off or preventing debate on most debatable questions. This is true whether debate is cut off by recognized motions or by arbitrarily bringing questions to vote without adequate opportunity for discussion.[3] Members cannot be expected to maintain interest in an organization if they are frequently denied the right to participate in its deliberations.

Bringing a Question to Vote

When it appears to the presiding officer that all of the members who wish to speak have done so, he inquires, "Is there any further discussion?" or "Are you ready for the question?"

These queries give notice to members that if they desire to speak they must claim the right promptly. The proper response to these queries is for members to answer "Question" if they wish to end discussion or to ask for recognition if they wish to speak. If no one responds to the queries, the presiding officer puts the question to vote.

The presiding officer should never hurry the vote unduly. He should pause long enough after the query, "Are you ready for the question," to enable an alert member to request recognition. If the presiding officer starts to put the question to vote prematurely, however, this does not cut off the right of a member to speak. A member, if reasonably prompt in claiming the privilege, can assert his right to debate at any time before the taking of the vote is completed and the result is announced. Debate is finally and completely closed by the announcement of the vote.

Discussion can be cut off only by a motion to vote immediately, or by a previously adopted limitation on debate. (See *Question! Question!*, p. 69.)

Informal Consideration

There are times when it is desirable to have discussion of a problem precede the proposal of a motion concerning it so that some agreement may be reached on the type and wording of the motion that is needed. There are also times when it is wise to set aside the formal rules governing discussion and debate. Both of these objectives may be accomplished by a motion to consider a particular motion, subject, or problem informally. Informal consideration permits freedom in the length and number of speeches, allows possible amendments and motions to be discussed together, and gives broader latitude in debate.

If no motion is pending and a motion for informal consideration carries, it permits consideration of a subject or problem before a motion concerning it is presented.

If a motion is already being considered by the assembly, the motion to consider the pending motion informally is an incidental motion. If it carries, the pending motion is considered informally until the members decide to take a vote on it. This vote terminates the informal discussion.

Sometimes an assembly wishes to consider a problem that is not sufficiently understood or formulated for a member to propose a clear and adequate motion covering it. There may not be time to refer the problem to a committee. Informal discussion often brings understanding and agreement and makes evident how the motion should be worded. Rather than offer a poorly thought-out motion, which will consume time and effort to perfect by amendment, it is better to consider the problem informally and then formulate a good motion.

For example, a member might say, "We realize that some action must be taken to raise more funds for this organization. I move that we consider informally the problem of fund raising." If this motion carries, the presiding officer opens the problem to informal discussion. When the problem is clarified and there appears to be a solution or a consensus, a member should offer a motion embodying the idea. This motion automatically terminates the informal discussion, and the motion is considered and voted on under the regular rules of debate. If no agreement on the problem is reached, informal discussion may be terminated by a motion to end the informal discussion.

Informal consideration has all the advantages and none of the drawbacks of the old complicated procedures of a committee of the whole.

Chapter 16

VOTES REQUIRED FOR VALID ACTIONS

Significance of a Majority Vote

The most fundamental rule governing voting is that at least a majority vote is required to take an action. A majority vote is the vote of more than half of the members voting, unless the term is otherwise qualified. Jefferson said, "Until a majority has spoken, nothing has changed." It is obvious that to permit fewer than a majority to decide for any group would subject the many to the rule of the few, and this would be contrary to the most basic democratic principle. Democratic peoples universally accept decision by majority vote.

If a majority agrees, that is an agreement by the body, since all members by the act of joining the organization have agreed that the majority should govern. (See *Relationship Between Members and Organization*, p. 221.)

Fewer than a majority should not be authorized to decide anything, and more than a majority should not be required for most decisions. Yet sometimes organizations adopt a rule that permits a mere plurality; that is, one vote more than any other candidate to elect an officer, or go to the other extreme of requiring a high vote on certain proposals. Under either of these rules the minority, not the majority, controls.

Any requirements permitting decisions by *less* than a majority vote (for example, by plurality) or requiring *more* than a majority vote (for example, a two-thirds vote on a proposal) are not valid unless they are included in the law, the rules of parliamentary law, or the bylaws.

Requiring More Than a Majority Vote

Some parliamentary writers have mistakenly assumed that the higher the vote required to take an action, the greater the protection of the members. Instead, the opposite is true. Whenever a vote of more than a majority is required to take an action, control is taken from the majority and given to a minority. For example, when a two-thirds vote is required, the minority need be only one-third plus one member to defeat the proposal. Thus, a minority is permitted to overrule the will, not only of the majority, but of almost two-thirds of the members. If a two-thirds vote is required to pass a proposal and sixty-five members vote for the proposal and thirty-five members vote against it, the thirty-five members make the decision. This is minority, not majority, rule.

The higher the vote required, the smaller the minority to which control passes. The requirement of a unanimous vote means that one member can overrule the decision of all the other members and thus exercise what amounts to a power to veto the action of the body.

Recognition that decision by a majority vote is an integral and vital element of democracy was forcefully and clearly stated by Thomas Jefferson in a letter to Baron von Humboldt in 1817:

> "The first principle of republicanism is that the *lex-majoris partis* is the fundamental law of every society of individuals of equal rights; to consider the will of the society enounced by the majority of a single vote, as sacred as if unanimous, is the first of all lessons in importance, yet the last which is thoroughly learnt. This law once disregarded, there is no other but that of force, which ends necessarily in military despotism."

Requiring Less Than a Majority Vote

The effect of deciding proposals or electing candidates by less than a majority vote is similar to requiring a higher vote than a majority. It takes away the power of decision from the majority and gives it to a minority.

Electing a candidate or deciding an alternative proposal by plurality vote (more votes than any other candidate or alternative proposal) means that officers are chosen by a minority and that they therefore do not have the support that is behind a candidate chosen by a majority. If there is a large number of candidates for an office, the candidate elected may be chosen by only a small fraction of the members of the organization. No candidate can be elected to office and no proposal can be decided except by a majority vote, unless the bylaws provide for a plurality vote.

Importance of Defining the Vote Required

Every organization should state in its bylaws the number of votes required to elect candidates and also the votes required for important decisions. Whenever the basis on which a vote must be computed is not defined in the law or bylaws, there is confusion as to the vote that is required. A majority vote means a majority of what? A two-thirds vote means two-thirds of what? Even a unanimous vote has several meanings.

The common term *majority vote* is often misinterpreted because the basis for computing the majority is not stated. For years parliamentary writers have talked about a majority vote with no clear or definite understanding of its many and varied meanings. There has been no parliamentary source that gives a complete statement of the different meanings of this important term. This confusion has resulted in hundreds of cases being taken into court for a judge to decide which particular majority vote is meant. Even justices of the Supreme Court of the United States have differed as to the correct interpretation of a majority vote when it was not properly defined.[1]

Therefore, whenever such terms as *majority, two-thirds, three-fourths,* or *unanimous* vote are used, they should be qualified by stating the basis on which the vote is to be computed.

Different Meanings of Majority Vote

A majority vote, or any other vote, may be qualified or defined in many ways. For example, in an organization consisting of 200 memberships (limited to 200 members) which currently has 180 members in good standing, with a quorum requirement of one-eighth of all the members, which is 23, if there are 150 present at a meeting and only 20 vote, a majority vote would be variously computed as follows:

1.	A majority of all the memberships	101
2.	A majority of the members in good standing	91
3.	A majority of the members present	76
4.	A majority of a quorum	13
5.	A majority of the legal votes cast	11

A *majority vote of all the memberships* is often required to take an action in organizations having a fixed number of memberships. When this rule is applied to a board of education of eight members, a majority is five. If there are two vacancies, reducing the actual number of members to six, the required vote is still five because a majority of the eight memberships of the board is necessary.[2]

A *majority vote of all the members* means a vote of more than half of all the members both present and absent.[3] Such a vote is often required in organizations where the members serve in a representative capacity, such as a house of delegates or an executive board.

A *majority vote of the members present* is sometimes required to take an action. Under this rule the failure of some members to vote does not reduce the number of affirmative votes required. If there are 150 members present, an affirmative vote of 76 is necessary to act, regardless of the number voting.

A *majority vote of the quorum,* or a majority of the number of members who are authorized to act for the organization, is the minimum number that a few organizations permit to make a decision for all the members. This is the vote required in most corporate boards of directors.

Majority of the Legal Votes Cast

A majority of the legal votes cast is the requirement that most commonly approves a motion or elects a candidate. When the term "majority" is not defined and no other type of majority is specified, the law holds that a majority of the legal votes cast is required. This legal decision has been agreed on to resolve some of the confusion that resulted when the basis for counting a majority is not defined. Unless it is qualified in some way, a majority vote means a majority of the legal votes cast. Unless stated otherwise, this is the meaning of majority vote when used in this book.

The legal theory under which the decisions of an organization may be made by a majority of those voting is that all the members have the right to vote if they wish to exercise that right. The members who fail to vote are presumed to have waived the exercise of their right and to have consented to allow the will of the organization to be expressed by those voting.[4] The members who do not vote cannot be presumed to favor either side.

It is possible for a majority to consist of only one vote. A member may propose a motion that is of little interest to other members and when the presiding officer calls for a vote, the proposer votes "aye" and no one votes "no." The question is carried because it received a majority of the legal votes cast. A single affirmative vote, when there are no other votes cast, has been held by the courts to carry a question because that vote is the majority of the legal votes cast.[5]

Plurality Vote

A plurality vote means more votes than the number received by any other candidate or alternative proposition. There can be a plurality vote only if there are more than two candidates for the same office or more than two alternative propositions. The candidate receiving the highest number of votes has a plurality, but he does not have a majority unless he receives a greater number of votes than the number cast for all his competitors combined; in other words, more than one-half of the total number of legal votes cast for the particular office. A plurality vote does not elect a candidate or carry an alternative measure except when the bylaws provide for decision by a plurality vote. For example, the result of a vote might be:

Mr. A	23
Mrs. B	22
Mr. C	21

The total number of votes is sixty-six. The first candidate has a plurality vote, but no candidate has received a majority vote (thirty-four votes). If election to office is by plurality vote and only one candidate is to be elected, the candidate receiving twenty-three votes is elected. If election requires the usual majority vote, no candidate is elected.

Unanimous Vote

A unanimous vote on a proposal is a vote in which all of the legal votes cast are on the same side, whether affirmative or negative.

A unanimous vote for a candidate for a particular office is a vote in which one candidate receives all the legal votes cast for that office.

The essence of a unanimous vote is that all of those who vote, vote on one side or for one candidate.[6] A proposal is adopted unanimously if one vote is cast for it and no vote is cast against it, or is defeated unanimously if no vote is cast for it and one vote is cast against it.

If the term "unanimous vote" is qualified in some way, the qualification determines the meaning of that particular unanimous vote. For example, the unanimous vote of "all the members of the board" means that all the members of the board must be present and that all of them must vote on the same side of a proposal.[7] A unanimous vote of all the "members present" means that all of the members who are present must vote and that all of them must vote on the same side of a proposal.[8]

A unanimous vote is an example of decision by a minority—in this case a minority of one—and is a violation of the democratic principle of decision by a majority. It gives "the minority an absolute, permanent, all-inclusive power of veto." In 1693 the court of the Kings Bench stated that "the major number must bind the lesser, or else differences could never be determined." The requirement of a unanimous vote is seldom necessary or wise.

When a vote is not unanimous, no additional vote can change the original vote to a unanimous vote.

Tie Vote

A tie vote on a *motion* means that the same number of members has voted in the affirmative as in the negative. Since a majority vote, or more than half of the legal votes cast, is required to pass a motion, an equal or tie vote means that the motion is lost because it has failed to receive a majority vote. A tie vote on a motion is not a deadlock vote that must be resolved; it is simply not a majority vote and the motion is lost.

A tie vote that constitutes a deadlock that must be resolved can occur only when two or more candidates, or two or more alternative propositions, are being voted on at the same time and two or more of them receive the same number of votes. Then no candidate has been elected and no proposal has been adopted. Such a tie vote results in a deadlock, and the vote must be retaken until the tie is resolved by voting or by some other method which the assembly may choose.

Vote of the Presiding Officer

No officer relinquishes any of his rights as a member by accepting office, except that the presiding officer of an assembly cannot propose motions or nominate candidates. The presiding officer has the same voting privileges as any other member.

At times the presiding officer may wish to refrain from voting publicly on a controversial issue. If he does not wish to vote, he can refrain from voting just as any other member.

There is a popular belief that the presiding officer votes to break a tie vote. If he is a member and has not already voted, he may vote to break a tie if he wishes to do so.[9] If the presiding officer has already voted, he cannot vote again unless the bylaws provide that he may vote a second time in case of a deadlock tie vote.[10] Nothing can compel a presiding officer to vote in any situation any more than a member can be compelled to vote.

Computing a Majority for Separate Questions

When more than one question is voted on at the same time, or on the same ballot, the votes cast on each question are counted separately. A majority of the legal votes cast on each particular question is required to approve that question.

In an election, when candidates for more than one office are voted on at the same time, a majority of the legal votes cast for each particular office is required to elect a candidate to that office.

Computing a Majority When Electing a Group

Frequently candidates for several positions or offices of *equal* rank, such as members of a board, committee, or group of delegates, are voted on at the same time. When the offices are of equal rank and there is no differentiation between them, the majority vote required to elect is computed differently.

When several equal positions are voted on simultaneously, the majority vote is based on the total number of *legal ballots cast for the group* of equal offices. Even if some ballots contain a vote for only one nominee, these ballots are counted in determining a majority of the total *ballots* cast.

To be elected to one of several offices of equal rank that are being voted on simultaneously and require a majority vote, a nominee must meet two requirements. He must:

1. Receive a majority vote based on the total number of legal *ballots* cast for all of the equal offices
2. Receive a vote that is high enough to place him within the number of offices to be filled

If he receives a majority vote and fails to rank high enough to place within the number of offices to be filled, he is not elected. Or, if he ranks among the highest candidates but does not receive a majority vote, he is not elected. For example, if five board members are to be elected at the same time and there are seven nominees for these five positions, the vote might result as follows:

Nominee	Vote
A	80
B	79
C	75
D	75
E	69
F	52
G	43

Six members received the necessary majority vote, but only the top-ranking five are elected. The two nominees who tied for third and fourth place are both elected. Therefore, there is no necessity to break this tie vote. However, had there been a tie between the fifth and sixth places, it would have been necessary to vote again and break this tie to determine which nominee is elected.

If only three of the nominees had received a majority vote, only those three would be elected; it would then be necessary to take another vote to fill the two remaining vacancies. Unless the assembly adopts a motion to the contrary, all nominees except the three already elected remain candidates on the second ballot.

Voting Separately for Equal Positions

Some organizations favor differentiating between equal positions by numbering each position and nominating candidates separately for each position. For example, A, B, and C might be nominated as candidates for Board Member 1, and D and E as candidates for Board Member 2. In this case, a majority of the legal votes cast for each particular position would be required to elect a candidate. However, this practice is not always satisfactory. When the positions are numbered, some candidates receiving a small number of votes may be elected because they have no strong opposition, while other candidates who receive a large vote may be defeated because they face strong opposition.

When Members Cannot Vote

While it is the right and usually the duty of each member to vote on every question, in ordinary assemblies he cannot be compelled to vote on any question. The proposer of a motion has the same right as any other member to speak for or against or vote for or against the motion that he proposed.

There are certain situations in which a member has no right to vote. As a general principle, no one may vote on a question in which he has a direct personal or financial interest.[11] Stockholders are an exception to this principle. For example, a member cannot legally vote on a motion awarding a contract to himself. The courts have recognized an exception to this rule when the organization is authorized to fix the compensation of its members. Otherwise, it would be impossible to vote to fix the compensation.[12]

A member may vote on a question involving the whole organization when others are joined with him or affected by the vote, even though he has a direct personal or financial interest. For example, every member has the right to vote on a motion that determines convention expenses to be paid to delegates by the organization.

When charges have been preferred against a member, he cannot vote on the charges. However, if other members are also named in the charges, all members can vote on the charges. This rule prevents a small proportion of members from gaining control of an organization by filing charges against the majority of the members.

Chapter 17

METHODS OF VOTING

Voting Is a Fundamental Right

A member of any democratic body has the right to express his will or preference in electing officers and in deciding propositions. The right to a voice in determining the will of an assembly is the most fundamental right of a member. The will of an assembly is determined by taking a vote.[1]

Voting in Meetings

When the method of voting on a motion or candidate is not prescribed in the bylaws, a method of voting may be proposed by any member and determined by majority vote of the assembly at any time before the vote on the motion or candidate is taken. The usual methods of voting in a meeting are:
1. Voice vote
2. Rising or raising hands
3. Roll call
4. Ballot

Voice Vote

Voting by voice is the most commonly used method of voting. The presiding officer determines the result of the vote by the volume of voices. When the presiding officer is in doubt as to how the majority voted, he may call for the vote again or he may call for a rising vote.

If any member feels that a vote is indecisive or that the presiding officer has not announced it correctly, he may interrupt, if he does so promptly, and call for a division of the assembly,[2] in order to verify the vote.

In taking a vote by any method the presiding officer must always call for the affirmative vote first and announce it first.

Rising Vote

A rising vote or a vote by raising of hands may be used by the presiding officer to verify an indecisive vote or in response to a call from a member for a division of the assembly. The vote on a motion requiring a definite number or proportion of votes, such as two-thirds, is usually taken initially by rising so that a count may be made.

When the rising vote is close, the members should be counted; they must be counted if a count is demanded by a member and if there is any doubt as to the result of the vote. The presiding officer usually asks the secretary to count the vote. In a convention or a large meeting he appoints several tellers to assist the secretary. Each teller counts a particular section of voters and reports to the secretary, who announces the number of votes for and against the motion. The presiding officer then repeats the totals and announces the result: "The vote is 148 affirmative, 150 negative. The motion is lost."

When visitors or others who are not entitled to vote are

seated with members, votes should be taken only by rising, raising hands, or by roll call.

Roll Call Vote

A recorded vote is often advantageous when members vote as representatives of others, for example, delegates, proxies, or members of governmental boards or commissions. A roll call vote is sometimes termed voting by "ayes and noes" or by "yeas and nays." A vote by roll call may be required by the bylaws or may be decided upon by a motion from a member. The presiding officer states the question on a roll call as follows: "The motion is ... Those in favor of the motion will vote 'Aye' as their names are called; those opposed will vote 'No.' The secretary will call the roll."

The names are called in alphabetical order, or in the numerical order of districts, or in some other appropriate order. The name of the presiding officer is usually called last. If a member does not wish to vote, he may remain silent or answer "present" or "abstaining." The secretary should always have lists of names ready for use in calling the roll. The original roll call record is inserted in the minutes.

Ballot Vote

Voting by secret ballot is the only method that enables members to express their decisions without revealing their opinions or preferences. The legal definition of a ballot vote is "the expression by ballot, voting machine, or otherwise, but in no event by proxy, of a choice with respect to any election or vote on any matter, which is cast in such a manner that the person expressing such choice cannot be identified with the choice expressed." [3]

Voting by secret ballot is usually required in elections and frequently in voting on important proposals. If a vote by ballot on a particular motion is not required by the bylaws, it may be ordered by a motion to vote by ballot on the particular question. If a vote by ballot is required by the bylaws, a motion to dispense with the ballot vote, or to suspend the provision requiring such a vote, is not in order unless this procedure is provided for in the bylaws. (See *Casting Ballot by Secretary,* p. 157.)

The presiding officer should give careful instructions as to how the members should prepare their ballots and he should ask before the voting begins whether anyone is without a ballot.

Voting by Unanimous Consent

Routine or noncontroversial questions are often decided by unanimous consent without taking a formal vote. When members are in agreement, this method saves time and expedites business. For example, if a member moves "That the calling of the roll be dispensed with," the presiding officer may respond, "It has been moved and seconded that the calling of the roll be dispensed with. Is there any objection?" If any member says, "I object," a vote must be taken on the motion.

The presiding officer may propose action by unanimous consent without any motion. He may proceed by assuming unanimous consent. For example, if a member asks to make an announcement at an unusual time, the presiding officer may say, "If there is no objection, Mr. M will be allowed to make an announcement now." Even when the presiding officer has announced that an action has been taken by unanimous consent, if any member immediately objects, the question must be stated and voted on.

Voting by Mail

In organizations whose members are scattered over a wide area or who work during different hours, provision is sometimes made for members to vote on important questions by mail. Voting by mail cannot be used unless it is authorized in the bylaws.

Voting by mail has certain disadvantages. When voting by mail the members do not have the opportunity to discuss or listen to debate on proposals or to amend them. In elections there is no opportunity to nominate candidates from the floor.

Voting by mail by some members who cannot attend a meeting and voting at a meeting or convention by those who attend cannot be combined successfully. Since proposals and amendments to bylaws can be discussed and amended at a meeting or convention, those voting by mail and those voting at a convention might each be voting on quite different proposals or amendments. Similarly, when candidates are being elected, those voting by mail would have no chance to nominate additional candidates from the floor.

An organization should choose between voting on proposals or amendments to the bylaws by mail and the right to discuss, amend, and vote on them at a meeting or convention. It should similarly choose between voting for candidates by mail and the right to nominate additional candidates from the floor.

Any method of voting by mail may be followed so long as it insures the voters full understanding of the issues to be decided. Unless the bylaws provide for a particular plan, a ballot containing proposed measures or amendments or a list of candidates is mailed to each member by the secretary together with directions from the elections committee for voting. Some organizations include with the ballot information concerning qualifications of candidates and arguments for and against proposals to be voted on.

The ballot must be marked and returned to the secretary within a specified time. The usual way to preserve secrecy is to require each member to seal his ballot in one envelope which is furnished him and which has no mark of identification on it. He encloses this in another envelope which bears his signature so that it may be checked against the list of signatures of members eligible to vote. The inner envelopes are delivered, still sealed, to the tellers or elections committee.

Voting by Proxy

Voting by proxy means that a particular member or person is authorized to cast the vote of an absent member in a meeting or convention. The term "proxy" may mean either the statement authorizing a member to cast the vote of the member signing it or the member who casts the vote. The proxy voter may cast as many votes as he holds proxies.

In profit corporations, where membership is based on the ownership of shares of stock and voting rights are unequal, voting by proxy is the approved method of deciding proposals and electing officers.

In nonprofit corporations or organizations, voting by proxy is legal in most states only if it is authorized by statute and provided for in the charter and bylaws of the organization. Directors or board members cannot vote by proxy in their meetings since this would mean the delegation of a discretionary legislative duty which they cannot delegate.

A proxy may be in almost any form as long as its meaning is clear. It may be limited to one meeting, or motion, or issue, or person, or time, or it may be unlimited. All proxies, however, must conform strictly to the provisions of the statutes and charters, and to the bylaws of the organization. The use of proxies in organizations where all members have an equal vote is ill advised and is never permissible unless specifically authorized by the bylaws, charters, or statutes.

Changing a Vote

When a vote is taken by a show of hands, by rising, or by roll call, a member may change his vote up to the time that the result of the vote is finally announced. After a vote by roll call has been announced, a member can change the record of his vote only by proof that an error was made in recording it. When a member has voted by ballot, he may not change his vote after the ballot has left his possession.

Announcing the Result of a Vote

It is the duty of the presiding officer to announce the result of the vote according to the facts.[4] However, an incorrect or untrue announcement of the vote cannot make the vote as cast by the majority illegal.[5] In case of a disputed vote, the courts will examine the facts to determine whether the vote as announced is correct.[6]

All Votes Binding During a Meeting

A few organizations follow the improper practice of taking an informal, test, or straw vote in meetings which they interpret to be a vote that is not binding. Such a vote is sometimes used to influence members to reach a consensus. A unity of opinion, if it is reached without coercion, is desirable; but informal votes cannot properly be taken during a meeting.

No body, board, or committee can, during its meeting, properly take a vote that is not binding. If an assembly wishes to vote to recess to determine the probable vote of the members, it may do so; but under the law all votes taken during a meeting are binding.[7]

Chapter 18

NOMINATIONS AND ELECTIONS

Choosing Organization Leaders

The process of nominating and electing officers is vital to every organization, because the abilities and talents of the leaders largely determine the achievements of the group.

Parliamentary law permits a wide latitude of choice in each step of the nominating and electing process. There is no one magic method, but there are certain procedures that experience has proved are better than others for obtaining good leaders.

Bylaw Provisions on Nominations and Elections

The procedure for choosing the officers of an organization begins with nominations and continues through the taking of office by those elected.

The bylaw provisions on nominations should include the offices to be filled, the eligibility and qualifications of candidates, the method and time of nominating, and the term of office. If a nominating committee is to be used, provisions for selecting its members, and determining their qualifications, instructions, duties, and reporting should also be included.

The bylaw provisions on elections should include the time, place, and method of voting, the notice required, a statement of who is eligible to vote, the vote required to elect, the method of conducting the election, and the time when the new officers take office. Some bylaws include a provision for special elections if needed to fill vacancies.

Nominations from the Floor

A nomination is the formal presentation to an assembly of the name of a member as a candidate for a particular office. If the bylaws do not provide the method for nominating officers, any member may propose a motion determining how nominations are to be made.

Unless the bylaws provide otherwise, nominations from the floor are always permitted even if the initial nominations are made by a nominating committee. When the presiding officer opens nominations from the floor, he may say: "Are there nominations [or further nominations] for the office of president?" Any member may then rise and, after recognition, say, for example, "I nominate Mr. A."

It is customary to permit a nominator to state his reasons for supporting the nominee. Nominations do not require seconds, but some organizations permit other members to give endorsing statements, which are called *seconding speeches.* If the report of a nominating committee states the qualfications and abilities of its nominees, a member who nominates from the floor may also state the qualifications and abilities of his candidate.

The presiding officer should repeat his request for further nominations and should pause to allow ample opportunity for members to present nominees. When there appear to be no further nominations for a particular office, he may declare nominations for that office closed, or ask for nominations for the next office without closing nominations; or some member may move that nominations for that office be closed. The presiding officer should not recognize a motion to close nominations or declare them closed, however, until members have had a reasonable opportunity to nominate.

A motion to close nominations or a declaration by the presiding officer closing nominations is not required. If nominations have been closed, they may be reopened by a motion to this effect until voting has begun.

Relying solely on nominations from the floor is usually not the most satisfactory method for securing the best candidates. The lack of time for considering qualifications, the tendency of nominees to decline nominations from the floor, and the resulting confusion often prevent the organization from securing the best leaders. A nominating committee, so long as it is fairly chosen and is representative, will usually select good candidates, but nominations from the floor should always be provided for as a safeguard.

Voting for Candidates Not Nominated

A member need not be nominated for an office, either from the floor or by a committee, to be elected to that office when the vote is taken by ballot or by roll call. Members may vote for anyone who is eligible, regardless of whether he has been nominated, by writing in the name of their choice on the ballot or voting for him on roll call. Any member receiving the necessary vote is elected, unless he declines to accept the office.

Selecting a Nominating Committee

A nominating committee is one of the most important committees of an organization because it can help to secure the best officers. Nomination of candidates by a committee has advantages. A committee has the time to study the leadership needs of the organization and to select candidates to meet these needs. It can interview prospective nominees, investigate their experience, qualifications, and abilities, persuade them to become candidates, and secure their consent to serve if elected. The committee is also able to apportion representation equitably among different groups and different areas.

A nominating committee should be a representative committee. Many organizations provide, for example, that if the nominating committee consists of five members, three of the members are elected by the membership, and the chairman and the fifth member are appointed by the governing board.

The members chosen by the board are usually current or recent members of the board who, by reason of their service, have a broad and up-to-date knowledge of the needs of the organization and of the leadership abilities of its members. The members of the committee elected by the membership usually reflect the viewpoint of the general membership.

Any plan by which experienced leaders choose some of the members of the nominating committee and the membership chooses the other members is usually effective in securing a committee that is both representative and knowledgeable.

The president should not appoint any members of the nominating committee, give the committee instructions, or take any part in its deliberations. This requirement protects both the president and the committee from accusations of favoritism or self-perpetuation. When a nominating committee is used, it is essential that the members be chosen wisely and democratically and that both the committee and the membership be protected by permitting nominations from the floor.

Duties of a Nominating Committee

A carefully chosen nominating committee should be permitted to use its judgment in selecting the candidates who will give the best service to the organization. It should choose the candidates on the basis of what is good for all the members and not on the basis that an office is a reward to be given to a deserving member. The committee may invite suggestions but should not be limited by them.

A few organizations use the nominating committee merely

as a computing group to which names from various areas or local groups are sent and the results tabulated. This type of committee does little more than compile a list of nominees based on the preferences stated by the various areas or local groups.

On the other hand, many organizations believe that the best leaders are secured by delegating to the nominating committee the duty to find and nominate the best candidates. The duties usually assigned to such a nominating committee are:

1. To study the problems and leadership requirements of the organization. For example, if the organization has financial difficulties, dissension, or a decreasing membership, it needs leaders who are capable of solving such problems. The particular needs of the organizations for the next term of office should be summarized in an introduction to the report of the nominating committee.
2. To select nominees who have the experience and the qualities that meet the needs of the organization.
3. To interview prospective nominees personally, by telephone, or by mail, and secure their consent to serve if elected.
4. To prepare a report containing the committee's analysis of the leadership needs of the organization, the names of the nominees, their experience and qualifications, and the reasons that the committee feels the candidates named can meet these needs.
5. To submit its report to the meeting or convention and for publication and distribution to the members.

Qualifications of Nominees

Qualifications for each office should be stated in the bylaws. No member can be a candidate for, or be elected to, an office for which he cannot qualify under the rules of the organization. The nomination of an unqualified member must be ruled out of order.

Nomination to More Than One Office

No member can accept nomination for or hold two incompatible offices. Some organizations in their bylaws combine two offices, thus, in effect, declaring them compatible. For example, the offices of secretary and treasurer are sometimes combined as secretary-treasurer. Membership on the governing board is usually compatible with other offices such as president or secretary. The fact that bylaws usually provide that the officers serve on the board is a determination of compatibility. Incompatibility does not consist of physical impossibility to perform the duties of both offices but lies in a conflict of interest between the duties of the two offices.[1]

If a member is nominated for two incompatible offices at the same election, he must choose the office that he prefers and decline the other nomination. Unless the bylaws provide otherwise, a member who holds an office may be a candidate for another office, but if he is elected to and accepts an incompatible office, he forfeits the former office.

Nominating-Committee Members as Candidates

Members who are likely to become candidates should not serve on a nominating committee. But members of the committee can become candidates. If they were barred from becoming candidates, supporters of one candidate might maneuver to place his prospective opponents on the nominating committee in order to disqualify them from candidacy. A member of a nominating committee who becomes a candidate should resign from the committee immediately.

Single and Multiple Slate

If an organization chooses a representative nominating committee carefully and democratically, it may be desirable to nominate a single candidate for each office. A single slate, meaning one nominee for each office, frequently offers certain advantages provided that nominations may also be made from the floor and that election by write-in votes is not forbidden.

In some organizations the belief persists that it is more democratic to have two or more nominees for each office in order that there may be a contest. This belief is probably based on the fact that national and state governments have a two-party political system and therefore have a candidate from each party for each office. There is a growing tendency for nongovernmental organizations to nominate a single slate.

There are many capable members who may be persuaded to take the responsibility of an office if they believe that the membership wishes them to do so. But often they will not engage in a contest with other members for the office.

When a nominating committee is required to submit the names of two or more nominees for each office, it often faces a dilemma. If the committee members decide, for example, that Mr. A can offer the best leadership as president, they are obliged to do either of two things. They may add another nominee who is not well qualified in the hope that Mr. A will be more certain to be elected, or they may add regretfully the name of Mr. B who is also well qualified, and sacrifice one of their two best potential leaders by defeat.

Defeated candidates seldom choose to run again. Thus, the services of many good leaders may be lost to the organization because they are sacrificed to furnish a contest. Few organizations can afford this waste of good leadership. There is no particular democratic purpose served by nominating additional members in order to defeat all but one of them.

In organizations that provide for a single slate, there are situations that make a contest for an office necessary or desirable. For example, if the members are seeking to decide an important policy or course of action and they do not wish to vote on the matter directly, they may decide it by nominating two or more candidates who represent substantially different opinions and voting on the candidates. Such an election is not simply a vote for the best qualified candidate for the office but is a vote to decide on the course of future action and on a candidate who is best qualified to carry out that action.

The single slate always should be safeguarded by the right of nominations from the floor and of write-in votes. If the nominating committee fails to express the will of the majority of the members in its selection of nominees, this should be rectified by adding nominees from the floor to provide a contest.

Election Committee

Organizations usually appoint an election committee which conducts the election. This committee should also be a representative committee. It supervises the preparation and printing of ballots, their distribution to voting members either at a meeting or convention or by mail, the collection and counting of the ballots, and the preparation of a report showing the results of the election.

Counting Ballots

The chairman of the election committee is responsible for seeing that ballots are counted accurately. One effective method of counting ballots is for one member to read the votes for all offices from each ballot while another member stands near enough to check the correctness of the reading. The votes are recorded by another member whose tabulation is also checked to insure accuracy. If a ballot has several offices to be voted upon, it is more efficient to divide the recording of the votes between two or more teams of recorders and checkers, each recording only the votes for one or two offices. While counting the votes, there should be silence except for the reading of the names. If there is a possible error, some member says, "Stop," and the vote is verified before proceeding.

In large organizations, where thousands of voters must be counted, the ballots are divided among many teams of readers, counters, and checkers and counted in the same way by each team. Votes are usually tallied in groups of five. Any member has a right to be present while the ballots are being counted.

Many organizations have developed effective methods of counting ballots, to meet their own needs. Any method is appropriate if it is accurate.

Determining Legality of Ballots

The legality of ballots is governed by the following rules:

1. A mistake in voting for a candidate for one office does not invalidate the vote for candidates for other offices on the same ballot.
2. A technical error, such as misspelling, or using a cross instead of a check, does not invalidate a ballot if the *intent* of the voter is clear.
3. A torn or defaced ballot is valid if the *intent* of the voter is clear.
4. Blank ballots or votes for ineligible persons are counted as illegal ballots.
5. If several nominees for equal offices are voted for in a group, a ballot containing fewer votes than the number of positions to be filled is valid. But a ballot containing votes for more than the number of positions to be filled is illegal for all the positions.

If the results of the count by the committee do not check, a recount must be made. If more ballots have been cast than there are members entitled to vote, and the result of the election could have been affected by the extra ballots, or if there has been any substantial violation of the right of members to vote in secret,[2] the vote must be retaken. If there are minor errors which could not change the result of the election, a vote need not be retaken.

Report of Election Committee or Tellers

The following example shows the essential requirements of a report of an election committee:

Report of Election Committee
January 19
Sacramento Farm Bureau

Qualified voters	340
Legal ballots cast	338
Illegal ballots rejected (ballots were blank)	2
President	
Legal votes cast for president	330
Illegal votes (cast for ineligible person)	1
Number of votes necessary to elect	166
Mr. A received	323
Mr. B received (write-in votes)	7
Secretary	
Legal votes cast for secretary	338
Number necessary to elect	170
Mr. D received	336
Mr. E received (write-in votes)	2
Board of Trustees (three to be elected)	
Number of legal ballots cast for trustees	331
Number of votes necessary to elect	166
Mr. F received	326
Mr. G received	318
Mr. H received	315
Mr. I received (write-in votes)	13

Signatures of Committee

The report must account for all ballots cast, both legal and illegal. If any ballots or votes are rejected as illegal, the number must be reported and the reasons for rejection must be given. The number of votes received by each candidate and the number of write-in votes for any member, qualified or unqualified, must be included in the report and must be read.

The chairman of the election committee reads the report without stating who is elected and hands it to the presiding officer. The presiding officer reads only the names of those who are elected and declares them elected.

The report is signed by all members of the election committee. Tally sheets are signed by those who kept them. All ballots, tally sheets, and records are delivered to the secretary of the organization who keeps them sealed until he is directed by the governing board to destroy them.

Vote Necessary to Elect

The vote necessary to elect should be fixed in the bylaws. Unless otherwise provided, the following rules govern:

1. When a candidate receives a majority of the legal votes cast for a single office, he is elected.
2. When a candidate receives a plurality of the legal votes cast (more votes than any other candidate), but not a majority, he is not elected unless there is a provision in the bylaws for election by plurality.
3. When election to an office requires a majority vote, but no candidate receives a majority vote, the requirement for a majority vote cannot be waived but the assembly may adopt motions to enable it to complete the election within a reasonable time. (See *Supplementing Procedural Rules by Motions,* p. 211.)

Casting of Ballot by the Secretary

Most bylaws provide for the election of officers by ballot vote. When there is only one candidate for an office, or a slate consisting of one candidate for each office, or when additional votes are necessary to secure a majority vote as required for an office, a member sometimes proposes a motion that the secretary be instructed to cast the ballot of the members for the candidate or slate. This motion deprives members of their right to write in the name of another member and to keep their choice secret, since they cannot oppose this motion without revealing that they favor some other member. If an organization wishes to provide that the secretary may be directed to cast a ballot for the assembly, this provision should be included in its bylaws. Unless the bylaws provide for the casting of a ballot for an uncontested candidate, the general provision requiring a ballot vote for all officers must be complied with. Many organizations direct the secretary by majority vote to cast the ballot of the assembly in certain situations to save time. If this is done in good faith, the action would probably be upheld legally.

The motion directing the secretary to cast a ballot, when permitted, requires a majority vote. It should not be stated as a motion "to cast a unanimous ballot," since this would require a unanimous vote.

If the motion for the secretary to cast a ballot carries, the secretary prepares a ballot as directed and, rising, says, "Mr. Chairman, by direction of the members I cast the ballot of the members for Mr. A for the office of president and for Mr. C and Mr. D for members of the board of directors." Then the presiding officer declares these members elected.

Motion to Make a Vote Unanimous

A unanimous vote means that all of the legal votes cast were cast on one side and that there were no votes cast on the other side. One common error is to suppose that a vote which is not unanimous can be made unanimous by adopting a motion to that effect by majority vote. Sometimes the candidate receiving the second highest number of votes or one of

NOMINATIONS AND ELECTIONS

his friends proposes a motion to make the vote unanimous for the elected candidate. This is only a complimentary gesture, and does not change the legal vote.

When Elections Become Effective

An election becomes effective immediately if the candidate is present and does not decline. If he is absent and has consented to his nomination, the election becomes effective as soon as he is notified. Unless some other time is specified in the bylaws, an officer assumes his office as soon as he is declared elected and no formal installation is necessary.

Sometimes the bylaws provide that the new officers should take office at a later date. The ceremony of installing officers does not determine the time at which they assume office unless the bylaws contain a provision that the new officers take office at the time of their installation.

Challenging a Vote

If a member desires to challenge the right of another member or members to vote, or the validity of a proxy, he should do so by presenting the challenge to the credentials committee or to the election committee. He should do this before the voting has begun or at least before the challenged vote is cast. If the right of a member to vote is challenged, the credentials committee or the election committee holds a hearing and decides the matter subject to an appeal to the assembly. If there is no election committee, a challenge is decided by the assembly.

Challenging an Election

An election may be challenged only during the time that it is taking place or within a reasonably brief time thereafter.[3] The grounds for challenging an election are usually that persons who are ineligible have voted, that procedures required for carrying out a fair election were not observed, that procedures or actions during the election were unauthorized or illegal, that there was gross negligence in conducting the election, or that the election requirements in the bylaws were not correctly interpreted or followed and that these violations could have changed the result of the election.[4]

When an election is challenged, an investigation is usually made by the board of directors or by a committee selected by them. The board or committee reports its recommendation to the meeting or convention for final decision. If the meeting or convention is no longer in session, the board of directors decides the matter and takes whatever action seems best. The board must report its action to the members.

When an election is challenged while it is in progress, it continues unless a decision is reached to stop the election and declare it void. If it is challenged after it is completed, the officers chosen at the election take office and remain in office until a decision on the challenge is reached.

If it can be proved that enough illegal votes were cast so that the results of the election could have been changed, the election should be voided. If illegal votes cast or illegal practices engaged in could not have changed the results of the election, the fact that there were illegal votes or practices does not void the election.

Chapter 19

OFFICERS

The President as Leader

The president or the head of an organization, whatever his title, usually has three roles—leader, administrator, and presiding officer. Each role calls for different abilities.

There are certain fundamental qualities that most good leaders have in common. One is the *ability to plan*—to sense what the members want and to help them crystallize their ideas. Another is the *ability to unite*—to rally members behind a plan and behind their leader. Perhaps the most important is the *courage to win*—to overcome all obstacles.

A good leader works with his members, and he keeps them happy while they are working. He has a power *with* people, not *over* them. Carrying out their will is a project in human collaboration, which the president leads.

An organization is not merely a group of people working toward some common aim. It is also a powerful medium through which members can realize their individual hopes. A competent leader forges ahead toward the collective goal, but he is not blind to individual aims.

A leader skilled in handling people recognizes that sentiment and tradition are important influences, both in welding people together and in dividing them. This human understanding is a basic factor in good leadership.

The President as Administrator

The most important duties of the president as administrator are to:

1. Act as chief administrative officer and legal head of the organization
2. Exercise supervision over the organization and all its activities and employees
3. Represent and speak for the organization to other organizations and to the public
4. Preside at business meetings
5. Appoint committees
6. Sign letters or documents necessary to carry out the will of the organization
7. Serve as chairman of the board of directors or governing board

The President as Presiding Officer

As presiding officer the president is the leader and representative of the entire assembly. Respect for his position is respect for the organization and for the members who have chosen him. He must maintain firm control of the meetings, yet always remember that he is the "first servant of the assembly."

Just as a judge exercises wide discretion in a courtroom, the presiding officer should exercise wide discretion in a meeting. He is not a robot, limited to mechanical responses, but must meet each situation with flexibility of judgment, common sense, and fairness to all members—acting always impartially and in good faith. For example, if a member moves to adjourn, and the presiding officer knows that there is important business that should be attended to, he should state this fact and ask the proposer of the motion for adjournment if he wishes to withdraw his motion. If the member refuses, the presiding officer should explain the business that needs attention before the vote on adjournment is taken.

During discussion the presiding officer has great latitude in carrying out his duties. He should assist members in exercising their rights and privileges. He should not act as a partisan advocate, but if he knows facts that no other member can present, he should state them in an unbiased manner. He should stimulate and encourage discussion. He should see that all sides of a controversial question are presented by asking if members wish to discuss a different viewpoint and by alternating the opportunity to speak between friends and foes of the question.

He should make sure that members understand all proposals and what their effect will be. If members do not understand, it is his duty to see that proper explanations are given.

A presiding officer should protect the group from improper conduct. He should warn obstructionists who are using dilatory tactics, and if they persist, deny them recognition. He should expose parliamentary trickery, prevent railroading, and promptly rule out discussion of personalities. He must keep the assembly in order at all times and act quickly to restore order at the first sign of disturbance.

A presiding officer must be firm and decisive, yet not dictatorial; courteous and patient, yet alert to insure progress. He must keep the meeting moving ahead so that business is accomplished and members maintain their interest; yet he must not appear to hurry the meeting unduly.

Presiding is an art that cannot be learned entirely from a book. The tactful presiding officer knows how to discourage courteously the member who talks too much or too often and how to encourage the shy member who speaks only when impelled by strong convictions. When an assembly is restive, he knows how to shorten discussion and how to make business move along; yet he senses when members are confused and when the business should move more slowly.

He must know parliamentary law and how to apply it. Associate Justice Felix Frankfurter described the ideal presiding officer when he wrote:

"He presided with great courtesy and with a quiet authority ... with great but gentle firmness. You couldn't but catch his own mood of courtesy.

"He never checked free debate, but the atmosphere which he created, the moral authority which he exerted, inhibited irrelevance, repetition, and fruitless discussion.

"He was a master of timing: he knew when discussion should be deferred and when brought to an issue. He also showed uncommon resourcefulness in drawing elements of agreement out of differences, and thereby narrowing, if not always escaping, conflicts." [1,2]

When the President Presides

The president, or in his absence the officer next in rank, should preside at all meetings at which business may be transacted. If no officers are present at a meeting, a senior member calls the meeting to order and presides until a temporary chairman is elected. At social or program meetings, the program chairman or another member may preside; but at business meetings the president, if present, must preside, and he cannot delegate this duty to another member.

The presiding officer does not leave the chair to present important facts that need to be presented. If a motion is directed at him personally, he asks the vice president to take the chair until the motion is disposed of. This is true whether the motion affects him favorably—for example, to award him a life membership—or adversely, as a vote of censure.

Although there is a principle that an officer does not give up his rights as a member by becoming an officer, the presiding officer cannot propose or second a motion or nominate a candidate while presiding. The president, or the regular presiding officer, presides during an election even though he is a candidate for office.

The President-elect

Some organizations elect a future president in advance of his term of office and assign him specific duties. In many organizations he is given responsibilities, such as coordinating and overseeing committees, that will familiarize him with the work of the organization. The president-elect is in training for the office of president and automatically becomes the president when the latter's term of office expires.

The president-elect usually assumes the duties of the president when that officer is absent or is incapacitated. He also presides when it is necessary for the president to leave the chair.

When acting in the place of the president, the president-elect has all the powers, duties, responsibilities, and privileges of the president.

The Vice President

The vice president assumes the duties of the president in case of the absence or incapacity of the president and becomes president on the death, resignation, or permanent incapacity of the president unless the bylaws provide differently.

The vice president has only a few responsibilities established by parliamentary law, but in practice he is usually assigned other duties by the bylaws. Vice presidents frequently direct departments of work or study, head important committees, serve on the governing board, and have other duties assigned to them.

The Secretary

The president and the elected secretary are recognized by the law as the legal representatives of the organization. The secretary has extensive duties. He is the chief recording and corresponding officer and the custodian of the records of the organization. In organizations in which employees perform these functions, the responsibility for seeing that they are properly carried out remains with the elected secretary. The secretary works under the direction of the president, and his instructions should come from the president.

The chief duties of a secretary are to:
1. Take careful and authentic notes of the proceedings of the meetings as a basis for preparing the minutes
2. Prepare and certify the correctness of the minutes and enter them in the official minute book

3. Read the minutes to the organization for correction and approval
4. Enter any corrections approved by the members in the minute book and initial them
5. Record and attest by his signature the approved minutes as the official minutes of the organization, with the date of approval
6. Provide the presiding officer or the assembly with the exact wording of a pending motion or of one previously acted on
7. Prepare a list of members and call the roll when directed by the presiding officer
8. Read all papers, documents, or communications as directed by the presiding officer
9. Bring to each meeting the minute book, a copy of the bylaws, rules, and policies, a list of the members, a list of standing and special committees, and a copy of the parliamentary authority adopted by the organization
10. Seach the minutes for information requested by officers or members
11. Assist the presiding officer before each meeting in preparing a detailed agenda
12. Preserve all records, reports, and official documents of the organization except those specifically assigned to the custody of others
13. Prepare and send required notices of meetings and proposals
14. Provide the chairman of each special committee with a list of his committee members, a copy of the motion referring the subject to the committee, and instructions and other documents that may be useful
15. Provide the chairman of each standing committee with a copy of all proposals referred to it, instructions, or material that may be useful

16. Authenticate official documents by his signature
17. Carry on the official correspondence of the organization as directed, except correspondence assigned to other officers

In addition to these duties, the secretary performs many lesser tasks such as calling attention to actions in the minutes that have not been carried out, and keeping a report book or file of all reports submitted, a correspondence file, and a book of adopted policies and procedures. He is responsible for calling attention to deadlines and the dates for taking certain actions.

The elected secretary does not forfeit any rights of membership by reason of holding office. He may propose motions, and discuss and vote on all measures.

The Corresponding Secretary

In some organizations the secretarial duties are divided between a recording secretary and a corresponding secretary. The corresponding secretary conducts the official correspondence for the organization as directed by the president or board, answers official letters, and maintains a correspondence file.

The Treasurer

The treasurer is responsible for the collection, safekeeping, and expenditure of all funds of the organization, and for keeping an accurate financial record. He should be chosen for his integrity and his knowledge of how to keep, or supervise the keeping of, financial accounts.

In organizations that delegate to employees the work of collecting, disbursing, and accounting for funds, the treasurer is still legally responsible for the performance of these duties and for the accuracy of his reports.

The treasurer collects and disburses funds only as directed by law, the bylaws, the membership, the board of directors, or other authority provided for in the bylaws. He does not have the power to borrow money or issue funds or checks except as he is authorized to do so by the assembly or bylaws. He usually has the responsibility of helping to prepare the budget.

The treasurer should report briefly on the finances of the organization at each membership and board meeting, answer any questions on financial matters, and submit a full report to the membership annually. (See *Report of Treasurer,* p. 214.)

The Member Parliamentarian

There are two types of parliamentarians. One is the employed consultant who has had training and professional experience in parliamentary law and who is not a member of the organization. (See *Parliamentarian,* p. 230.)

The other is the parliamentarian appointed from the membership by the president to assist him. The member parliamentarian should be a source of information on parliamentary procedure, but, like all parliamentarians, he has no authority to enforce his ideas or to make rulings.

A competent member parliamentarian can be a valuable aid to the presiding officer and to the other officers and members.

The Sergeant at Arms

The sergeant at arms, under the direction of the presiding officer, helps to maintain order and decorum at meetings. He acts as doorkeeper, directs the ushers, and is responsible for the comfort and convenience of the assembly. In small organizations he performs these duties personally, but in large organizations he has a staff of assistant sergeants at arms.

Honorary Officers

Some organizations provide in their bylaws for honorary officers and members. Honorary titles are created as a compliment to those on whom they are conferred; such honorary titles generally carry with them the right to attend meetings and to speak but not to propose motions, vote, or preside. Holding an honorary office does not prevent a person who is a member from exercising any of his rights or from holding a regular office.

Powers and Liabilities of Officers

The actual powers and duties of officers are stated in the bylaws and sometimes in statutes and charters. In addition, officers have the implied power to do whatever is necessary to carry out the functions and duties of their office.[3] For example, a president who has the duty of appointing a committee has the implied power to fill a vacancy on the committee or to remove and replace a member who fails to perform his duties.

An officer or director of an incorporated organization is not liable for debts or losses of the corporation if he performs his duties with ordinary care and is not guilty of fraud or bad faith.[4]

Delegation of Authority by Officers and Boards

Both officers and members should understand their responsibilities in delegating to other members or employees the powers, duties, and responsibilities assigned to them by the law or the bylaws.

The basic principle of the delegation of powers, duties, and responsibilities is that the members, officers, boards, or committees delegating authority retain full responsibility for the performance or exercise of the powers, duties, and responsibilities that they have delegated. They also are responsible for negligence and its consequences in the exercise of the delegated authority.

There are two general types of powers, duties, and responsibilities—legislative and administrative. *Legislative* powers and duties provided for by statute or bylaws, either expressly or by implication, cannot be delegated, except in profit-making corporations where most duties are delegated to the board. For example, if the bylaws provide that an organization elect its officers by a ballot vote of the delegates at the annual convention, the assembly of delegates cannot delegate this duty to its board of directors.

Administrative powers and duties are of two kinds—discretionary and ministerial. *Discretionary* powers and duties are those that depend on a special trust in the officer, board, or committee member and involve personal reliance on his wisdom, integrity, and discretion. An example of a discretionary duty is the appointment of committees by the president or the certification of minutes by the secretary.

Discretionary powers and duties assigned to a particular officer or board by statute, charter, or bylaws can never be delegated.[5] For example, a board of directors of a nonprofit corporation cannot delegate its power to borrow money. The board of directors can authorize a committee or an employee to investigate the best rates and sources for borrowing money, but the final decision must be made by the board.

Ministerial powers or duties are those that require simply carrying out specifically described duties that do not call for the use of discretion but involve only the faithful performance of a mechanical or clerical function. Ministerial powers and duties can be delegated freely to members or employees.[6] For example, a secretary has the ministerial duty of sending out notices of a meeting already authorized and can delegate this duty to members or employees.

A committee may delegate some of its powers and duties to a subcommittee, but the committee remains responsible for all actions of its subcommittees.

Powers and duties should be delegated carefully and with the knowledge that the responsibility for supervising their exercise and execution remains with those making the delegation.

Term of Office

The bylaws should define the term of office of all officers, directors, and committees. Bylaws sometimes limit the number of terms that a member may hold an office. This provision is intended to prevent domination of the organization by a few members. However, a limitation on terms often works out to be more a limitation on the right of members to elect whom they please than a limitation on a member to continue to hold office. The deciding principle should be, not the right of every member to have "a turn" regardless of his ability, but the overall good of the organization.

Many organizations favor a short term of office, which brings officers up for review by election frequently. If the members are alert and interested, it is often unnecessary and disadvantageous to limit the number of terms to which a member may be elected because "one year is too long for a poor officer and too short for a good one."

When there is a provision in the bylaws restricting the number of terms to which a member may be elected to a particular office, a member who fills a vacancy in that office for a partial term is not barred from being elected to a full term or terms of his own, unless the bylaws provide otherwise.

When eligibility to hold a certain office includes a requirement that a member must have served a term in another office, serving for half or more of a term to fill a vacancy ordinarily fulfills the requirement.

Officers are not always elected with the regularity or at the precise time prescribed by law or the bylaws. The ordinary rule in such an event is that the incumbents continue to hold office until their successors are elected or appointed.

Vacancies

The bylaws should include rules governing vacancies. A vacancy in an office, board, or committee usually occurs because of the death, resignation, or departure of the member from the locality, and in these instances there is no question that a vacancy exists.

There is sometimes uncertainty when a vacancy occurs by reason of discovery of the ineligibility of an officer after he has been elected, or when there has been an abandonment of the office, an implied resignation, or prolonged neglect or inability to act. If there is a question as to whether or not an office is vacant, the board or the members should declare the office vacant to clear the record before a member is chosen to fill the vacancy.

Declaring a vacancy is not a means of removing an officer. An office cannot be declared vacant when there is an incumbent willing and able to perform the duties of the office.

A vacancy is filled by the same authority that selected the officer, director, or committee member unless the bylaws provide otherwise. A special election is sometimes called to enable the members to fill a vacancy.

Some bylaws provide that the officer who is next in rank automatically moves up to fill a vacancy. Other bylaws require the board of directors to fill vacancies not otherwise provided for. If this duty is delegated to the directors or to any other group except the membership, the member chosen to fill the vacancy serves only until the next election at which the vacancy can be filled by the membership.

Vacancies in elective offices must not be ignored or concealed. Members should be informed promptly of a vacancy, and the vacancy should be filled as soon as possible. If the board of directors or the president knows that there is, or is about to be, a vacancy, this knowledge cannot properly be withheld until after a meeting, convention, or election at which the members could have elected someone to fill the vacancy; to do so would permit the president or board to fill the vacancy by appointment.

Neither officers nor members should try to outwit the provisions of the bylaws by maneuvering to fill vacancies in elective offices by appointment. No member should accept an elective office with the intention of resigning in order to create a vacancy and thereby permit the appointment of another member to the office.

Removal of Officers

An organization has an inherent right to remove an officer or director from office for valid cause.[7] It also has the right to suspend an officer or director from office. The bylaws should provide for procedures for removal or suspension.[8] These procedures are quite different from those for the disciplining or expulsion of a member.

Officers, directors, or committee members can be removed by the same authority that selected them. The power to select carries with it the power to remove. An elected officer or director can be removed by vote of the members.[9] An appointed officer or committee member can be removed by the authority that appointed him.

The common *valid* causes for removal from office are:
1. Continued, gross, or willful neglect of the duties of the office

2. Failure or refusal to disclose necessary information on matters of organization business
3. Unauthorized expenditures, signing of checks, or misuse of organization funds
4. Unwarranted attacks on the president or refusal to cooperate with him [10]
5. Misrepresentation of the organization and its officers to outside persons
6. Conviction of a felony
7. Membership in subversive organizations

Examples of conduct that are *not valid* grounds for removal from office are:

1. Poor performance as an officer due to lack of ability
2. Negligence that is not gross or willful
3. A tendency to create friction and disagreement
4. Mere unsuitability to hold office

The procedures for suspending or removing officers must provide adequate notice to the accused officer, a fair hearing, the right to counsel, and a reasonable opportunity to defend himself.[11]

An officer who complains of improper removal or a member who believes that he has been disciplined improperly must show that he has exhausted the procedures for relief afforded by the organization before he appeals to the courts. If proper procedures are followed, the courts will seldom interfere with the removal of an officer for valid cause.[12]

Chapter 20

COMMITTEES AND BOARDS

Importance of Committees

Committees perform the bulk of the work of organizations. Through the use of committees the responsibilities of an organization are apportioned among its members. Work to be done is delegated to committees and proposals are formulated by committees for final decison by the whole assembly. The meetings of many groups are concerned largely with the consideration of committee reports and recommendations. Usually the conclusions of committees are accepted as the conclusions of the organization.

Committees are too valuable to be misused. They should not be burial grounds for unpleasant issues, or a method of rewarding members and distributing titles to friends, or a device for giving everybody something to do. Membership on a committee should never be used to placate chronic troublemakers.

No committee should be appointed unless it is needed. Members of a committee that has no real work soon recognize this fact and lose interest in the organization.

Advantages of Committees

A committee has many advantages that enable it to work more efficiently than the larger parent organization. Some of these are that:
1. Greater freedom of discussion is possible.
2. More time is available for each subject.

3. Informal procedure can be used.
4. Better use can be made of experts and consultants.
5. Delicate and troublesome questions may be settled without publicity.
6. Hearings may be held giving members opportunity to express their opinions.

Standing Committees

A standing committee does any work within its particular field that is assigned to it by the bylaws or referred to it by the organization or the board. Its term of service is usually the same as the terms of the officers. Standing committees provide ever-ready and experienced groups to which work may be referred at any time. They handle many tasks that need to be carried out regularly. A membership committee, which investigates and passes on applications for membership, is an example of a standing committee.

An organization may provide for and fix the duties of as many standing committees as it finds useful. The name, method of selecting members, usual duties, term of office, and requirements for reports of each standing committee should be included in the bylaws.

Special Committees

A special committee, sometimes called an *ad hoc* committee, performs some specific task and automatically ceases to exist when its final report is disposed of. If the organization votes to delegate additional work to a special committee, it continues until the new assignment is completed and another report is submitted. A committee to arrange the annual banquet is an example of a special committee.

Both the board of directors and the president have the inherent power to appoint special committees to assist them at any time, and to delegate investigative, planning, or routine administrative duties to them. These committees report only to the authority that appointed them. (See *Delegation of Authority,* p. 169.)

Committees for Deliberation

Committees may be classified according to the nature of their assignments into committees primarily for deliberation and committees primarily for action. It is vital that a committee appointed for deliberation and investigation or which performs discretionary duties be representative of all important elements and groups within the organization. The report of a representative committee will reflect the opinions of the whole organization and has a good chance of being approved. A nominating committee and a committee to determine the location for a new clubhouse are examples of committees that should be representative.

Committees for Action

A committee for action carries out a particular task already decided on. Such a committee does not function well unless it is composed of members who favor the job to be done. A committee to raise an endowment fund is an example.

Selection of the Committee Chairman

A committee chairman should be chosen for his ability to plan and direct the work of his committee and to function well with its members. Unlike the presiding officer of an assembly, the chairman of a committee takes an active part in its discussion and deliberations.

If no committee chairman is elected or appointed, a chairman may be selected by the committee from its own membership. If no chairman is designated, the member first named calls the committee together and presides during the election of a chairman. There is no parliamentary rule requiring that the member who proposes the creation of a committee be appointed as chairman or member of it, and there is no rule that bars him.

Selection of the Committee Members

Members of standing committees are usually appointed by the president with the approval of the governing board. The advice and suggestions of board members enable the president to utilize the talents of a larger number of members effectively.

It is often advisable to consult a prospective committee chairman regarding the selection of the other members of his committee, particularly if the committee has a difficult assignment.

Ex Officio Members of Committees

The bylaws of some organizations provide that the president or other officers, because of the particular office they hold, are automatically members of certain boards or committees. Such members are termed *ex officio* members. An ex officio member is not elected or appointed to a committee, but becomes a member when he is elected or appointed to a particular office. When an ex officio member ceases to hold office, his membership on the committee terminates and his successor in the office replaces him on the committee. The president and other officers are usually ex officio members of the board of directors. The treasurer is usually an ex officio member of the finance committee.

An ex officio member has all the rights, responsibilities, and duties of any other member of the committee, including the right to vote. He is not, as is commonly believed, merely a consulting or advising member. He is a full-fledged working member of the committee; consequently a president cannot be expected to serve effectively as an ex officio member of all committees. If it is desirable to have the president or some other officer act as consultant or advisor to a particular committee, he should be made an advisory or consulting member rather than an ex officio member.

Powers, Rights, and Duties of Committees

The powers, rights, and duties of each standing committee and of important special committees that are appointed periodically should be provided for in the bylaws. The powers, rights, and duties of other special committees should be provided for in the motion creating them or in the instructions given to them. Since no committee has inherent powers, rights, or duties, these must be delegated to it by the creating or appointing authority. Even an executive committee or board of directors has no powers and no duties except those delegated to it by the bylaws or by vote of the membership. (See *Delegation of Authority*, p. 169.)

All committees are responsible to and under the direction and control of the authority that created them. Standing committees are responsible to and under the control of the voting body and the governing board when it is acting for the voting body in the intervals between meetings. Special committees appointed by the membership, governing board, or the president are responsible to the appointing authority.

Any subject or duty that has been assigned to a committee may be withdrawn at any time and assigned to another committee or considered by the body. Any proposal or assignment of work to a standing committee may be withdrawn by the governing body unless it is assigned exclusively to the committee by the bylaws. Any special committee may be dissolved by the authority that created it.

The members of a committee may be replaced by the appointing or electing authority. A member of a committee who is unable or fails to perform his duties should be removed and notified of his removal by the president or by the body that appointed the committee, and another member should be chosen to replace him.

A committee cannot represent the organization to any outside person or organization except when clearly authorized to do so. Unless there is specific authorization given a committee to collect, hold, or disburse funds, all funds should be collected, held, and disbursed through the regular financial channels of the organization.

A committee has the right to appoint subcommittees of its own members to which it may delegate authority and which are directly responsible to the committee. Subcommittees report only to the committee that created them.

Working Materials for Committees

The secretary should furnish each committee with specific instructions on the work it is expected to do, and with all helpful information in the possession of the organization, such as:

1. A list for each member of the committee members with addresses and telephone numbers
2. A statement of the motion, problem, or task referred to the committee
3. Any instructions to the committee from the membership, governing board, or president
4. A statement of the duties, powers, and financial limitations of the committee
5. Available information that will be helpful to the committee—for example, reports of former similar committees

6. Policies, rules, or decisions of the organizations relating to the committee's work
7. The nature of the report desired and the date it is due

It is the duty of the secretary of the organization to provide these materials for each committee. If the secretary of the organization does not provide the materials, it is the duty of the chairman of the committee to secure them for his committee members.

Committee Meetings Limited to Members

Since committees and boards of directors often consider business of a confidential nature, which should not be discussed at a meeting of the membership, the law protects the privacy of a committee. No officer, member, employee, or outside person has the right to attend any meeting of a board or committee except by invitation of the committee.

If the committee wishes to invite a staff member, consultant, or other person, it may vote to do so, but otherwise all meetings of boards or committees are limited strictly to members of the committee. To further protect the privacy of the proceedings of a board or committee, its minutes are open to no one except members of the committee.

Procedure in Committee Meetings

The chairman should submit suggested plans for work to the committee for consideration at its first meeting. The chairman often talks over plans and a division of duties with his members even before the first meeting.

Meetings of a committee are called by the chairman. In case of his inability or failure to act, a meeting may be called by a majority of the members of a committee.

A majority of the members of a committee is a quorum and

a majority of the legal votes cast is necessary to take any official action.

Simple and informal procedure is desirable in a committee meeting. Committees follow the ordinary rules of procedure only in so far as they are appropriate to the committee's situation. In committee meetings it is not necessary to stand when making a motion, or to limit the length of speeches, and no seconds are required.

Motions must be accurately stated, discussion confined to the motion or subject, and only one person permitted to speak at a time. In large committees considering controversial subjects, it may be necessary at times to be as formal and to apply parliamentary rules as strictly as in the assembly itself. Most committees find it helpful to keep minutes for the information and convenience of their members.

Committee Hearings

A committee hearing is a meeting during which a committee listens to the viewpoints of members and sometimes of experts on the subject assigned to it. At the end of the hearing the committee, with only its members present, agrees on the conclusions and recommendations that it will present to the membership for their guidance in making the final decision.

Most committee hearings are open to all members of the organization. However, hearings for the purpose of considering matters of discipline, finance, or other subjects that should be decided without publicity that might be harmful to the organization or to a member are open only to members of the committee assigned to conduct the hearing.

The Board of Directors

Few organizations have time in their meetings for the members to plan, discuss, and decide all the matters necessary to carry on the work of the organization. Consequently, the

COMMITTEES AND BOARDS

members provide in the bylaws that a small elected group acting as the representatives of all the members shall carry on the work of the organization during the intervals between meetings of the membership. The group is called the board of directors, executive board, board of trustees, or by some other name meaning the governing board.

A governing board is generally composed of the elected officers of the organization, who are members ex officio, and of directors elected by the membership. Usually the president and secretary of the parent body are the chairman and secretary of the governing board. The law refers to all members of the governing board as officers, but the term "officers," as used in this book, does not include the members elected to the board.

The duties, responsibilities, and powers of the board of directors should be clearly defined in the bylaws. Such a board is usually delegated the duty and power of acting for the membership in the intervals between meetings,[1] except that certain powers are vested exclusively in the members and that the membership can overrule the board.[2] The final authority of any organization remains in its "members assembled." Any action of a governing board can be rescinded or modified by the membership, except when the matter has been specifically delegated to the board in the bylaws or when the matter acted on no longer remains within the control of the organization. The board also has specific duties and responsibilities assigned to it.

All members of a governing board share in a joint and collective authority which exists and can be exercised only when the group is in session.[3] Members of a board have no greater authority than any other member of the organization except when the board is meeting. Officers and members to whom specific duties are assigned perform the duties of their office or assignment in addition to sharing in the group authority and duties of the board.

Business transacted at a board meeting should not be discussed except with other directors, unless and until the information has been issued to all members or to the public by the proper authority. The minutes of a board are open only to its members, because the board considers many matters that cannot be discussed outside of the board without injury to the organization or to its members.

Most organizations give continuity to the board by staggering the dates of election of members to the board so that there are always experienced members on the board.

The Executive Committee of the Board

Since many boards cannot meet on short notice, it is customary to provide for a small executive committee of the governing board. A board of directors has the inherent power to appoint an executive committee from its own membership.[4] This committee, usually made up of the president and two or three other officers, is delegated the power to act for the board, within limitations, when it is not meeting.

The specific powers and duties of this committee should be provided for in the bylaws. Some organizations give the executive committee extensive power to act for the board. Others limit it to acting on emergency matters or on recurring matters that must be disposed of promptly.

An executive committee reports to the board at its next meeting or by mail, and its actions are reviewed and included in the minutes of the board.

The Committee of the Whole

When a parliament, a house of Congress, or a state legislature wishes to act informally on a matter, it sometimes resolves itself into a committee of the whole. This requires the body to vote on the motion to become a committee of the whole, vote on a proposal or report, adjourn the committee, reconvene as the original body, read the report of the committee of the whole, and vote on it as the original assembly. This complicated procedure for a committee of the whole has been discarded by the Senate of the United States and by most organizations. Its purpose is achieved quite simply by a motion to consider a matter informally. (See *Informal Consideration,* p. 128.)

Chapter 21

COMMITTEE REPORTS AND RECOMMENDATIONS

Form of Committee Reports and Recommendations

Committee reports usually include:

1. A statement of the question, subject, or work assigned to the committee, and any important instructions given to it.
2. A brief explanation of how the committee carried out its work
3. A description of the work that the committee performed or, in the case of a deliberative or investigating committee, its findings and conclusions

A committee report should be as brief as possible, consistent with clarity. It should give the background necessary to an understanding of any recommendations the committee is making for decision by the assembly. Credit is given to anyone rendering unusual or outstanding service to the committee, but the report does not give special mention to those who only perform their expected duties.

Recommendations from the committee should be attached

to the report but should not be included in it. Each recommendation must be in the form of a motion or resolution to be presented, discussed, and acted on as a separate motion by the voting body. If opinions and recommendations are included in a report, and the report is approved, they are binding on the organization. Such a blanket commitment is dangerous.

Agreement on Committee Reports

The report and the recommendations of a committee must be agreed on at a meeting of the committee. The committee members must have the opportunity to hear all the different viewpoints on the questions involved and to discuss them freely with each other. Otherwise, the report cannot state the collective judgment of the committee. The approval of a committee report or recommendation by members of the committee individually and separately, without a meeting, is not valid approval unless specifically authorized by the body creating the committee.

When it is difficult or impossible for the members of a committee to meet, the bylaws or a motion may authorize the committee to agree on a report without a meeting. A report may be prepared by the chairman and submitted by mail to the members for their suggestions and approval. Every member of the committee must have the opportunity to review the proposed report and to present his objections or changes. Members who approve, sign the report and the recommendations and, if a majority sign, the report becomes the report of the committee.

When a report in its final form has been considered and approved by a majority vote at a committee meeting, it is signed by the chairman and the members who agree with it if they wish to do so. A member may withdraw his approval of a report at any time before it is presented. A member who agrees to a committee report with exceptions or reservations may indicate the portions with which he does not agree and sign the report, signifying his approval of the remainder.

Presentation of Committee Reports

At the time in the order of business for committee reports, the presiding officer calls for each report in turn. Standing committees usually report first in the order in which they are listed in the bylaws and are followed by special committees in the order of their appointment. The order of presenting reports, however, should be flexible to meet the needs of the particular meeting, and the order of presentation may be varied by majority vote or unanimous consent. A committee report is presented by its chairman or some member of the committee designated by him. He may introduce the report with a brief explanation if it is necessary to an understanding of the report. If a committee report is long, usually only a summary of it is presented.

In conventions or annual meetings of large organizations, committee reports usually are printed in advance and distributed to members by mail or at the convention. In this case, the committee chairman makes such explanatory statements as are needed and presents only the recommendations of the committee.

Consideration of Committee Reports

A committee report, after being presented to an assembly, is open for comment, questions, or criticism, but the members of the committee and their motives may not be attacked.

A committee report cannot be amended except by the committee, since no one can make the committee say anything it does not wish to say. A committee report, after it is presented, may be disposed of in any of the following ways:

188 COMMITTEE REPORTS AND RECOMMENDATIONS

1. The report may be filed. This is the usual method for disposing of a committee report. It may be filed automatically or ordered filed by a motion, or the presiding officer may announce, "The report will be filed," and proceed to the next item of business. A report that is filed is not binding on the assembly but is available for information and may be considered again at any time. An expression of thanks to the committee may be combined with a motion to file the report.
2. A subject and the report covering it may be referred back to the committee if further study, modifications, or recommendations are needed.
3. Consideration of a committee report may be postponed definitely to a more convenient time.
4. A report may be adopted. This commits the assembly to all the findings and opinions contained in the report and to any recommendations that might be included in it, but not to any recommendations submitted separately. A committee report can be adopted in part or with exceptions or reservations. The word "accept" is sometimes used instead of adopt, but the word "adopt," which cannot be misunderstood, is preferable. A motion "to receive" a committee report is meaningless, since an organization cannot refuse to receive and hear the report of its authorized committee. Since the adoption of a committee report binds the assembly to everything in the report, organizations are wise to file reports instead of adopting them.
5. A final or annual financial report from a treasurer or finance committee is referred to the auditors by the presiding officer without a motion. No final financial report is adopted without an accompanying report from the auditors certifying its correctness.
6. If a financial report concerns proposed or future ex-

penditures only, as in a budget, it is treated as any other financial recommendation of a committee.

Record of Committee Reports

When a committee member has presented a report, he hands it to the secretary for filing in a special book or file reserved for committee reports. A committee report is not included in the minutes unless the assembly votes that a brief summary be included.

Reports of standing committees are usually filed in chronological order under the name of each committee. Reports of special committees are usually filed in alphabetical order according to the subject or name of the committee.

The minutes of each meeting should state what reports were presented, by whom, the disposition of each report, and record the page or file number where the particular report may be found.

Minority Reports

If any members of a committee disagree with the report submitted by a majority of the committee members, they may submit a minority report signed by members who agree to it. More than one minority report may be submitted. A minority report can be presented only immediately after the majority report. A minority has the right to present and read a report, even though a motion is pending to dispose of the majority report, but the minority report is not considered unless some member moves to substitute it for the report of the majority. If the motion to substitute carries, the minority report becomes the official report of the committee and the majority report is filed for reference. If the motion to substitute fails, the minority report is filed for reference.

Presentation of Committee Recommendations

Recommendations may be acted on separately when they are presented with the committee report, postponed to a definite time, or taken up under new business. When several recommendations are interrelated and have not been printed or sent to the members previously, they should all be read before considering and voting on the individual recommendations.

Whenever the assembly desires to consider the recommendations, the chairman of the committee reads the first recommendation of the committee and moves its adoption.

The motion should be stated in a form that will allow the assembly to vote directly on the proposal itself, not on whether to agree or disagree with the recommendation of the committee. For example, if a committee recommends "that a membership drive should be held in the spring of each year," the motion should be stated to the assembly as "I move that a membership drive be held in the spring of each year." This statement of the proposal allows the assembly to consider, apply motions (for example, the motion to amend), and to vote directly on the actual proposal. This motion is much clearer than a motion such as "I move that we concur with (adopt, reject, accept, approve, or agree with) the recommendation of the committee."

A well-stated motion requiring a decision directly on the proposal prevents the confusion caused by such motions as, "I move that we approve the recommendation of the finance committee rejecting the proposal of the treasurer to modify the system of keeping financial records." It is impossible to amend or affect this motion in any way that will reach the original proposal, even though the members may wish to do so. The original motion should be stated: "I move that the treasurer be authorized to modify the present system of keeping financial records." The presiding officer or the chairman of the committee would then state for the information of the members that the original motion had been proposed by the treasurer and that the finance committee recommends a "no" vote on it.

After a motion embodying a recommendation has been stated to the assembly, it is considered and acted on as any other main motion.

Chapter 22

CONVENTIONS AND THEIR COMMITTEES

General Structure of Conventions

A *convention* of an organization is the series of consecutive meetings when members and delegates assemble to transact important business, consider developments in the organization's particular field, exchange ideas and experiences, and enjoy the fellowship of others who share a common interest.

Every member of an organization is entitled to attend the convention, but in most organizations the voting on issues is done by the delegates or by a smaller elected legislative body such as a house of delegates. In most international, national, and state conventions reports and certain general issues are brought before a voting body composed of the elected delegates of the various constituent and component groups, affiliates, chapters, or branches of the parent body. Usually these larger organizations provide that most of the enormous volume of business shall be transacted by a smaller legislative body.

Instruction of Delegates

Voting delegates to a convention may be instructed, partially instructed, or uninstructed by the group they represent. Usually the local groups meet and talk over issues to be voted on by their delegates at the convention. Thus the delegate becomes familiar with the opinions of the group he represents.

Except in unusual circumstances, it is not wise to give delegates explicit instructions as to how they must vote. If the delegate is simply a messenger carrying a vote, it is more economical to send a telegram.

At a convention a delegate learns new facts and listens to the arguments of delegates from different localities and with differing viewpoints. Frequently he finds that a proposal is changed so completely by amendments adopted at the convention that it is really a different proposal. He realizes that the members of the group he represents, had they heard the discussion and the amendments, would have instructed him quite differently.

The first duty of a delegate is to vote for what he believes is best for the organization as a whole; his second duty is to vote for what is best for the particular group that he represents. He is first a legislator for the whole organization and second a spokesman for his particular group. The delegate should understand thoroughly how the members of his group feel about the proposals to be voted on but should be trusted to follow his own best judgment in evaluating and voting on measures as they are finally presented for decision.

Convention Committees

Committees common to most conventions are the credentials, rules, and bylaws committees. Many larger organizations also have some form of reference committee.

The *credentials* committee must report before any item of business is presented to the voting body, so that it is known which members are entitled to vote and how many members make up the voting body. This committee examines the credentials of each member or delegate, authorizes the issuance of the badge or card admitting members to meetings, and prepares a list of the members who are entitled to vote.

At the first business meeting the credentials committee gives a preliminary report listing the delegates, alternates, and members who make up the various classes of membership in attendance at the convention. As soon as this report has been adopted by the convention, it becomes the official list of delegates and members of the convention and determines the voting strength (number of members eligible to vote) of the convention. Supplementary reports are usually given daily as new members or delegates present their credentials and are certified by the credentials committee. A final report is given at the concluding business meeting.

The *rules* committee usually submits its report after that of the credentials committee. Since the rules ordinarily vary only slightly from one convention to the next, the report of the rules committee listing the proposed rules frequently is published and distributed to members beforehand.

Convention rules are adopted by a majority vote and can be suspended by the same vote. They ordinarily cover such subjects as seating of delegates and alternates, length of speeches, and privileges of nonvoting members.

The committee on *bylaws* receives and reviews amendments to the bylaws sent in by members or by constituent groups, and usually may propose amendments of its own. The committee makes recommendations, if it wishes, approving or disapproving each proposed amendment and giving the reasons for its decision. The committee can revise or combine several similar amendments, with the permission of their proposers. The committee cannot kill any proposed amendment by failing to report it to the voting body. If the committee were given the power to decide which amendments should be presented to the voting body and which should be withheld, it would have the power to control amendments to the bylaws.

Use of Reference Committees

The reference committees of various organizations differ in details but their purposes and methods are fundamentally the same. The duty of a reference committee is to hold a hearing on each proposal assigned to the committee at which any member may speak, to investigate each proposal thoroughly, and to recommend to the voting body what action should be taken on it.

There is not time during most conventions for delegates to consider proposals sufficiently to vote intelligently; nor is there always time to hear all delegates wishing to speak on particular proposals nor for all important business to be transacted. Reference committees can solve all of these problems. By dividing the work of hearing, investigating, and making recommendations on proposals among a number of small representative groups, the organization provides opportunities for not only delegates but also for other members to present their views on proposals. Also the voting body is able to transact an enormous amount of business with a thorough understanding of the facts about each proposal.

Reference committees are usually appointed by the presiding officer of the voting body. Each reference committee should be representative and is usually composed of from three to seven respected members experienced in the committee's particular field.

Most organizations require that all proposals for consideration by the voting body be submitted by a certain date in advance of the convention. Special provision is made for emergency proposals to be submitted during the convention. Proposals in the form of motions or resolutions usually may be submitted by constituent or component groups, or committees or boards of the organization and in some groups by individual members. Recommendations from standing or special committees and proposed amendments to the bylaws or policies are also referred to appropriate reference committees. Some organizations also refer all reports of officers and committees to reference committees for study, evaluation, and comment.

In larger organizations each reference committee has a general field of work, such as finance or service to members. In smaller organizations all proposals usually are divided among three or four general reference committees. In some small organizations, the regular standing committees serve as reference committees at their convention.

As soon as possible after the opening of the convention each delegate is given a list of all the proposals submitted, including the name of the reference committee to which each proposal has been referred, and the time and place of the hearing on it.

Hearings must be scheduled with care to insure that the more important proposals in a particular field or in related fields are not set for the same time. Members interested in several proposals should be able to attend hearings on each.

If a proposal comes within the field of interest of more than one reference committee it may be referred to several reference committees. Each reference committee holds hearings and reports on the proposal from the viewpoint of its particular field of interest, or several committees may hold a joint hearing. When there is a joint hearing, each committee usually submits its own recommendations to the voting body.

Duties of Reference Committees

The primary duty of a reference committee is to recommend to the voting body an appropriate course of action on each proposal that has been referred to the committee. This duty requires that a committee hold a hearing open to all members interested in a particular proposal.

The committee then should evaluate each proposal referred to it; consider all relevant comments or recommendations on it that are sent to it by the board of directors, the board of trustees, the bylaws committee, or other groups of the organization; weigh all statements made during the hearing; obtain as much available information and advice as possible; and recommend the best course of action to be taken by the voting body on the proposal.

A reference committee must make a recommendation to the voting body on each proposal assigned to it. The committee may not "pigeonhole" or fail to return a proposal for any reason; the voting body must receive the proposal and dispose of it.

Hearings of Reference Committees

During a hearing the members of a committee usually are seated at a table in the front of the room. They listen to comments and opinions of all members. The committee members may ask questions to be sure that they understand the opinions being expressed, or may answer questions if a member seeks clarification; however, the committee members cannot enter into arguments with speakers or express opinions during the hearing. The committee listens carefully and evaluates all opinions presented so that it may provide the voting body with a carefully considered recommendation.

The chairman of the reference committee presides at the hearings and facilitates discussion. As far as possible all who wish to speak should be heard and a few persons should not be permitted to monopolize the discussion. The committee may limit the length of time assigned to each speaker. The chairman cannot permit motions or votes at the hearing, since its objective is only to receive information and opinions; decisions of any sort during the hearing would hamper the reference committee in its private deliberations.

After the hearing, the committee holds a meeting with only its members present to discuss and evaluate the proposals and opinions expressed by the members and to vote on its recommendation to the voting body. A minority recommendation may also be submitted.

Reports of Reference Committees

Reference committees may call on officers, staff members, or experts in order to gain as much information as possible on which to base their recommendations. A reference committee may recommend amendments to proposals that have been referred to it and may submit proposals of its own. It may make an explanation of the reasons for the committee's decision before offering its recommendations. It may recommend that a proposal be adopted, rejected, amended, or otherwise disposed of.

The recommendation of the reference committee is usually a deciding factor in determining the decision of the voting body. The great influence exercised by the committee, however, is advisory, and it is important that every voting body have the opportunity to consider all proposals submitted to it and to make the final decision on them.

Chapter 23

MINUTES

Importance of Minutes

Accurate, concise, and complete minutes are of vital importance to an organization. They are the official history and permanent record of the proposals, reports, and decisions of the members.[1] Minutes are invaluable for reference, and the courts give them great weight as evidence. Auditors depend on them for proof of authorization for important expenditures.

Responsibility for Minutes

The elected secretary working under the direction of the president is responsible for taking notes on all actions at business meetings, preparing minutes from these notes, reading the minutes to the assembly, recording any corrections, and certifying the minutes by his signature when the organization has approved them.[2] If a verbatim record is taken, the secretary is still responsible for the preparation and accuracy of the official minutes that he prepares from it. These are discretionary duties which he cannot delegate. The members of an organization or board are responsible for pointing out errors and approving the minutes.

The secretary is the official custodian of the minutes. The minutes of an organization are open to inspection by members at any reasonable time. Minutes of a board or committee meeting are available only to members of the board or committee.

Preparing Minutes

The secretary should prepare the minutes as soon after a meeting as possible. He signs the minutes certifying that, to the best of his knowledge, they are an accurate record of the proceedings of the meeting. Insuring the accuracy of the minutes is a discretionary duty which the secretary cannot delegate. An employee may prepare them under the direction of the secretary but cannot sign them.

Reading and Correction of Minutes

The presiding officer calls on the secretary to read the minutes at the proper place in the order of business. The reading of the minutes may be postponed or dispensed with for the current meeting by a motion to this effect. However, organizations should not make a practice of postponing or dispensing with the reading of minutes since delay makes it more difficult for members to detect errors.

After the secretary has read the minutes, the presiding officer asks, "Are there any corrections to the minutes?" He should pause after this question. When corrections are suggested, they are often approved by unanimous consent. The presiding officer may say, "If there is no objection, the error pointed out by Mr. A will be corrected."

If there is disagreement on a proposed correction, the presiding officer, without waiting for a motion, may take a vote to decide whether the correction should be made.[3]

The secretary makes minor corrections in ink immediately and initials each one. Any substantial correction is made as an appendix to the minutes that are being corrected. A reference to the appended correction is inserted at the place to which the correction applies. The statement of the corrections is recorded as approved actions of the body in the minutes of the meeting at which the corrections were made. If an error in the minutes is discovered at a later time, the error may be corrected by the assembly regardless of the lapse of time. The correction and final approval of the minutes are the duty of the assembly.

If the organization has a standing committee on minutes, this committee usually corrects the minutes and reports to the organization at regular intervals. On the certification of the minutes committee that the minutes are correct, the body may approve the minutes by unanimous consent or by majority vote.

After the minutes have been entered in the minute book, no corrections except in spelling or punctuation may be made unless they have been approved by the assembly.

Some organizations send copies of minutes to members after each meeting in order that members may study them and be prepared to bring up any corrections at the next meeting.

Approval of Minutes

If there are no corrections—or after all corrections have been made—some member may move to approve the minutes as read, or as corrected, or the presiding officer may take a vote on their approval, or he may state: "If there are no further corrections, the minutes are approved as corrected."

Before the assembly has approved the minutes, they are merely the secretary's record. When the minutes have been approved, and the secretary has certified them as the official approved minutes by writing the word "Approved" at the end of the minutes and signing his name with the date, they become the *official* minutes of the organization. Some organizations require that the president also sign,[4] and some direct the president and the secretary to initial each page of the minutes.

What Minutes Should Contain

Minutes vary greatly according to the needs of different organizations. In general, minutes are a record of all actions and proceedings but not a record of discussion. The opening sentences must record the date, hour, and place at which the meeting was called to order, the type of meeting (regular, special, or adjourned), the name of the presiding officer, and the fact that a quorum was present. The minutes of a special meeting should also include a copy of the notice or call for the meeting.

The minutes record all motions or resolutions, whether passed or lost, with the name of the proposer, usually the name of the seconder, and the way in which each motion was disposed of. The exact wording of all motions should be recorded. It is not sufficient to state that a motion "was amended and finally adopted." When a vote is taken by division which is counted, or by ballot, the number voting on each side is recorded. The record of each member's vote on a roll call is entered in the minutes. No member can have his views or protests on a motion recorded in the minutes unless a motion permitting such action is passed by majority vote.

Each report should be recorded with the name of the member presenting it, the action taken on the report, and the reference to the file where the report may be found. An important report is sometimes summarized briefly in the minutes and the file reference given for the complete report.

The statements of business transacted should be specific. A statement such as "letters were read" or "reports were given" is of no value. Each letter read should be identified or summarized briefly and the action on it, if any, recorded.

Minutes kept by committees are often more detailed than the minutes of the meetings of the organization because committee minutes frequently serve as the basis for the committee's report. Minutes of committee hearings frequently list those who speak for or against proposals and summarize the facts presented by each speaker.

What Minutes Should Not Contain

The secretary should never include any of his personal opinions, interpretations, or comments in the minutes. Descriptive phrases, such as "an able report," or "a heated discussion," have no place in a factual record of business.

Adverse criticism of members should never be included except in the form of a motion censoring or reprimanding a member. Praise of members should appear only in the form of officially adopted votes of thanks, gratitude, or commendation.

The Minute Book

An exact copy of the official, approved minutes should be entered in a suitable record book and kept in a safe place. If a loose-leaf book is used, the minutes should be bound at the end of each year. An index to each year's minutes by subject, date, and page is useful. It is also important to keep in the minute book copies of the charter, bylaws, rules, policies, and procedures of the organization for quick reference in meetings. (See *Model Minutes*, Appendix, p. 253.)

Chapter 24

CHARTERS, BYLAWS, AND RULES

Types of Charters

An organization looks to the law as its highest source of guidance on procedure and to its charters and bylaws as the next-ranking sources. Charters are of two types [1]—charters of incorporation from government and charters from a parent organization. Many organizations hold charters of both types. The charter from government ranks above the charter from a parent organization.

The charter of an incorporated organization is a grant,

usually by a state government, to a group of persons of the right to incorporate and to operate for specific purposes under the laws governing profit or nonprofit corporations. In some states this charter is termed the *articles of incorporation.* The charter of a nonprofit corporation usually contains its name and business address, a statement of the purposes of the organization, and provisions for members, a governing board, and officers.

The charter should provide for its own amendment by the membership, subject to the approval of the governmental body that issued the charter. No amendment to the charter or articles of incorporation is effective until it has been approved by the membership and also by the governmental authority that granted the charter. Amendments to charters are adopted by the same rules and procedures as amendments to the bylaws.

The charter from a parent organization is a certificate issued to a group of persons giving them the right to operate as a subsidiary unit of the parent organization. The regional organization holding the charter is subject to the provisions in the charter or bylaws of the parent organization that relate to its constituent and component organizations.

Constitution and Bylaws

Some organizations adopt both a constitution and bylaws. The constitution establishes the fundamental framework [2] of the organization, and to amend it usually requires a higher vote than the bylaws. The bylaws supplement these fundamental provisions and are easier to amend.

Most organizations combine the provisions of a constitution and bylaws in one document called bylaws. A single document is more practical because all provisions relating to one subject are in one place.

Drafting Bylaws

Good bylaws alone do not make an effective organization; they are an outline of its structure. However, suitable bylaws are necessary to enable an organization to function well.

Bylaws should be concise and are best arranged in outline form. Many organizations keep their bylaws simple and brief by including only essential provisions and supplementing them with adopted procedures.

The best bylaws are those which are written to meet the needs of the particular organization. A provision that works well for one organization may be entirely unsuitable for another. Bylaws should be custom-made to fit each individual organization.

Adoption of the Original Bylaws

When the presiding officer calls for the report of the committee appointed to draft the bylaws, the chairman first moves the adoption of the proposed bylaws in order to bring them before the assembly for consideration and discussion. The presiding officer states the motion, "It has been moved and seconded that the bylaws be adopted. The chairman will read the first section."

The chairman reads the first section of the first article and the presiding officer calls for discussion, questions, or amendments to it. If an amendment to the section is proposed, the presiding officer states it to the assembly and after discussion it is voted on, but only amendments, not articles or sections, are voted on at this time. The presiding officer then calls for the reading of the next section and follows the same procedure. When the reading and amendment of all the bylaws are completed, the presiding officer asks, "Are there any further amendments to the bylaws? Is there any further question or discussion?"

When all proposed amendments have been voted on and when no one rises to discuss the bylaws further, the presiding officer takes the vote on the motion to adopt the bylaws.[3] A majority vote only is required for their adoption.

When Bylaws Go into Effect

The bylaws go into effect immediately with the announcement of the vote adopting them unless the motion to adopt provides that the bylaws, or some portion or provision in them, is not effective until a later date. For example: "I move that the bylaws be adopted as amended, with the reservation that Article IX, Section 4, that provides for regular monthly meetings, will not go into effect until January 1 of next year."

When a good set of bylaws has been drafted and adopted, an organization should try not to clutter them with unimportant amendments. The bylaws committee should strive to give the new bylaws a chance to be tested thoroughly before proposing amendments. Amendments, unless vital, should be withheld until a number of changes can be made at one time, or until a revision is needed. Important constructive work is often neglected at annual meetings and conventions because so much time is devoted to unimportant amendments to the bylaws, rules, or procedures.

Provisions for Amending Bylaws

It is good practice for an organization to include in its bylaws specific requirements covering the following:
1. How and by whom amendments to bylaws may be initiated and proposed
2. The form in which proposed amendments should be stated
3. The date before which proposed amendments must be received by the organization

4. The required notice to members of proposed amendments
5. The vote required to adopt the amendment

Proposing Amendments to Bylaws

In many local groups, any member may rise while new business is being considered and give notice that he is proposing an amendment to the bylaws simply by stating the proposed amendment. He then gives a copy of it to the secretary.

Some groups provide that the proposed amendment is then given to the bylaws committee, which studies it and reports the recommendation of the committee to the voting body. A few groups limit consideration of amendments to the annual meeting.

State, national, and international groups ordinarily require that amendments be proposed by constituent or component groups or by a committee or a board of the parent organization. These organizations require that proposed amendments be sent to the bylaws committee by a certain date preceding the convention. The bylaws committee usually considers and makes recommendations on each amendment. The proposed amendments are published with the committee's recommendations on them; also included are notice of the date and time that the amendments are to be considered and voted on, and notice of any hearings to be held on them. (See *Notice of Proposed Actions,* p. 108.)

Form for Proposed Amendments to Bylaws

Unless the bylaws provide differently, a proposed amendment should be stated in such language that, if adopted, it may be incorporated directly into the bylaws and should be sent in this form as a notice to all members.

CHARTERS, BYLAWS, AND RULES 207

The following is a simple method of stating a proposed amendment:

Amendment I.

Proposed Amendment to Article VI, Section 1 of the Bylaws.

"To Amend *Article VI, Board of Directors, Section 1, Membership,* by striking out the words 'three members elected by the House of Delegates' and inserting in their place the words 'five members elected by the Assembly.'

"If *amended,* the section will read: *Section 1, Membership,* 'The Board of Directors consists of the President, Vice President, Secretary, Treasurer, Immediate Past President, and five members elected by the Assembly.'"

Considering Amendments to Bylaws

At a meeting or convention, when the time arrives for considering the proposed amendments, the chairman or some other member of the bylaws committee reads the first proposed amendment as it is stated in the notice and moves its adoption. Since a proposed amendment to the bylaws is a main motion, it may be amended, and amendments to that amendment are also in order. These amendments to the proposed amendment require no previous notice and require only a majority vote for their approval, even though the proposed motion to amend the bylaws may require previous notice and a higher vote.

When the required notice has been given concerning a proposed amendment to the bylaws, the law holds that the subject covered by the amendment has been opened to change and gives the assembly wide discretion in amending the proposed amendment. Parliamentary law, however, provides that:

1. The proposed amendment must be germane to the section to which it applies

2. No amendments can be proposed that cannot reasonably be implied by the notice given on the proposed amendment to the bylaws

If an organization wishes to restrict further the extent or type of amendments to proposed amendments to the bylaws, it must include provisions for the additional restrictions in the bylaws.

Since notice of the proposed amendment to the bylaws has been given, the members are aware that the particular amendment and the subject that it covers will be open to amendment without further notice at the meeting. For example, if a proposed amendment to a section of the bylaws entitled *Classes of Membership* adds a new provision establishing an additional type of membership—associate membership—members know that the proposed amendment may itself be amended by providing or changing the qualifications, rights, or privileges of the proposed class of associate members. Amendments pertaining to other classes of membership are not in order, since notice does not state or imply amendments to any class of membership except associate membership.

An amendment to another part of the bylaws not specified in the notice is admissible only if it is reasonably implied by the amendment as stated in the notice. Using the same example, if the original amendment provided for the creation of an associate membership class, the necessity of fixing the dues for associate members would reasonably be implied, although the subject of dues is covered in another part of the bylaws and might have been omitted unintentionally in the proposed amendment. An amendment providing the dues for associate members would therefore be admissible.

If a provision in a proposed amendment conflicts with a provision already in the bylaws, the conflicting provision in the bylaws can also be amended, to conform to the newly adopted amendment without additional notice.

Vote Required on Amendments to Bylaws

The vote required to amend the bylaws varies from a majority vote to perhaps a two-thirds vote of the legal votes cast or a two-thirds vote of the delegates at a convention.

Since the adoption of the original bylaws requires only a majority of the legal votes cast, it would seem logical that an amendment to them might be made after proper notice by the same requirement of a majority vote. Some organizations also provide that to meet emergencies the bylaws may be amended at a convention without notice, but this procedure usually requires a high vote.

Revision of Bylaws

After bylaws have served for a considerable period of time, it may be necessary to amend many portions of them. The simplest method, when extensive changes are required, is to select a special committee for this purpose or instruct the bylaws committee to study the bylaws and submit a revision. The report of a special revisions committee or of a bylaws committee is a revision when it proposes a substantial number of changes that may affect considerably the structure of the organization, or a rewriting of the form of the bylaws for clarity or reorganization.

A copy of the proposed revision with notice of the date when it will be considered and voted on should be sent to each member in advance of the meeting or convention. Any necessary explanation should be inserted before the provision to which it applies. A revision proposes, in effect, a new set of bylaws, and the revision is presented, considered, and voted on under the same procedures as those followed for the adoption of the original bylaws. The original bylaws, which are still in effect, are not before the assembly for consideration. A revised set of bylaws requires only a majority vote for adoption.

A revised set of bylaws automatically becomes effective immediately after the vote adopting the new revision. It is possible, however, to provide in the motion to adopt the revised bylaws that certain portions of them should not become effective until a later specified time.

Interpreting Bylaws and Rules

Organizations frequently have difficulty in agreeing on the interpretation of their own bylaws and rules. It is wise to assign the duty of interpreting the bylaws and rules to the committee on bylaws or to the board of directors. The interpreting group may seek the advice of an attorney or a parliamentarian.

Special and Standing Rules

Organizations sometimes adopt rules of procedure that add to or vary from the rules of parliamentary law as stated in their parliamentary authority. The rules that are temporary and intended to meet a current or special situation are termed *special* rules. The rules that are intended to stand until revoked are termed *standing* rules. Organizations have the right to adopt special or standing rules by majority vote without notice and to abolish them in the same manner.

Parliamentary Authority

The rules and procedures contained in the parliamentary authority adopted by an organization are intended to cover all parliamentary situations not already provided for in the

CHARTERS, BYLAWS, AND RULES

law or the charters, bylaws, or other rules adopted by an organization.

The adopted parliamentary authority is provided for in the bylaws. This provision is best stated as follows: "The current edition of *Sturgis Standard Code of Parliamentary Procedure* governs this organization in all parliamentary situations that are not provided for in the law or in its charter, bylaws, or adopted rules."

Detailed Procedures

There are many minor details of procedure that are necessary to carry out the provisions of the charter, bylaws, and adopted rules. These detailed procedures should not be included in the bylaws as they will add length and confusion. These procedures adopted by an organization are called *adopted procedures*. They are changed more frequently than the bylaws or more important rules and require only a majority vote to adopt or to change. They should be classified under suitable headings, for example, "Procedures of Election Committee."

Supplementing Procedural Rules by Motions

An organization has the inherent power to take any action that is not in conflict with law, its charter, bylaws, or adopted rules. This includes the power to adopt motions regulating the conduct of its current business. Since many situations arise that are not covered by rules, it is essential that the details of transacting business be determined by motions. During the course of proceedings, motions are frequently necessary to facilitate the method, manner, or order of transacting business.

For example, if a committee has submitted five recommendations relating to the same subject, and the chairman has moved that the first recommendation be adopted and it is being considered, some member might move that the fifth recommendation be considered and decided first because it states a general policy on which the other four recommendations depend.

The power of an organization to adopt any motions for the conduct of current business is particularly important during elections. For example, when there are several candidates for an office and no candidate receives the required majority vote, it is often impractical to require that successive votes be taken until one candidate receives the necessary majority vote. An organization has the power to adopt motions to enable it to complete the election within a reasonable time. Organizations sometimes vote, for example, to drop the candidate having the lowest vote from the list of candidates, after each successive vote. Or an organization may decide to reopen nominations for the office in order to secure a candidate on whom a majority can agree. Organizations have wide leeway in adopting motions to determine the conduct of pending business.

Adopted Policies

Bylaws define the structure of an organization. Policies define the beliefs and philosophy. Both are equally binding on the organization. Organizations frequently adopt policies that are as important in determining the action of the group as are its bylaws or other rules. Policies are usually formulated to meet recurring problems that come up for decision. Most successful businesses have written policies that have developed from experience and that guide their operations. Many organizations develop policies that have an equally powerful influence on their effectiveness.

Once a policy has been developed and adopted, it sets a

standard for judging and deciding all new proposals dealing with the subject or situations covered by the policy. If a proposal is contrary to an adopted policy of the organization, it is not in order and is not considered.

Organizations that use policies as guiding principles should provide in their bylaws for their adoption, vote required, and the method for amending and reviewing them. Some organizations review their policies each year to see whether changes or new policies are required. Many organizations provide for a standing committee on policies which maintains a list of currently effective policies, considers and makes recommendations on proposed policies, reviews all policies annually, and interprets them when requested.

Policies should not be included in the bylaws but should be compiled separately and stated appropriately. The following are examples of policies:

1. "This association believes that because its fundamental purpose is to educate, its programs should always include speakers representing both sides of any controversial or political subject and that equal time should be given each speaker."

2. "We adhere to a policy of raising our professional standards by strict screening of applicants for membership. The professional character of our organization can best be advanced by gradually increasing, but never lowering, the eligibility requirements of applicants for membership."

3. "This organization believes that current services to members is its most important function. Our policy is that dues should not be saved, accumulated, or invested for future use, but that all revenue from dues should be used to provide a constantly improving and expanding current program of services to our members."

4. "This organization adheres strictly to the policy that no member may give gifts or gratuities to any employee of the organization."

Chapter 25

FINANCES

Setting Up Financial Records

Every organization, large or small, should establish and maintain an appropriate accounting system for its funds. A good system for controlling finances saves time and money. Therefore, it is wise for even a small organization to consult an accountant when it is establishing or revising its financial records.

Report of the Treasurer

At each regular meeting the treasurer should give a brief report or summary of the collections and expenditures and call attention to any unusual items. When the treasurer has given his report, the presiding officer should inquire whether there are any questions about the treasurer's report.

The treasurer should make a complete report annually. All members should receive copies of this report, the auditor's certification, and any recommendations made by the treasurer or auditor.

If an organization has a finance committee, it should report at least annually, giving a realistic picture of the financial situation and problems of the organization and of any contemplated proposals or plans involving finances.

Report of the Auditor

Organizations should have an audit at least once a year. An auditing committee composed of members is helpful but is not the best financial safeguard of the organization's finances. Better results can be obtained if the members of the committee are trained in keeping financial records.

The auditor should be selected by vote of the governing board or membership. The treasurer and staff members concerned with finances should have no voice or part in selecting the auditor or the type of audit.

Certified and licensed public accountants are authorized by law to express professional independent opinions on the financial statements of an organization. They may also be requested to provide comments on important financial expenditures, methods, safeguards, and on the integrity of the accounting system and practices.

An auditor's report is an opinion on the treasurer's report. There are two main types of report that auditors provide:

1. The standard *short-form* report consists of two paragraphs expressing the auditor's opinion on the financial statements. The short-form report usually is adequate for most organizations. The standard form, if no exceptions are indicated, means that in the auditor's opinion the treasurer's report reflects fairly the current financial condition and results of operations of the organization, in conformity with generally accepted accounting principles applied on a basis consistent with that of the preceding year. If an exception is expressed in the opinion, the reasons for the exception should be carefully investigated.
2. The *long-form* report, in addition to the contents of the short-form report, describes and explains in detail the significant items in the financial statements. It may

also include further explanations of the audit procedures performed by the auditor. The long-form report is more expensive and most organizations consider it unnecessary unless the board of directors or the management of the organization need detailed financial information that is not otherwise available.

Financial Safeguards

Among the financial safeguards set up by some organizations are: The adoption of a budget, the requirement of authorization for purchases, strict supervision of officers, committees, or employees who collect or expend funds or incur financial obligations, an annual audit, and a blanket bond covering all members and employees who have access to organization funds.

Most organizations prepare and adopt a budget of estimated collections and expenditures. A budget is an estimate only. Adoption of a budget does not mean that the organization must observe its provisions unless required to do so by the rules of the organization. More often, the budget is a financial guide. Some groups require the authorization of the governing board or the membership for any expenditure in excess of the amount provided for in the budget. They also provide that any expenditure not included in the budget requires the same authorization.

A few organizations provide that proposed expenditures above a nominal amount require a purchase order or some other form of authorization and that unusual and particularly large expenditures require authorization by vote of the board of directors or of the membership.

Only members and employees specifically authorized should be permitted to commit the organization to an expenditure. If an authorized representative purchases goods or services in the name of the organization, the bill must be paid by the organization regardless of whether the members later vote to pay or not to pay it.

Instructions to any committee should state how much money, if any, the committee is authorized to spend. Unless a committee is authorized to collect, hold, or expend funds, all funds should be collected, held, and expended through the regular financial channels of the organization.

Chapter 26

LEGAL CLASSIFICATIONS OF ORGANIZATIONS

Meeting to Form an Organization

Since it is difficult for a large assembly to formulate plans, a small group or committee of founders should meet to consider and come to decisions on such questions as the purposes of the proposed organization, its legal form (temporary or permanent, profit or nonprofit, incorporated or unincorporated), types of membership, financing, policies, temporary officers, and affiliation with other organizations.

At the organizing meeting one of the group calls the meeting to order and nominates or calls for nominations for a temporary chairman.[1] If additional persons are nominated, a vote is taken on each until one candidate receives a majority vote. This nominee is then declared the temporary presiding officer, and calls for nominations for a temporary secretary who is elected in the same manner. The presiding officer then requests a member of the group to explain the purpose of the proposed organization. Someone may then present a motion or resolution for forming the organization.

A resolution for forming a *temporary* organization might read:

"*Resolved,* That this assembly form a temporary organization, to be known as the Waterfront Preservation Committee, for the purpose of protesting against the action of the County Board of Supervisors in authorizing a freeway along the waterfront; and be it further

"*Resolved,* That a committee attend the next meeting of the County Board of Supervisors to present a signed protest against this freeway; and be it further

"*Resolved,* That a copy of this resolution with the reasons for our opposition and a list of our officers be sent to each newspaper in this county."

A motion to form a *permanent* organization might read:

"I move that we organize as the Sharon Civic Association."

If this motion carries, some member moves to appoint a committee to draft bylaws; or if the bylaws have already been prepared, they are presented. As soon as the bylaws have been adopted, permanent officers are elected and the organization is complete. (See *Adoption of Bylaws,* p. 204.)

If the members decide to seek a charter as a unit of an already-existing organization, they select or authorize the presiding officer to appoint a committee to carry out this procedure.

Temporary and Permanent Organizations

An organization may be established as either a temporary or a permanent organization. A temporary organization may exist for a few meetings or even a single meeting. It dissolves automatically as soon as the members accomplish the purpose for which they organized. An example of a temporary organization is an organization to elect a candidate to office.

A permanent organization is one formed with the intention of functioning over a considerable period of time, indefinitely, in perpetuity, or until it is dissolved.

Incorporated and Unincorporated Organizations

The founders of a new organization or the members of an older organization who wish to reorganize must decide whether they wish to incorporate or to remain unincorporated. Those nonprofit, unincorporated organizations that are rather loosely structured and operated only under a set of their own rules are termed *associations*. These associations are sharply limited with regard to tax exemption, property holding, and gift-receiving powers. Most organizations, whether local, state, national, or international in scope, are incorporated. The chief advantages of incorporation are:

1. The organization holds a charter from government. Usually this is granted by the state in which the organization incorporated. It operates under the guidance and protection of the state laws governing corporations.
2. The purposes of the organization and the powers necessary to carry out these purposes have legal recognition.
3. The individuals or member groups are able to work with greater effectiveness and scope by joining their resources and efforts.
4. The organization exists permanently until dissolved, even though its membership changes.
5. The corporation is recognized as a legal entity apart from its individual members and thus can do business and hold property of any kind in its own right.

6. Officers, directors, and members are free from personal liability for debts of the organization.
7. The name and seal of the organization are legally protected.

Nonprofit Organizations

Almost all voluntary organizations are nonprofit groups. The first requirement of a nonprofit corporation is that its purposes be ethical, social, moral, or educational. The activities of a nonprofit organization may be charitable, political, social, governmental, or educational in character. The second requirement is that any income or profit of the organization must be used solely to carry out its legal purposes and cannot be distributed as profit to its members. The organization cannot pay dividends or other remuneration to its members. It can, however, pay reasonable compensation or salaries for services rendered.

A nonprofit organization may receive profit incidental to its operations, but that profit must be used for the purposes for which the organization exists. For example, a state medical association having tax exemption as a nonprofit organization might receive considerable profit from some of its activities; this money could not be distributed as pecuniary gain to its members, but it could be expended for educational or other purposes that would benefit its members and the public.

A nonprofit organization, whether incorporated or not, may apply to both the federal and state government for tax-exempt status.

Chapter 27

RIGHTS OF MEMBERS AND OF ORGANIZATIONS

Relationship Between Member and Organization

When a member joins an organization, he enters into a contract between himself and the organization. No particular procedure is necessary to establish this relationship so long as a mutual understanding as to membership is reached.[1] Some organizations require members to sign the bylaws or go through an initiation ceremony, whereas others provide that an applicant becomes a member the moment his application is approved.

When a person joins an organization, he accepts the organization as it then is. The charter, bylaws, and other rules of the organization as they then exist are a part of the contract binding both the member and the organization.[2]

However, the rights of members do not necessarily remain unchanged. Privileges of members may be taken away by decision of the voting body, or other privileges may be added. Fees and dues can be changed, and assessments levied if provided for in the bylaws, but vested rights, those that have been acquired as a result of the contract between the member and the organization, cannot be taken away.[3]

All changes in the rights and privileges of members and all changes in the rules of the organization must be made according to the provisions for making such changes contained in the bylaws or parliamentary law.[4]

Rights of Members

A member of an organization has, in addition to his rights as a person, associational or natural rights, property rights, and parliamentary rights—all of which are protected by law. His rights as a member of the organization are known as associational rights.[5] These rights are different in each organization because they depend on the provisions of its bylaws. A member's associational rights stem from interest in his position and status as a member of the organization. For example, a member has the right to fair and equitable treatment from the other members of the organization.

In addition to associational rights, a member usually has property rights.[6] He may own an interest in the clubhouse, for example.

A member also has the following fundamental rights under common parliamentary law, subject only to any specific limitations contained in the bylaws:

1. To be sent notices
2. To attend meetings
3. To present motions
4. To speak on debatable questions
5. To vote
6. To nominate
7. To be a candidate for office
8. To inspect official records of the organization
9. To insist on the enforcement of the rules of the organization and of parliamentary law
10. To resign when he chooses
11. To have a fair hearing before expulsion or other penalties are applied
12. To receive or have the right to inspect an up-to-date copy of the bylaws, charter, rules, and minutes of the organization

RIGHTS OF MEMBERS AND OF ORGANIZATIONS

13. To exercise any other rights or privileges given to the members by the law, by the bylaws, or by the rules of the organization

The rights of a member may vary depending on whether he is a regular member, an associate member, a life member, or some other type of member. If any of the associational, property, or parliamentary rights of a member are violated, he may seek to enforce his rights by legal action against the organization. As a general principle, however, courts will not adjudicate such actions until the member has exhausted the means provided him for enforcing his rights under the bylaws of the organization.[7]

Rights of Organizations

An organization itself has rights. These rights are exercised by the decision of a majority of its members. Some of the fundamental rights of an organization are:

1. To carry out its purposes and to exercise any of the rights or authority granted it by law
2. To change its purposes, if permitted by law and its charter, to merge with another organization, or to dissolve
3. To establish eligibility requirements and procedures governing the admission of members,[8] and to grant or refuse membership according to the law and its adopted rules [9]
4. To establish and to amend, through changes in its bylaws, the rights, privileges, and obligations of its members either by extension or limitation
5. To delegate authority, within legal limits, to officers, boards, committees, and employees
6. To select its officers, directors, and committee members and to suspend or remove them for valid cause

7. To discipline or expel members in accordance with the law and with its bylaws
8. To hold property and to defend or enter into litigation in its own name if it is incorporated

Relationship of Individual and Organizational Rights

The rights of each member are definite and are protected by law; they must, however, be regarded in relation to the rights of the other members and of the organization. In order to assert his rights, a member must choose the proper time and must follow the proper procedure. For example, a member has the right to present any proposal to the assembly. But he cannot attempt to exercise this right at a special meeting by proposing a motion that is not stated in the call for the special meeting.

Similarly, a member has the fundamental right to be heard on any debatable question before the assembly. However, if the member attempts to discuss the question when it has not yet been presented, or for a second time when others desire to speak, or when some other member has the floor, or after debate has been terminated by a motion to vote immediately, he cannot assert his right to discuss.

If the rights of an individual member or a minority of members conflict with the rights of the majority of the assembly, the rights of the majority ultimately must prevail. For example, a minority has the right to be heard. But if the minority attempts to be heard when a majority wishes to adjourn, its right must give way to that of the majority.

The right of members to oppose ideas and candidates does not extend to the right to undermine the organization itself. If after the majority has made a decision some members continue to oppose to the point where the organization has difficulty in functioning or is in danger of being destroyed, the governing board or the membership should protect the organization by taking proper disciplinary action.

Discipline and Expulsion of Members

Procedures for the discipline and expulsion of members should be included in the bylaws. However, every organization has the inherent right to discipline, suspend, or expel a member for valid cause, even if provisions for doing so are not included in the bylaws.[10]

Discipline may consist, for example, of requiring a member to appear before the governing board and explain his actions or pay a fine, or a member may be reprimanded or suspended from membership for a limited time.

A membership can be terminated and a member expelled because of his violation of an important duty to the organization, a breach of a fundamental rule or principle of the organization, or for any violation stated in the bylaws as a ground for expulsion.[11] In general, termination of membership is justified if a member fails or refuses to work within the framework of the organization.

In addition, an organization has the implied power to expel a member for violation of his duties as a citizen. For example, a member may be expelled if he is convicted of a criminal offense that would discredit the organization.

A proceeding to expel a member must not violate any rule of the organization or any of the member's rights under the law.[12] The primary requisites for expulsion proceedings are due notice and fair hearing.[13]

The essential steps for imposing severe discipline or expelling a member are:
1. *Charges:* Charges in affidavit form stating the alleged violations and preliminary proof should be filed with the secretary.
2. *Investigation:* The proper committee should investi-

gate the charges promptly and, if it decides that a hearing is warranted, set a date and notify the secretary.

3. *Notification:* The secretary should send the accused member a registered letter at least fifteen days before the date of the hearing, containing a copy of the charges, the time and place of the hearing, and a statement of his right to be present at the hearing, to defend himself, to be represented by an attorney, and to receive a copy of any transcript.

4. *Hearing:* In conducting the hearing the committee should preserve decorum and fair play, restrict evidence and testimony to the written charges, and uphold the right of the accused member to defend himself, to cross-examine witnesses, and to refute the charges against him.

5. *Decision:* The hearing committee should within a reasonable time make findings of fact on the essential points at issue, recommend a decision of guilt or innocence, and send a copy of the recommended decision and findings of fact to the accused member and to the secretary.

6. *Penalty:* If the member is found guilty of the charges, the board of directors should recommend a penalty to the membership meeting. The decision may be approved by a majority vote of the legal votes cast at the meeting.

Some organizations permit a member who has been expelled to apply for readmission after a certain period of time.

Resignations

A member has the right to resign from an organization at any time that he desires.[14] A provision in the bylaws that he must have paid his dues before he resigns cannot prevent him from resigning. There is no practical way in which any organization can compel a delinquent member to continue as a member against his will, nor can it persist in assessing and collecting dues from him. A resignation becomes effective immediately, unless some future time is specified by the member, and no acceptance of it is necessary to make it effective.

An officer or a director may resign from his office at his pleasure. A resignation need not be written, and it may be implied,[15] as when a member moves out of the jurisdiction of the organization and is no longer eligible for membership. A resignation does not require acceptance since the officer resigning can determine his own action. A bylaws provision that an officer holds office "until his successor is elected"[16] does not prevent him from resigning nor can it be used to force him to serve against his will. A resignation effective at a future date may be withdrawn until it has been accepted or until the effective date of the resignation;[17] if, however, the resignation is intended to become effective immediately, it cannot be withdrawn.[18]

After an officer or director has resigned, either orally or in writing, he cannot simply resume his office if he changes his mind. A person who has resigned from an elective office can be restored to that office only by re-election, or by reappointment if he held an appointive office. After he resigns, an officer or director continues to be liable for acts he committed or concurred in before his resignation.

Chapter 28

STAFF AND CONSULTANTS

The Executive Secretary

Most large organizations and many local groups employ a chief administrator who is variously called executive secretary, executive director, or manager. He is chosen by the governing board and is responsible to the board.

This administrator needs an extensive knowledge of planning for and administering voluntary organizations, and experience with business methods; in addition, he needs the ability to adapt to a constantly changing group of employers. He should have the skill and the willingness to assist officers, committees, and members, and to direct credit and appreciation to the members rather than to himself. He must stand aloof from the politics and rivalries of members and his devotion must be to the over-all good of the organization.

He directs the administration of the organization, employs all staff members with the approval of the governing board, and performs all duties assigned to him by the voting body, the governing board, or the president; as the need arises, he also performs many more tasks that are within the administrative policies already established by the group.

A competent and loyal executive secretary is the greatest single asset of any organization. He provides continuity of policies, work, and progress in associations whose leaders are changing frequently and whose members are busy with their own occupations.

The Accountant

An organization that handles any considerable amount of money needs the assistance of an accountant. He can save the organization time and money by establishing or revising its accounting system so that it meets the particular needs of the group. He may audit the financial records and prepare the tax reports. If he is a licensed or certified public accountant, he can comment on the significance of various items in his own auditing report.

The Consultant to Nonprofit Organizations

Business corporations are concerned primarily with profit and operate entirely with paid employees. Such organizations, therefore, can benefit materially from the assistance of management and business consultants. Nonprofit corporations or organizations, on the other hand, operate on principles, psychology, and policies that, except in the work of their business offices, are almost the opposites of those followed by profit-making organizations. Nonprofit corporations and organizations are concerned with professional, educational, or political objectives, work almost entirely with unpaid volunteers, and therefore require the services of consultants who are trained in the fundamentals of working with such groups.

A good consultant to nonprofit organizations, in addition to understanding parliamentary procedure, must know the basic principles on which such organizations function effectively. He must have a broad knowledge of many types of organizations, large and small, of their structures, objectives, and problems; and be able to offer solutions for their problems. He must know how to develop bylaws, rules, and policies that meet the needs of the particular organization. He must be able to offer solutions for problems of finances, services to members, communications, dissension, education of members, tax exemption, foundation possibilities, the practical working-out of different types of organizational structures, and the relationships between world, national, and state organizations and their constituent and component groups.

The Attorney

An organization needs the help of an attorney on all important legal matters. Situations in which an attorney's services are essential include:

1. Decision on the type of organizational structure that legally is best suited to the purposes of a new organization; for example, association, society, nonprofit corporation, profit corporation, or a type of foundation
2. Incorporating the organization
3. Establishing a foundation for the organization
4. Entering into or altering an important contract
5. Transactions involving the purchase, lease, or sale of real property or important personal property
6. The merger or the dissolution of the organization
7. Expulsion of a member
8. Initiation or defense of litigation

The Parliamentarian

A competent parliamentarian can be helpful to any organization, and in large organizations his services are essential to effective operation.

The parliamentarian is usually chosen by the president, works under his direction, and cooperates with him as requested. The parliamentarian also aids and advises the governing board, committees, members, and staff members. In

STAFF AND CONSULTANTS

most organizations he is retained on an annual basis. He can be of greater assistance if those who need his services consult him in advance as to the best methods for handling problems. Before a meeting or convention he can assist in planning for it. After a meeting he can advise on the problems that arise in carrying out the decisions of the membership.

At a meeting or convention the parliamentarian usually sits next to the president, cooperating with him in whatever way the presiding officer requests or finds helpful. The parliamentarian cannot make rulings, but he advises the presiding officer, who does make rulings. If a question is asked, the parliamentarian may explain the answer to the president only, or, if the president directs, he may reply so that all the members may hear him. If the presiding officer asks the parliamentarian to explain a procedure to the members, he does so. He should not offer unsolicited advice unless a serious error is being made; then he unobtrusively calls the mistake to the attention of the presiding officer.

The more capable and experienced a presiding officer is, the better he understands the value of a good parliamentarian and how to use his services. The more a presiding officer knows about parliamentary law, the more he appreciates the fact that a parliamentarian can relieve him of responsibility for procedural problems and details so that the presiding officer is free to concentrate on reactions and concerns of members and on the over-all progress and tone of the meeting. Thus he can proceed with confidence and poise.

The parliamentarian is responsible for seeing that no procedural details are overlooked, for anticipating parliamentary strategy, and for being certain that all parliamentary requirements are observed. He is also responsible for giving an opinion or advice and for explaining a problem when requested.

The parliamentarian is in somewhat the same position as an attorney; he offers advice when requested, knowing full well that the president and the members can accept or ignore that advice as they choose. A competent parliamentarian is not an advocate of causes or a representative of the point of view of divergent groups within the organization. Rather, he is retained to help the members do what they wish to do, and to find a valid way of accomplishing, if possible, the legitimate purposes that the organization seeks to achieve.

It is clear that the parliamentarian cannot perform his duties properly unless he is competent to deal with the many problems that may arise. Since there are no state licensing laws for parliamentarians as there is for teachers and members of other professions, a parliamentarian must be selected on the basis of his own competence and experience. In addition to understanding common parliamentary law, he must know the statutory law, if there is any, that applies to the particular organization with which he is working. He need not consult lawbooks to acquire this knowledge if he follows a parliamentary authority that is based on the law. The fact that an organization has adopted a parliamentary book that is not legally correct does not absolve the parliamentarian or the organization from observing the law.

Many parliamentary problems involve several rules and principles. A parliamentarian must be able to reconcile the conflicting principles and rules of parliamentary law that may be involved in a particular situation or in answering a particular question. When he is asked a question, he must apply the principles and the rules and give his considered opinion. He works on the principle that he has been retained as an authority and should neither argue nor seek to prove the correctness of his opinion by quoting from books, any more than a doctor would cite a medical authority in his diagnosis of a patient's illness. He explains his opinion if there is need to do so.

APPENDIX

GOVERNMENTAL BOARDS, COUNCILS,
COMMISSIONS, AND COMMITTEES

LABOR ORGANIZATIONS

SUGGESTED BYLAW PROVISIONS
FOR A LOCAL ORGANIZATION

MODEL MINUTES

REFERENCES

DEFINITIONS OF PARLIAMENTARY TERMS

GOVERNMENTAL BOARDS, COUNCILS, COMMISSIONS, AND COMMITTEES

Governmental Bodies and Parliamentary Law

Local, state, and national governmental bodies (except state legislatures and Congress, which have their own systems of specialized rules) operate under the common law of parliamentary procedure. All these bodies, whether primarily legislative, administrative, or quasi-judicial, or whether they combine these functions, must comply with any constitutional, statutory, or charter enactments on procedure that apply to them and must also conduct their business in strict accord with common parliamentary law.

Parliamentary law applies somewhat differently to governmental bodies and to voluntary organizations. The powers of voluntary organizations arise from agreement of the members and can be changed by the members. The powers of governmental organizations do not reside in the members themselves and can be changed only by the authority that established them. The powers of governmental bodies are delegated to them by constitution or statute.

The boards, councils, commissions, and committees of government have an even greater obligation to observe correct parliamentary law than do voluntary organizations. They have a responsibility to the public and their decisions, more widespread and permanent in effect, have greater impact, both moral and financial.

Every governmental body has an inherent right to regulate its own procedure subject to the provisions of the constitution, statutes, charter, or other controlling authority. Although governmental bodies have the right to adopt special rules governing some of their procedures, none of these adopted rules can conflict with the law or with public policy.[1] For example, when a charter provides that interested citizens shall be heard by the council, the council cannot require instead that objections be submitted in writing.[2]

Because of the differing responsibilities and legal status of these public bodies, some parliamentary rules that apply to them differ from common parliamentary law, or are supplementary to it. The principles explained here apply unless a statute or an adopted rule of the body provides differently.

The statutory law that controls the procedure of governmental bodies differs in detail in the various states, counties, cities, and districts. However, there are basic principles and rules that apply only to governmental bodies and that are common to all of them.

This section of the appendix alerts such bodies to the parliamentary principles that apply particularly to them and that the law considers important. It also explains the more important parliamentary principles and rules that differ from or are in addition to the common parliamentary law as applied to voluntary organizations, and as explained in this book. The material presented here is intended only for members of governmental bodies.

Organization of Governmental Bodies

A board, council, commission, or committee of government must organize with a presiding officer and a recording officer before it can undertake any business. Usually such bodies reorganize annually and elect officers periodically as the law provides.

A statute may designate the presiding officer and other officers, as when an elected mayor is the ex-officio presiding officer of a city council. Frequently the law authorizes governmental bodies to elect their own officers from their membership, as when a board of education selects its own president and secretary.

If two or more of these bodies meet together as a *joint body*, they must organize as a joint body and choose a presiding officer and a recording officer. If two or more bodies meet as *separate bodies* holding a *joint meeting*, they do not organize jointly, but they cannot take legal action except as separate bodies.

Notice Requirements

A governmental body must adhere strictly to all statutory, parliamentary, or adopted requirements regarding notice of all regular and special meetings, hearings, and of matters requiring notice if its actions are to be legal. If notice of any meeting or hearing is intentionally or negligently withheld from a member or from others to whom notice is due, the proceedings of that meeting are invalid.[2] Similarly, if notice of any proposal requiring notice is intentionally or negligently withheld from a member, action taken on the proposal is invalid. Notice of special meetings must state the particular subjects to be discussed and the specific proposals to be voted on.

In certain instances the law requires governmental bodies to give public notice of those meetings and hearings that are open to the public; for example, a budget hearing. Some proposals require notice to persons who have a particular interest in the business to be considered at the meeting or hearing; thus, a board of supervisors must send notice to all property owners within the boundaries of a proposed new improvement district. Many governmental bodies also are required to publish notice of the time and place of their regular meetings. All such requirements regarding notice must be fulfilled if the actions of the body are to be valid.

A defect in notice to members can be overcome only if all the members of the body (or all the persons affected) are present and vote to waive the defect.[3] However, no waiver by the members can validate actions taken at a meeting if the actions are invalid for any other reason.

Quorum

The quorum of governmental bodies is usually fixed by statute or ordinance or by an adopted rule of the body. If it is not thus determined, the rule of common parliamentary law governs and a quorum consists of a majority of the members of the body. (See Quorum Requirements, p. 113.) The most common statutory requirement for a quorum is that it consist of a majority of the positions or memberships of the body. This requirement is not changed by vacancies or disqualification of members.[4]

When two or more bodies come together in a joint meeting but do not organize as one joint body, the quorum is a majority of each body computed separately. When two or more bodies meet and organize as one joint body, the quorum is a majority of the members of the joint body.[5]

If there is not a quorum present at the time set for the meeting, the body cannot be called to order; legally, there can be no meeting until a quorum is present. If there is not a quorum, those present cannot fix a time for another meeting. If a special meeting is desired, the procedure for calling such a meeting must be complied with; otherwise, there can be no meeting until the next regular meeting.

If at any time in a meeting a quorum ceases to be present, the presiding officer or some member should immediately raise the question of no quorum, and the question of the presence or absence of a quorum should be determined immediately and recorded in the minutes. If at a later date a question of the lack of a quorum at the time of taking a particular action is raised, the courts will presume that a quorum continued to be present if the minutes show that a quorum had been present previously at the meeting and do not show by a vote, roll call, or statement that a quorum had ceased to be present at the time of taking the particular action. (*See* Presumption of a Quorum, p. 115.)

Minutes

All actions taken by governmental organizations must be fully and accurately recorded in their minutes.[6] The minutes are the primary evidence of actions taken by the body; they determine whether proposals were adopted and state specifically what the proposals were. When ordinances, laws, or rules are printed separately, they may be identified in the minutes by subject, name, and number instead of being included in full.

The final legal responsibility for correcting and approving the minutes rests solely with the members of the body.[7] If the district attorney, for instance, is assigned the duty of correcting the minutes of a board of freeholders, the responsibility for correcting and approving them as the correct and official minutes of the body still rests with the members.

If during a meeting an employee records a verbatim report from which the minutes are later prepared, the members are still responsible for the accuracy of the minutes, and the secretary whose duty it is to sign them cannot finally attest them until after they have been prepared, corrected, and approved by vote of the body.

Only then does this record of actions become the official minutes of the body. An employee may prepare the minutes, but only the secretary of the body may attest them after their approval by the body.

Minutes of governmental organizations, with the exception of closed hearings or meetings to consider such matters as the hiring or dismissal of employees, or sale or purchase of property, are a part of the public record and are available to the public at reasonable times.

Presiding Officer

The presiding officer in a governmental body is usually a member and has all the rights and duties of the other members. He has the right to introduce motions or proposals and to speak and vote on them while he is presiding. Since each member of these bodies often is elected or appointed to represent a segment of opinion or a geographical area, the group represented by the presiding officer would be deprived of representation if he did not have the same rights as other members.

Powers and Duties of Members

The powers and duties of most boards, commissions, councils, and committees are joint powers and duties that can be exercised only when the body is meeting. Individual members do not have authority to act individually and independently, because of the fact that they are members of the body. An exception to this principle is when specific duties or powers are assigned by statute or delegated by vote of the body to a certain member or members or to a committee of the body.

The legislative and administrative powers and responsibilities, when vested in such a body, may be exercised only in the meetings of the body.

No member of a governmental body has the right to speak or act for it unless specifically authorized by law or by the body. Ex officio members of these bodies have the same rights and duties as the other members of the body unless the law provides differently.

A governmental body cannot delegate any discretionary powers or duties to any other persons or groups, not even to a committee of its own members or officers or to its individual members. It can assign ministerial or administrative duties or powers that do not require the exercise of discretion but merely involve the faithful performance of acts. Public bodies are more severely restricted than voluntary organizations in delegating their authority or discretionary power. (*See* Delegation of Authority by Officers, p. 169.)

No Seconds Required

Seconds to motions, resolutions, or ordinances cannot be required in governmental bodies and no proposal can be ruled out of order for want of a second. Because of the small size of many governmental groups—in a board consisting of three members, for example—to require a second would be to require that any proposal must receive the support of two-thirds of the members before it could be considered.

Some governmental bodies adopt a rule requiring seconds to motions, resolutions, or ordinances, but it is doubtful that such a rule would be upheld by the courts. It is hard to conceive of the courts denying the right of a representative in a legislative or administrative body to propose a motion or measure and have it considered and voted on by the body.

Voting

The vote required on different types of proposals is usually specified by statute. The required vote for most proposals is a majority of the members or memberships of the body. A majority of the memberships means, for example, that a board having twelve positions, two of which are vacant, requires a majority of seven. If there is no statute or adopted rule specifying the vote required, the rule of common parliamentary law governs; that is, decision by the majority of the legal votes cast.

Unlike voluntary organizations, governmental boards, councils, commissions, and committees cannot limit their powers by adopting a rule requiring more than a majority vote to pass an ordinance, or enactment, or a nonprocedural motion. Any requirement in excess of a majority vote to take such actions is illegal and may be disregarded.[8]

A member of a governmental body may refrain from voting. However, the members of such bodies are under a strong obligation to vote on all motions, because decision-making is one of the primary discretionary duties of the office to which they were elected or appointed. A public officer should refrain from voting only when there is a conflict of interest between his personal interest and the interest of the body of which he is a member. The circumstances in which there are conflicts of interest are defined in detail by the statutes of most states.

A member of a governmental body cannot vote on a measure in which he has a direct personal or financial interest, except in a situation where all other members have the same direct personal or financial interest. For example, a member of a commission could not vote on a motion to fix the sum of money allotted for expenses if he were the only member planning to attend a convention, but if all the other members planned to attend the convention and were joined with him in the motion to fix the sum allotted for expenses, all of them could vote on the motion. If this were not true, in many instances governmental bodies could not act on matters involving public interest. A member of a governmental body cannot vote by proxy or by absentee ballot.

When a governmental body is required to vote on a question, the body cannot delegate this duty to anyone else nor can it direct the secretary to cast a ballot for a particular candidate or measure.

Vacancies

Vacancies in appointive bodies are filled by the original appointing power. Elective bodies sometimes have the right by law to fill vacancies until the next election, at which time the voters elect a person to fill the office. In some instances a special election is called.

Removal of Members

Congress and state legislatures are granted by their constitutions the power to judge the election and qualifications of their members and to remove them under certain conditions and procedures. Governmental boards, councils, commissions, and committees do not have this authority, however, nor have they inherent power to discipline or remove their own members.

Statutory law provides procedures by which both appointed and elected members of governmental bodies can be removed for valid cause. Grounds for such removal are usually gross neglect of duty, incompetence, dishonesty, or conviction of a felony or other serious crime.

Appointive members of these public bodies, who hold office at the pleasure of the appointing power, can usually be removed at any time by the appointing power.

Elected members of governmental boards, councils, commissions, and committees can usually be removed only by those who elected them. States that have the recall procedure usually make its provisions applicable to elected members of these bodies.

Parliamentary Authority

Governmental bodies have the right and duty to supplement statutory procedures or those of their adopted rules by the adoption of a book on parliamentary law. This parliamentary authority governs the procedure of the body in all situations not otherwise provided for by law or by the adopted rules of the body.

Rights of Citizens Attending Meetings

Citizens have the right to attend the meetings of most governmental bodies and they may be permitted to address the body on subjects relevant to its business. However, citizens must observe all the rules and regulations of the body regarding attendance and addressing its members.

Members of the public attending the meetings of governmental bodies do not have the right to interrupt or heckle. They have the right only to seek permission to be heard or to ask questions in accordance with whatever provisions for hearing public opinions or answering questions are fixed by law or have been adopted as rules of the body. They also have the right to submit written petitions, protests, and requests for hearings.

LABOR ORGANIZATIONS

Unions Have Additional Parliamentary Rules

The members of labor organizations have a most favorable and unique relationship to parliamentary law. They have all the rights and privileges established by common parliamentary law; in addition they are the only group for which Congress has enacted a statute that restates some of the principles of common parliamentary law and establishes additional specific parliamentary safeguards. Including these parliamentary provisions in the Labor-Management Reporting and Disclosure Act of 1959 [1] has raised these principles and rules of common parliamentary law and the specific rules established for labor organizations to the highest rank, that of statutory law.

Members of labor organizations must know and observe the rules of common parliamentary law as explained in this book. In addition, they must know and observe the specific parliamentary provisions contained in this statute. This section of the appendix separates the *parliamentary provisions* from the many other provisions of the statute, rewords them for simplification and clarity, and states them in language that makes them suitable for inclusion in union bylaws.

Bylaws Should Include Statutory Provisions

The subjects covered by these parliamentary provisions are the same as the subjects usually contained in a well-drawn set of bylaws (or constitution and bylaws). Every union, therefore, should include a simplified version of the parliamentary provisions of the statute in its bylaws (or constitution and bylaws) so that all parliamentary provisions will be in one document that is readily available to all members.

The parliamentary provisions of the statute do not constitute a complete set of bylaws (or constitution and bylaws). They are the framework to which each union can add the many provisions that make a particular set of bylaws suitable to the distinctive needs of the particular group. There is no model set of bylaws that will suit every labor organization, or even every local union in the same international group. Any set of bylaws (or constitution and bylaws) is effective in direct proportion to its suitability and fitness to serve the particular needs of the organization adopting it.

The bylaw provisions given here are worded for use by local unions, but the explanatory statements show any differing provisions that should be used for labor organizations other than local unions. The parliamentary provisions of the statute are sometimes expressed in simpler words, but the meaning has not been changed. Each local union should include in its constitution and bylaws (or bylaws) all of the provisions printed in *italic* type. It should then supplement these required provisions by adding qualifications, limitations, or other provisions as its members may choose. The statute leaves intact the right of a union to fix and enforce duties and obligations applying to its members. Any parliamentary provision may be added to those required by the statute provided it meets the following three requirements:

1. The provision must be a *reasonable* one. For example, the statute provides that any member in good standing may be a candidate for union office. A particular union might add the provision to its bylaws that a candidate must have been a member of that union for a specified time (for example, two years) or must have worked in the trade for a certain period of time (for example, two years). These would be reasonable provisions. However, the union could not add a provision that in order to be a candidate for office a member must have attended every meeting for the last five years. This would be an *unreasonable* provision, and therefore illegal.

2. The provision must be *uniformly imposed*. This means that the provision must be applied to all members equally and in the same manner. For example, if a union has a provision that any member who is tardy at a business meeting must pay a fine of one dollar, the fine must be collected from *all* members who are tardy, and not from some members only.

3. The provision cannot be *in conflict* with any provision of the statute. For example, the statute provides that every member must be given notice of an election by letter or by publication prominently displayed in the official news organ of the union, mailed to him at his last known address at least fifteen days in advance of any election. A provision that notice of an election may be given merely by posting notice on the bulletin boards at all places where union members are employed would be in conflict with this provision of the statute. Such a provision, therefore, would be null and void.

The statements that are included in the remainder of this section in italic type could be included in union bylaws just as they are stated. The statements that are in regular type are explanatory only and should not be included in the bylaws.

Provisions to Include in Union Bylaws

BILL OF RIGHTS

1. **Equal Rights and Privileges.** *Every member has rights equal to every other member. These rights include the right to receive notices, attend meetings, nominate, take part in discussion, vote, and to exercise all of the rights and privileges granted by the organization to its members.*
2. **Freedom of Speech and Assembly.** *Every member has the right to meet with other members and to express his views, arguments, and opinions on candidates and proposals.*
3. **Dues, Fees, and Assessments.** *Every member has the right to protection against increases in the rates of dues or initiation fees and against the levying of assessments. The members control any increase or levy through the specific voting procedures as stated in these bylaws in Article (   )—Voting.*
4. **Right to Sue.** *Every member has the right to initiate or participate in legal actions in any court or administrative body regardless of whether a labor organization or its officers are involved, to be a witness in any governmental proceedings, and to petition or to consult legislators.*

5. **Safeguards Against Improper Disciplinary Action.** *Every member has the right to protection against arbitrary or unfair disciplinary action such as fines, suspension, or expulsion (except for nonpayment of dues). He is protected by the procedures in Article( )—Discipline and Expulsion of Members—of these bylaws requiring that he must be served with written notice of the specific charges against him, given a reasonable time to prepare his defense, and afforded a full and fair hearing.* (See Discipline and Expulsion of Members, p. 225.)

6. **The Right to Information.** *Every member has the right to information concerning the rules, actions, and other matters affecting the membership of this organization. This local organization must:*
   A. *Keep its members informed on the provisions of, or amendments to, all statutes applying directly to labor organizations.*
   B. *Forward, upon request, a copy of each collective bargaining agreement to those members whose rights are directly affected by it.*

   Labor organizations, other than local unions, must forward a copy of each such agreement to constituent locals having members directly affected, and also keep copies of these agreements on file and available for members to consult.

   C. *Make available to its members the operational and financial information in the report required to be submitted to the Secretary of Labor and also permit any member who has just cause to do so to examine any books, records, and accounts necessary to verify the report.*

   Reports filed with the Secretary of Labor by unions and employers are public information and must be furnished to any person at cost of publication, and a file of these reports must be maintained at designated agencies as directed by the Secretary of Labor.

   D. *Permit any candidate to inspect, but not make copies of, the list of names and addresses of all the members working under union security shop agreements.*
   E. *Make available to each member an up-to-date copy of the bylaws (or constitution and bylaws) adopted by this organization, and send copies to the Secretary of Labor.*

These rights have been interpreted, clarified, and extended in their application by court decisions and by administrative rulings. The emphasis given to these particular rights by including them in a federal statute does not mean that there are not other vitally important rights that belong to union members and to members of all organizations. (*See* Rights of Members, p. 222.)

MEMBERSHIP

This organization establishes the following qualifications, eligibility requirements, and rules for becoming a member and for retaining membership: (list)

These requirements may differ in each organization. The rules established must be reasonable, uniformly applied, and may not be in conflict with any provision of a statute.

OFFICERS, AGENTS, AND OTHER REPRESENTATIVES

The officers of this organization are: (list)

The term officers *when used in these bylaws means any officer provided for in the constitution and bylaws who is authorized to perform the functions of president, vice president, secretary, treasurer, or other executive functions, and any member of the executive or governing board.*

Since the officers occupy positions of trust, they have a special responsibility to the members to act in good faith in the conduct of all affairs of the organization and in their relations to the union and the membership.

All officers must be bonded individually by a corporate surety company for not less than 10 per cent of the funds they annually handle.

No officer, agent, or employee may receive any loan from the organization that is in excess of $2,000 nor may he receive money or gifts of value intended to influence him in his actions as a representative of employees. (*See* Powers and Liabilities of Officers, p. 169.)

THE EXECUTIVE BOARD

The executive board has the power and the authorization to act for the organization between meetings. The "members assembled" can always rescind, repeal, or amend any action of the executive board, except when the action is no longer within the control of the members, or when the action has been specifically assigned as a power or duty to the executive board. (See The Board of Directors, p. 182.)

ELIGIBILITY FOR NOMINATION AND ELECTION

1. *Candidates may be nominated from the floor or they may be nominated by petition of (state number or proportion of members).*
2. *Write-in votes for members who have not been nominated are permissible.*
3. *Any member in good standing is eligible to be a candidate unless he is disqualified by having been convicted of any of certain criminal offenses or is disqualified after a fair hearing on a challenge for cause.* See Sec. 504. (a). Labor-Management Reporting and Disclosure Act of 1959.

TIME OF ELECTIONS

This organization elects officers every ( ) years at its annual meeting.

A local union must hold an election at least once every *three* years. General committees, system boards, joint boards, joint councils, or other intermediate bodies must elect at least once every *four* years. National or international unions must hold an election at least once every *five* years.

TERM OF OFFICE

All officers hold office for a term of ( ) years.

There is no statutory restriction against members re-electing an officer if they wish to do so.

CAMPAIGN REQUIREMENTS

This union and its officers must comply without discrimination with all reasonable requests from candidates to distribute campaign literature to all members in good standing at the candidate's expense.

No funds from an employer or from a union may be used to promote the candidacy of any member.

VOTING IN ELECTIONS

Every member must be given notice by letter or by publication prominently displayed in the official news organ of the union, mailed to him at his last known address, at least fifteen days in advance of any election.

LABOR ORGANIZATIONS

Any member in good standing may vote and otherwise support the candidate of his choice without penalty or reprisal, and he cannot be disqualified from voting by delay or default in payment of checked-off dues.

All elections must be conducted by secret ballot.

Votes must be counted and the results published separately for the local organization. All ballots and election records, including the voting list, must be preserved for at least one year.

In an election at a convention, the reports of the credentials committee, the tally sheets, and the report of the tellers or election committee must be preserved for at least one year.

The election committee must provide adequate safeguards to insure a fair election. Any candidate may have an observer at the polls and at the counting of ballots. (*See* Counting Ballots, p. 154.)

CHALLENGING AN ELECTION

Any member may challenge an election for irregularities that could have affected the outcome of the election. When a member has exhausted the remedies provided by the constitution and bylaws of this organization or of a parent organization against irregularities in an election, or has had no decision after three months, he may file with the Secretary of Labor a complaint based on his challenge.

To exhaust the remedies within an organization means to try all the means provided by the bylaws of the organization to enforce a right or to redress an injury. (*See* Challenging an Election, p. 159.)

REMOVAL OF OFFICERS

Any officer may be removed for serious misconduct. Before removal an officer must receive a written copy of the charges against him, must be given a reasonable time to prepare his defense, and must be given a fair hearing with opportunity to refute the charges and to question witnesses. (*See* Removal of Officers, p. 123.)

VOTING REQUIREMENTS

Voting on Officers, Delegates, and Those Exercising Executive Duties

Voting on officers, delegates, and others who have executive duties must be by secret ballot, and a majority of the legal votes cast is required to elect.

VOTING ON INITIATION FEES, DUES, AND ASSESSMENTS

No increase may be made in the initiation fees or rate of dues and no assessment may be levied, except by:

1. *A majority vote of the legal votes cast by members in good standing, voting by secret ballot, at a general meeting after reasonable notice has been given of the proposal, or*
2. *A majority vote of the members in good standing, in a membership referendum conducted by secret ballot.*

In *national* and *international* unions and *other labor organizations* no increases in the initiation fees or rate of dues may be made and no assessment levied except by: (1) a majority vote of the legal votes cast by the elected delegates voting at a regular convention or at a special convention held after thirty or more days written notice to each local union, *or* (2) a majority vote of the members in good standing in a membership referendum conducted by secret ballot, *or* (3) a majority vote of the members of the executive or other governing board provided this authority is contained in the bylaws. This action by a board is effective only until the next regular convention.

DISCIPLINE AND EXPULSION OF MEMBERS

Members may be disciplined by fine, suspension, or expulsion according to the provisions of this constitution and bylaws that provide the grounds for such discipline and state the requirements for notice, hearing, judgment, and appeals. (*See* Discipline and Expulsion of Members, p. 225.)

In addition to the subjects contained in the Taft-Hartley and the Labor-Management Reporting and Disclosure Act of 1959, the bylaws of a local organization must provide for such important matters as defining the geographical area and classification of work of the organization, its quorum, the duties of officers, and the obligations of the members to the organization.

All the rights that are stated or created by the Labor-Management Reporting and Disclosure Act of 1959 have remedies provided in the bylaws of the union to enforce them. After these remedies have been exhausted, administrative and legal remedies are open and available to every member to protect him in the assertion and exercise of his rights. The protection and enforcement of the rights of members and of the union are the duty of the organization.

SUGGESTED BYLAW PROVISIONS
FOR A LOCAL ORGANIZATION

ARTICLE I Name

ARTICLE II Purposes
(If the purposes are stated in a charter, they need not be repeated in the bylaws.)

ARTICLE III Membership
    A. Classes of membership with eligibility requirements, rights, and privileges of each class (active, associate, honorary, etc.)
    B. Requirements of parent organization if group holds a charter from higher organization
    C. Procedure for membership application and certification

ARTICLE IV Officers
    A. List of officers of organization
    B. Method of selection
    C. Duties of each officer

ARTICLE V Board of directors
    A. Membership
        1. Ex-officio members (usually the officers of the organization)
        2. Elected members: qualifications
    B. Officers of board
        1. Qualifications
        2. Selection
    C. Duties and responsibilities of board (usually the duty and power to act for the organization between meetings of the organization)
    D. Executive committee of board
        1. Membership
        2. Duties

E. Meetings of board
F. Reports of board and executive committee

ARTICLE VI Meetings
- A. Annual: notice, business to be conducted, order of business
- B. Regular: notice, usual order of business
- C. Special: how called, notice

ARTICLE VII Committees
- A. Standing committees: list of standing committees, number of members, selection, duties, powers, meetings, reports
- B. Special committees: provisions for selection

ARTICLE VIII Finances
- A. Budget preparation and adoption
- B. Dues: How determined, when delinquent
- C. Auditor: How selected, type of report
- D. Surety bond for officers and employees

ARTICLE IX Terms of office
- A. Length of term of officers and board members
- B. Staggering of terms

ARTICLE X Elections
- A. Time and method of nominating
- B. Nominating committee: duties and report
- C. Time and method of election
- D. Vote necessary to elect

ARTICLE XI Quorum
- A. Meetings of organization
- B. Meetings of board

ARTICLE XII Discipline and expulsion of members
- A. Grounds for action
- B. Investigation, hearing, final decision
- C. Reinstatement

ARTICLE XIII Parliamentary authority
- A. Provision for adoption
- B. Scope of application

ARTICLE XIV Policies
  A. Provisions for adoption
  B. Vote required for adoption and amendment

ARTICLE XV Amendments to bylaws
  A. Notice, form
  B. Method of consideration, vote required

MODEL MINUTES

September 15, 1972

THE LOUISVILLE DENTAL SOCIETY, INC.

Call to Order

The regular meeting of the Louisville Dental Society, Inc., was called to order on Wednesday, September 12, 1972, at 7:30 P.M. in the auditorium of the Medical Arts Building by President A. B. Coxwell. A quorum was present.

Minutes
Correction

Approval

The minutes of the May 12th meeting were read by the Secretary, John Atkinson. Frank Jordan called attention to an error in omitting the name of James Skaggs from the Dento-Legal Committee. The correction was made, and the minutes were approved as corrected.

Reports
President

President Coxwell reported that a two-day Leadership Institute was planned for January 16–18, to be held at the Audubon Country Club. He asked all members to reserve the date. *Good Committee Techniques* is the subject.

Treasurer

J. L. Walker, Sr., Treasurer, gave the following summary of collections and expenditures from July 1, 1971, to June 30, 1972:

Treasurer's Report

Receipts, 1971–72
  A.D.A., K.D.A., and Local Dues
    400 @ $100.00 $40,000.00
    Bank Budget Plan   1,500.00
              TOTAL $51,500.00
  Balance on Hand, June 1, 1971   3,500.00
                          $55,000.00

Disbursements
  A.D.A., K.D.A.
    400 @ $80.00 $32,000.00
  National Children's Dental
    Health Week   2,000.00
  Brown Hotel   100.00
  Clinicians' Expense   4,000.00
              TOTAL $38,100.00

Receipts on Hand $55,000.00
Disbursed   38,100.00
Balance on Hand, July 1, 1972 $ 6,900.00

Clinic Committee

A. P. Williams, Chairman of the Clinic Committee, reported on the Summer Clinic held at the University of Louisville.

Program Committee

Ed Buechel, Chairman of the Program Committee, reported that a program listing the meetings and events of the coming year was being printed and would be mailed to each member on January 1.

MODEL MINUTES

Unfinished Business

The President called attention to the fact that a motion to contribute $1,500.00 to the Cleft Palate Clinic of the Kentucky Dental Association, Inc., which was being discussed at the last meeting and which was interrupted by adjournment, should be acted upon.

MOTION
Donation to Cleft Palate Clinic

The motion is "That $1,500 be donated to the Cleft Palate Clinic of the Kentucky Dental Association, Inc." Motion carried.

New Business
MOTION
Permitting Advertisers

It was moved by Burke Coomer, seconded by Bert Williams, "that the editor of the Bulletin be permitted to secure advertisers to help meet the cost of publication."

AMENDMENT

It was moved by Arnold Kirk, seconded by Bert Watts, "that the motion be amended by adding the words 'and that a committee of five be appointed to assist the editor.'" Amendment carried. Motion carried.

INFORMAL DISCUSSION
New Office

It was moved by Bob Thomas, seconded by Burke Coomer, "that the question of securing a new office for the society be discussed informally." Motion carried.

MOTION
Lease

The discussion continued for an hour and was terminated by a motion presented by John Atkinson, seconded by Duke Hannett, "that the Secretary be directed to sign a lease for six connecting rooms in the Starks Building." Motion carried.

MOTION TO ADJOURN

Moved by Harry Ritter, seconded by Hugh Nichols, "that the meeting adjourn." Motion carried.

Adjournment		The meeting adjourned at 10:08 P.M.

John Atkinson
Secretary

CORRECTION The word "approved," which was omitted before the word "advertisers" in the motion permitting advertising in the Bulletin, was added.

J. A.

October 10

APPROVED
as corrected
Oct. 13, 1972

John Atkinson,
Secretary

A. B. Coxwell
President

REFERENCES

Chapter 1 THE SIGNIFICANCE OF PARLIAMENTARY LAW

1. Douglas, William O., "Procedural Safeguards in the Bill of Rights," *Journal of the American Judicature Society*, vol. 31 (6): 166–70 (Apr. 1948).
2. McNabb v. U.S. (1943) 318 U.S. 332, 347.
3. Cannon, Clarence, "Rules of Order," *Encyclopaedia Britannica*, Vol. 19 (1964), 632B–634.

Chapter 3 PRESENTATION OF MOTIONS

1. City of Galveston v. Morton (1883) 58 Texas 409.
2. Shoults v. Alderson (1921) 55 Cal. App. 527, 203 Pac. 809.

Chapter 6 RULES GOVERNING MOTIONS

1. Wood v. Town of Milton (1908) 197 Mass. 531, 84 N.E. 332.
2. Hill v. Goodwin (1876) 56 N.H. 441.

Chapter 7 MAIN MOTIONS

1. El Paso Gas Co. v. El Paso (1899) 22 Tex. Civ. App. 309, 54 S.W. 798.
2. State ex rel. Burdick v. Tyrrell (1914) 158 Wis. 425, 149 N.W. 280; State v. Miller (1900) 162 Oh. St. 436, 57 N.E. 227; Regina v. Donoghue (1858) 15 Up. Can. Q.B. 454.
3. Brown v. Winterport (1887) 79 Me. 305, 9 Atl. 844.
4. Cushing, Luther S., *Lex Parliamenteria Americana: Elements of the law and practice of Legislative Assemblies in the United States of America,* Sec. 1266, Little, Brown & Company, Boston, 1856.
5. Crawford v. Gilchrist (1912) 64 Fla. 41, 50 So. 963.
6. Schiefelin v. Hylan (1919) 174 N.Y.S. 506; Brown v. Winterport (1887) 79 Me. 305, 9 Atl. 844.
7. Tetley v. Vancouver (1897) 5 B.C. 276.
8. Naegely v. Saginaw (1894) 101 Mich. 532, 60 N.W. 46; Stockdale v. School District (1881) 47 Mich. 226, 10 N.W. 349.

Chapter 8 SUBSIDIARY MOTIONS

1. Wood v. Town of Milton (1908), 197 Mass. 531, 84 N.E. 332.
2. Zeiler v. Central Ry. Co. (1896) 84 Md. 304, 35 Atl. 932.
3. Heron v. Riley (1930), 209 Cal. 507, 289 Pac. 160.
4. Hood v. City of Wheeling (1920), 85 W. Va. 578, 102 S.E. 249; State v. Cox (1920) 105 Neb. 175, 178 N.W.913.
5. Casler v. Tanger (1929) 234 N. Y. Supp. 571.
6. Terre Haute Gas Corporation v. Johnson (1942) 221 Ind. 499, 45 N.E. (2d) 484; Commonwealth v. Cullen (1850) 13 Pa. 133, 53 Am. Dec. 450.
7. People v. Davis (1918) 284 Ill. 439, 120 N.E. 326.
8. Wright v. Wiles (1938) 173 Tenn. 334, 17 S.W. (2d) 736, 119 A.L.R. 456.

Chapter 9 PRIVILEGED MOTIONS

1. Ex parte Mirande (1887) 73 Cal. 365, 14 Pac. 888; Donogh v. Hollister (1890) 82 Mich. 305, 46 N.W. 782.
2. State v. McKee (1890) Oregon 120, 35 Pac. 82; Dingwill v. Detroit (1890) 82 Mich. 568, 46 N.W. 938.
3. Choate v. North Fork Highway Dist. (1924) 39 Idaho 483, 228 Pac. 885; Rolla v. Schuman (1915) 189 Mo. App. 252, 175 S.W. 241.

Chapter 10 INCIDENTAL MOTIONS

1. State v. Lasher (1899) 171 Conn. 540, 42 Atl. 636; Proctor Coal Co. v. Finley (1895) 98 Ky. 405, 33 S.W. 188.

258 APPENDIX

2. Capito v. Topping (1909) 65 W. Va. 587, 64 S.E. 845; State v. Alt (1887) 26 Mo. App. 673.
3. State v. Lasher (1899) 171 Conn. 540, 42 Atl. 636.
4. State v. Ellington (1895) 117 N.C. 159, 23 S.E. 250, 53 A.M.S.R. 580, 30 L.R.A. 532.

Chapter 11 NOTICE OF MEETINGS AND PROPOSALS

1. People ex rel. Carus v. Matthiessen (1915) 193 Ill. App. 328, 109 N.E. 1056.
2. Haines v. Readfield (1856) 41 Me. 246.

Chapter 12 MEETINGS

1. Tandy and Fairleigh Tobacco Co. v. Hopkinsville (1917) 174 Ky. 189, 192 S.W. 46; Coon Valley v. Spellum (1926) 190 Wis. 140, 208 N.W. 916.
2. People ex rel. Loew v. Batchelor (1860) 22 N.Y. 128.
3. Hayden v. Noyes (1824) 5 Conn. 391.

Chapter 13 QUORUM

1. Brown v. District of Columbia (1888) 127 U.S. 579, 32 L. Ed. 262; State v. Porter (1888) 113 Ind. 79, 14 N.E. 883; In re Gunn (1893) 50 Kan. 155, 32 Pac. 948; Ellsworth Woolen Mfg. Co. v. Faunce (1887) 79 Me. 440, 10 Atl. 250; Dingwall v. Common Council (1890) 82 Mich. 568, 46 N.W. 938; Boggess v. Buxton (1910) 67 W. Va. 679, 69 S.E. 367.
2. People v. Wright (1902) 30 Colo. 439, 71 Pac. 365; State v. Porter (1888) 113 Ind. 79, 14 N.E. 883; Swan v. Indianola (1909) 142 Iowa 731, 121 N.W. 547.
3. Seiler v. O'Maley (1921) 190 Ky. 190, 227 S.W. 141.
4. Fisher v. Harrisburg Gas Co. (1857) 1 Pear. (Pa.) 118.
5. Morrill v. Little Falls Mfg. Co. (1893) 53 Minn. 371, 55 N.W. 547; State v. Riechmann (1911) 239 Mo. 81, 142 S.W. 304; Kimball v. Marshall (1863) 44 N.H. 465.
6. State v. Paterson (1871) 35 N.J.L. 190; Gildersleeve v. Bd. of Education (1860) 17 Abb. Pr. (N.Y.) 201.
7. People v. Wright (1902) 30 Colo. 439, 71 Pac. 365; State v. Porter (1888) 113 Ind. 79, 14 N.E. 883.
8. Enright v. Heckscher (1917) 240 Fed. 863, 153 C.C.A. 549; Burton v. Lithic Mfg. Co. (1914) 73 Ore. 605, 144 Pac. 1149; Federal Life Ins. Co. v. Griffin (1912) 173 Ill. App. 5.
9. Shugars v. Hamilton (1906) 122 Ky. 606, 92 S.W. 564; Dafoe v. Harshaw (1886) 60 Mich. 200, 26 N.W. 879.
10. State v. Ellington (1895) 117 N.C. 159, 23 S.E. 250, 53 Am. S.R. 580, 30 L.R.A. 532; Christoffel v. United States (1949) 338 U.S. 84; United States v. Bryan (1950) 339 U.S. 323.

REFERENCES

11 Pollard v. Gregg (1914) 77 N.H. 190, 90 Atl. 176; Ralls v. Wyand (1914) 40 Okla. 323, 138 Pac. 158.

Chapter 15 DEBATE

1 People v. American Inst. (1873) 44 How. Pr. (N.Y.) 468.
2 Commonwealth v. Cullen (1850) 13 Pa. State 132, 53 Am. Dec. 450.
3 Terre Haute Gas Corp. v. Johnson (1943) 221 Ind. 499, 45 N.E. (2d) 484.

Chapter 16 VOTES REQUIRED FOR VALID ACTIONS

1 United States v. Ballin (1892) 144 U.S. 1, 12 Sup. Ct. 507, 36 Law Ed. 321.
2 State v. Bandel (1906) 121 Mo. App. 516, 97 S.W. 222.
3 Cascaden v. City of Waterloo (1898) 106 Iowa 673, 77 N.W. 333.
4 Martin v. Ballenger (1938) 25 Cal. App. (2d) 435, 77 Pac. (2d) 888.
5 Launtz v. The People (1885) 113 Ill., 137, 55 Am. Rep., 405; Walden v. Vanosdal (1891) 131 Ind. 388; State v. Green (1881) 37 Ohio St., 227; Attorney General v. Shepard (1889) 62 N.H. 384; Somers v. City of Bridgeport (1891) 60 Ct., 521.
6 State v. Stephens (1916), 189 S.W. 630, 631. 195 Mo. App. 34.
7 Crickenberger v. Town of Westfield (1904) 58 A. 1097. 71 N.J.L. 467.
8 Coxon v. Inhabitants of City of Trenton (1909), 78 N.J.L. 26, 73 Atl. 253, 254.
9 O'Neil v. O'Connell (1945) 300 Ky. 707, 189 S.W. (2d) 965; Frost v. Hoar (1932) 85 N.H. 442, 160 Atl. 51.
10 O'Neil v. O'Connell (1945) 300 Ky. 707, 189 S.W. (2d) 965.
11 Hartford A & I Co. v. City of Sulphur (1941) (CCA. 10th) 123 Fed. (2d) 566; Caffey v. Veale (1944) 193 Okla. 444, 145 Pa. (2d) 961.
12 Coles v. Williamsburgh (1833) 10 Wend. (N.Y.) 659; Oconto County v. Hall (1879) 47 Wis. 208, 2 N.W. 291.

Chapter 17 METHODS OF VOTING

1 Landers v. Frank St. Methodist Church (1889) 114 N.Y. 626, 21 N.E. 420.
2 State v. Ellington (1895) 117 N.C. 159, 23 S.E. 250, 53 Am. S.R. 580, 30 L.R.A. 532.
3 Labor-Management Reporting and Disclosure Act of 1959, Definitions sec. (k).
4 City of Chariton v. Holliday (1883) 60 Iowa 391, 14 N.W. 775.

5 Ibid.
6 State v. Hutchins (1891) 33 Nebr. 335, 50 N.W. 165.
7 Conrad v. Stone (1889) 18 Mich., 640.

Chapter 18 NOMINATIONS AND ELECTIONS

1 People ex rel. Chapman v. Rapsey (1940) 16 Cal. (2d) 636, 107 Pac. 2nd 388.
2 People v. Goodall (1917) 203 Ill. App. 189.
3 In re George (1924) 238 N.Y. 513; 144 N.E. 776.
4 Appon v. Belle Isle Corp. (1946) 29 Del. Ch. 122; 46 A (2d) 749.

Chapter 19 OFFICERS

1 Frankfurter, Felix, *Of Law and Men*, Harcourt, Brace and World, Inc., New York, 1956, p. 119.
2 Ibid., p. 140.
3 New York Mortgage Co. v. Garfinkel (1931) 258 N.Y. 5, 179 N.E. 33.
4 Goff v. Emde (1928) 32 Ohio App. 216, 167 N.E. 699.
5 Dewey v. Nat. Tank Maintenance Corp. (1943) 233 Iowa 58, 8 N.W. (2d) 593.
6 Gerrish Dredging Co. v. Bethlehem Steel Corp. (1923) 247 Mass. 162, 141 N.E. 867.
7 Abberger v. Kulp (1935) 156 Misc. 210, 281 N.Y. Supp. 373.
8 Whyte v. Faust (1924) 281 Pa. 444, 127 Atl. 234.
9 Kiel v. Medart Mfg. Co. (1932) Mo. App. 46 S.W. (2d) 934.
10 Gutman Silk Corp. v. Reilly (1919) 178 N.Y.S. 189 A.D. 258; 457.
11 Piedmont Press Assn. v. Record Publ. Co. (1930) 156 S.C. 43, 152 S.E. 721.
12 State ex rel. Blackswood v. Brast (1925) 98 W. Va. 596, 127 S.E. 507.

Chapter 20 COMMITTEES AND BOARDS

1 Templeman v. Grant (1924) 75 Colo. 519, 227 P. 555; Berkeley County Court v. Martinburg and P. Turnpike Co. (1922) 94 W. Va. 246, 115 S.E. 448.
2 Commercial Nat. Bank v. Weinhard (1904) 192 U.S. 243, 24 S. Ct. 253, 48 L. Ed. 425.
3 Harris v. Harris (1930) 137 Misc. 73, 241 N.Y. Supp. 474.

Chapter 23 MINUTES

1 Black's Law Dictionary (4th Ed. 1951). West Publ. Co., St. Paul, Minn.

2 Dendinger v. J. D. Kerr Gravel Co. (1925) 158 La. 324, 104 S. 60.
3 Glencoe Board of Education v. Trustees of Schools (1798) 174 Ill. 510, 74 Ill. App., 401.
4 Hornaday v. Goodman (1928) 167 Ga. 555, 146 S.E. 173.

Chapter 24 CHARTERS, BYLAWS, AND RULES

1 Witherspoon v. State (1925) 138 Miss. 310, 103 So. 134.
2 Landes v. State (1903) 160 Ind. 479, 67 N.E.
3 Arizona Southwest Bank v. Odum (1931) 38 Ariz. 394, 300.

Chapter 26 LEGAL CLASSIFICATIONS OF ORGANIZATIONS

1 People v. Albany, etc., R. Co. (1869) 1 Lans. (N. Y.) 308, 55 Barb. 344.

Chapter 27 RIGHTS OF MEMBERS AND OF ORGANIZATIONS

1 Austin v. Searing (1857) 16 N.Y. 112, 69 Am. Dec. 665.
2 Brotherhood of Railroad Trainmen v. Williams (1925) 211 Ky. 638, 277 S.W. 500; Des Moines City Railway Co. v. Amalgamated Assn. of S. and E. Ry. Employees (1927) 204 Iowa 1195, 213 N.W. 264.
3 Marshall v. Pilots' Assn. (1902) 18 Pa. Sup. Ct. 644, but see (1903) 206 Pa. 182, 55 Atl. 916.
4 Hall v. Morrin (1927) Mo. App. 293 S.W. 435; Hillery v. Pedic Society of State of N.Y. (1919) 179 N.Y. Supp. 62, 189 App. Div. 766.
5 Berrien v. Pollitzer (1947) 83, U.S. App. D.C. 23; 165 F. (2d) 21, Noted, 33 Cornell Law. Q. 579 (1948); 36 Geo. L. 692 (1948); 34 Va. L. Rev. 352 (1948); 34 Yale L. p. 999 (1949).
6 Loubat v. LeRoy (1886) 40 Hun. (N.Y.) 546; Smith v. Decks (1929) 197 N.C. 355, 148 S.E. 464.
7 Snay v. Lovely (1929) 276 Mass. 159, 176 N.E. 791.
8 Simons v. Berry (1924) 205 N.Y. Supp. 442, 210 App. Div. 90.
9 Harris v. Thomas (1920) 140 Tex. 183, 217 S.W. 1068.
10 Elfer v. Marine Engineers' Ben. Assn. (1934) 179 La. 383, 154 So. 32.
11 State v. Seattle Baseball Assn. (1910) 61 Wash. 79, 111 Pac. 1055.
12 Dingwell v. Amalgamated Assn. of Street Ry. Employees (1906) 4 Cal. App. 565, 88 Pac. 597.
13 Evans v. Brown (1919) 134 Md. 519, 107 Atl. 535.
14 Arnold v. Burgess (1934) 272 N.Y. Supp. 534, 231 App. Div. 364.
15 University of Maryland v. Williams (1938) 9 Gill & J. (Md.) 365.

16 In re McNaughton's Will (1908) 138 Wis. 179; 118 N.W. 997; 120 N.W. 288.
17 In re Fidelity Assur. Assn. (1941) 42 F. Supp. 973; revd. on other gds., 129 F. (2d) 442; Affd. 318 U.S. 608; (63 Sup. Ct. 807.)
18 Levi & Co., Inc. v. Feldman (1946) 61 N.Y. Supp. (2d) 639.

GOVERNMENTAL BOARDS, COUNCILS, COMMISSIONS, AND COMMITTEES

1 Werts v. Rogers (1894) 56 N.J.L. 480, 20 Atl. 726; Hodges v. Keel (1913) 108 Ark. 84, 159 S.W. 21.
2 State v. Jersey City (1855) 25 N.J. (1 Dutcher) 309.
3 Kidder v. McClanahan (1921) 126 Miss. 179, 88 So. 508.
4 Moore v. City Council of Perry (1903) 119 Iowa 123, 93 N.W. 510; Holton v. Bd. of Education (1933) 113 W. Va. 590, 169 S.E. 239.
5 Saterlee v. San Francisco (1863) 23 Cal., 315; Buffington Wheel Co. v. Burnham (1883) 60 Ia., 493 McCracken v. San Francisco (1860), 16 Cal., 591; McDermott v. Miller (1883) 45 N.J.L. 215; Fisher v. Harrisburg Gas Co. (1857), Pears (Pa.) 118.
6 State v. Patterson (1871) 35 N.J.L. 190, 194; Kimball v. Marshall (1863), 44 N.H., 465, 468; Beck v. Hansom (1854) 29 N.H. 213.
7 San Luis Obispo Co. v. Hendricks (1886) 71 Cal. 242, 11 Pac. 682.
8 State v. Dixie Finance Co. (1926) 152 Tenn. 306, 278 S.W. 59.
9 Commonwealth v. Mayor of Lancaster (1836) 5 Watts (Pa.) 155; Heiskell v. Mayor of Baltimore (1885) 65 Md. 125, 57 Am. Rep. 308; Gosler v. Corp. of Georgetown (1821) 6 Wheat. 597; City of Chariton v. Holliday (1883) 60 Ia. 391.

LABOR ORGANIZATIONS

1 Labor-Management Reporting and Disclosure Act of 1959.
2 Ibid., Title I.
3 Labor-Management Relations Act 8 (b) (1)A.

DEFINITIONS OF PARLIAMENTARY TERMS

Adhere To be attached to and dependent on; pending amendments *adhere* to the motion to which they are applied.

Ad-hoc Committee A special committee chosen to do a particular piece of work only.

Adjourn To officially terminate a meeting.

Adjourned Meeting A meeting that is a continuation at a later specified time of an earlier regular or special meeting. The continuation is legally a part of the same meeting.

Adjournment Sine Die (without day) The final adjournment terminating a convention or series of meetings.

Administrative Duty A duty requiring only the faithful performance of acts or functions already determined; a ministerial duty.

Adopt To approve by vote and give effect to a motion or a report.

Affirmative Vote The "yes" vote supporting a motion as stated.

Agenda The official list of items of business planned for consideration during a meeting or convention.

Apply A motion is said to *apply* to another motion when it may be used to alter, dispose of, or affect the first motion.

Approval of Minutes Formal acceptance, by vote of the members or by unanimous consent, of the secretary's record of a meeting, thus making the record the official minutes of the organization.

Assembly A meeting of the members of a deliberative body.

Ballot Vote The expression by ballot, voting machine, or otherwise, but in no event by proxy, of a choice with respect to any election or vote taken on any matter, cast in such a manner that the person expressing the choice cannot be identified with the choice expressed; i.e., a secret ballot.

Bylaws The set of rules adopted by an organization defining its structure and governing its functions.

Chair The presiding officer or chairman of a deliberative body.

Challenging a Vote Objecting to a vote on the ground that the voter does not have the right to vote.

Challenging an Election Objecting to an election on the ground that it is not being conducted properly.

Charter An official grant from government of the right to operate as an incorporated organization, or an official grant from a parent organization of the right to operate as a constituent or component group of the parent organization.

Common Parliamentary Law The body of rules and principles that is applied by the courts in deciding litigation involving the procedure of organizations. It does not include statutory law or particular rules adopted by an organization.

Constituent or Component Groups Subordinate groups making up a parent state, national, or international organization and chartered by it.

Convene To open a meeting or convention, usually a large and formal one.

Debate Formal discussion of a motion or proposal by members under the rules of parliamentary law.

Delegation of Authority An assignment by one person or group to another person or group of the authority to act for the first person or group in certain matters that are lawful and capable of being delegated.

Demand An assertion of a parliamentary right by a member.

Dilatory Tactics Misuse of procedures or debate to delay or prevent progress in a meeting.

Discretionary Duty A duty that usually cannot be delegated to another because members rely on the special intelligence, skill, or ability of the person chosen to perform the duty.

Disposition of a Motion Action on a motion by voting on it, referring, postponing, or in some way removing it from the consideration of the assembly.

Ex-officio Member One who is a member of a committee or board by reason of holding another office; a treasurer is often an *ex-officio member* of the finance committee.

Executive Session A term used by committees of the United States Senate to mean a meeting with representatives of the executive branch of government to transact executive business that is not to be transacted publicly. Commonly used to mean any meeting of a committee or organization which only members may attend unless others are requested by the body to attend.

Floor (as in *have the floor*) When a member receives formal recognition from the presiding officer, he *has the floor* and is the only member entitled to make a motion or to speak.

DEFINITION OF PARLIAMENTARY TERMS

General Consent An informal method of disposing of routine motions by assuming unanimous approval unless objection is raised.

Germane Amendment An amendment relating directly to the subject of the motion to which it is applied.

Hearing A meeting of an authorized group for the purpose of listening to the views of members or others on a particular subject.

Hostile Amendment An amendment that is opposed to the spirit or purpose of the motion to which it is applied.

Illegal Ballot A ballot that cannot be counted because it does not conform to the rules governing ballot voting.

Immediately Pending Question The last-proposed of several pending motions and therefore open for immediate consideration.

Incorporate To form a group into a legal entity chartered by government and recognized by law as having special rights, duties, and liabilities distinct from those of its members.

Informal Consideration Consideration and discussion of a problem or motion without the usual restrictions on debate.

Inherent Right A right or power that is possessed without being derived from another source.

In Order Permissible and correct from a parliamentary standpoint at a particular time.

Invariable in Wording When a motion can be worded one way only and so is not subject to amendment, it is said to be invariable in wording.

Majority A number that is more than half of any given total.

Majority Rule Rule by decision of the majority of those who actually vote, regardless of whether a majority of those entitled to vote do so.

Majority Vote More than half of the number of legal votes cast for a particular motion or candidate, unless a different basis for determining the majority is required.

Meeting An official assembly of the members of an organization during which there is no separation of the members except for a recess, and which continues until adjournment.

Member in Good Standing Any person who has fulfilled the requirements for membership in the particular organization and who has neither voluntarily resigned nor been suspended or expelled from membership.

Minority Any number that is less than half of any given total.

Minutes The legal record of the actions of a deliberative body that has been approved by vote of the body.

Motion A proposal submitted to an assembly for its consideration and decision; it is introduced by the words, "I move...."

Multiple Slate A list of offices and candidates containing the names of more than one nominee for an office or offices.

Nomination The formal proposal to an assembly of a person as a candidate for an office.

Nonprofit Corporation A corporation whose basic and dominant purposes are ethical, moral, or social, and which distributes no profit to its members.

Objection The formal expression of opposition to a proposed action.

Order of Business The adopted order in which the various classifications of business are presented to the meetings of an assembly.

Out of Order Not correct, from a parliamentary standpoint, at the particular time.

Parliamentary Authority The code of procedure adopted by an organization as its parliamentary guide and governing in all parliamentary situations not otherwise provided for in the charter or bylaws.

Pending Question Any motion that has been proposed and stated to the assembly for consideration and that is awaiting decision by vote.

Plurality Vote A larger vote than that received by any opposing candidate or alternative measure.

Policy An adopted statement of a belief, philosophy, or practice of an organization.

Precedence The rank or priority governing the proposal, consideration, and disposal of motions.

Precedent A course of action that may serve as a guide or rule for future similar situations in the particular organization.

Procedural Motion A motion that presents a question of procedure as distinguished from a substantive proposition.

Proposal or Proposition A statement of a motion of any kind for consideration and action.

Proxy A signed statement authorizing a person to cast the vote of the person signing it. Proxy may also refer to the person who casts the vote.

DEFINITION OF PARLIAMENTARY TERMS

Putting the Question The statement, by the presiding officer, of a motion to the assembly for the purpose of taking the vote on it.

Qualified Motion A motion that is limited or modified in some way in its effect by additional words or provisions "I move we adjourn *at four o'clock.*"

Question Any proposal submitted to an assembly for decision.

Quorum The number or proportion of members that must be present at a meeting of an organization to enable it to act legally on business.

Railroading To push a motion through so rapidly that members do not have opportunity to exercise their parliamentary rights.

Recognition Formal acknowledgment by the presiding officer of a particular member, giving him the sole right to speak or to present a motion.

Renew a Motion To present again a motion previously lost at the same meeting or convention.

Request A statement to the presiding officer of some right that a member desires to exercise. A request can amount to a demand; for example, a call for division.

Resolution A formal motion, usually in writing, and introduced by the word "Resolved," that is presented to an assembly for decision.

Restricted Debate Debate on certain motions in which discussion is restricted to a few specified points.

Ruling Any pronouncement of the presiding officer that relates to the procedure of the assembly.

Second After a motion has been proposed, the statement "I second the motion" by another member who thus indicates his willingness to have the motion considered.

Seriatim Consideration by sections or paragraphs.

Single Slate A list of offices and candidates containing the name of only one candidate for each particular office.

Special Committee A committee that is selected to do a particular piece of work, and that ceases to exist when its work is completed.

Specific Main Motion A main motion that is so frequently used that it has acquired a specific name to distinguish it from the general main motion; for example, the motion to rescind.

Standing Committee A committee that has a fixed term of office and that performs any work in its field assigned to it by the bylaws or referred to it by the organization, the board, or the presiding officer.

Statute A law passed by a legislative body, as a *statute* of Congress.

Statutory Law Law that is enacted by legislative bodies.

Substantive Motion A motion that states a concrete proposal of business as opposed to a procedural matter.

Substitute Motion The form of amendment that offers a new motion on the same subject, as an alternative to the original motion.

Teller A member appointed to help conduct an election and help count the votes.

Term of Office The duration of service for which a member is elected or appointed to an office.

Tie Vote A vote in which the affirmative and negative votes are equal on a motion, or a vote in an election in which two or more candidates receive the same number of votes. A motion receiving a tie vote is lost, since a majority vote is required to take an action. Candidates receiving a tie vote may be voted on until one is elected or the assembly votes to break the tie in some other way.

Unanimous Consent Deciding a routine motion or taking a procedural step without voting on it. If anyone objects, a vote must be taken.

Unanimous Vote A vote without any dissenting vote. One adverse vote prevents a unanimous vote.

Unfinished Business Any business that is postponed definitely to the next meeting or that was pending and interrupted by adjournment of the previous meeting.

Viva voce Vote A vote taken by calling for "ayes" and "noes" and judged by volume of voice response; sometimes called a "voice vote."

Waiver of Notice Act of relinquishing the right to have had notice of a proposal or meeting. Also may refer to the statement proving the relinquishment of notice.

Write-in Vote A vote for someone who has not been nominated, cast by writing in on the ballot the name of the person.

INDEX

*Index Prepared by Paul Mason
Parliamentary Consultant to State Legislatures*

Accountant:
   importance to organization, 229
   (*See also* Auditor)
Ad hoc (special) committees, 176–177
Adhering amendments, 55
Adhering motions, 46, 72
Adjourn, motion to, 79–83
   to adjourned meeting, 81, 111–112
   completion of business before, 80–81
   and dissolution (adjournment *sine die*), 81–82
   effect of, 83
   form of, 79–80
   and motion to recess, difference between, 77–78
   in order of precedence, 21, 83
   at previously fixed time, 82–83
   purpose, 79
   qualified and unqualified, 80
   rules governing, 83
   voting on, 82
Adjourned meeting, 111–112
   adjournment to, 81
   notice of, 108

Adjourned meeting (*Cont.*):
   order of business, 111–112
Adjournment, 120
   to adjourned meeting, 81
   business interrupted by, 83
   completion of business before, 80–81
   and dissolution (adjournment *sine die*), 81–82
   in order of business, 120–121
   at previously fixed time, 82–83
   and recess, difference between, 77–78
   voting on, 82
   (*See also* Adjourn, motion to)
Adjournment *sine die,* 81–82
Administrative powers and duties, 170
Adopted procedures, 211
Agenda, 117
   (*See also* Order of business)
Amend, motion to, 19, 49–57
   effect of, 57
   filling blanks in, 54
   form of, 49–50
   purpose, 49
   rules governing, 57
   (*See also* Amendments)

Amendability of motions, 27–28, 30–31
Amendments, 49–57
  of actions already taken, 19, 56
  by addition, 49
  adhering, 55
  of bylaws (*see* Bylaws, amendments to)
  of charters, 203
  debate on, 53–54
  by deletion, 50
  may be hostile, 52
  must be germane, 51–52
  rank of, 52–53
  with restrictions, 51
  by substitution, 50
    of new motion, 50, 54
    of words, 50–51
  vote required, 56
  voting on, 55–56
  what motions can be amended, 27–28, 51
  withdrawing and accepting, 54–55
  (*See also* Amend, motion to)
Announcements, in order of business, 120
Annual meeting, 107
Appeal, motion to, 84–86
  effect of, 86
  form, 84
  interrupting speaker for, 25–26
  purpose, 84
  rules governing, 86
  statement:
    of member's reason for, 85
    of presiding officer regarding, 85
    of question by presiding officer, 85
  vote on, 85–86
  when taken, 84–85

Assembly:
  privileges of, 75
  request for division of (*see* Division of assembly)
Association, defined, 219
Attorney, organization's need for, 230
Auditor:
  report, 215
    long form, 215–216
    short form, 215
  services to organization, 215
Authority, parliamentary (*see* Parliamentary authority)

Ballots, 142–143
  casting by secretary, 157–158
  counting, 154–155
  legal definition, 142
  legality, determining, 155–156
  in mail vote, 143–145
  secret, as fundamental right, 2
  tally sheets, 157
  (*See also* Vote)
Board of directors (governing board), 182–184
  delegation of authority by, 169–171, 179
  duties of, 183–184
  executive committee of, 184
  membership of, 183
    continuity of, 184
    ex officio, 178–179, 183
  notice of meeting, 106–108
  powers of, 183–184
    bylaws must define, 183
    belong to group only, 183
  (*See also* Committees and boards)
Board of trustees (*see* Board of directors)

INDEX

Boards (*see* Committees and boards)
Budget, 216
(*See also* Finances)
Business:
  completion before adjournment, 80–81
  interrupted by adjournment, 83
  new, 120
  order of (*see* Order of business)
  unfinished (*see* Unfinished business)
Bylaws, 203–211
  adoption of original, 204–205
  amendments to, 205–209
    amending, 207
      majority vote only required, 207
      notice not required, 207
    considering, 207–208
    form for, 206–207
    notice of, 207
    proposing, 206
    provisions for, 205–206
    vote required on, 209
  committee on, 193
  constitution and, 203
  drafting, 204
  interpreting, 210
  and parliamentary authority, 210–211
  revision of, 209–210
  rules and procedures supplementing, 211
  as source of parliamentary rule, 5
  suggested outline for local organizations, 250–252

Call for meeting (*see* Notice, of meetings)
Call to order, 117
Candidates (*see* Nominees)
Chairman:
  of committees, 177–178
  presiding officer (*see* Presiding officer)
Challenging, 159–160
  of election, 159–160
  of vote, 159
Charters:
  amendment of, 203
  as source of parliamentary rules, 5
  types of, 202–203
Commissions, governmental, 235–242
Committees and boards:
  for action, 177
  advantages of, 175–176
  board of directors (*see* Board of directors)
  on bylaws, 193
  chairman, selection of, 177–178
  convention, 192–197
  for deliberation and recommendation, 177
  election, 154–157
  ex officio members, 178–179, 183
  executive, of board of directors, 184
  governmental, 235–242
  hearings of, 182
  importance of, 175
  instructions to, 59–60
    (*See also* Refer to committee, motion to)
  meetings of:
    limited to members, 181
    notice of, 108
    procedure in, 181–182
  members:
    ex officio, 178–179, 183

Committees and boards (*Cont.*):
members (*Cont.*):
selection of, 178
minutes of (*see* Minutes)
nominating (*see* Nominating committee)
powers, rights, and duties of, 179–180
recommendations of:
form of, 185–186
presentation of, 190–191
reference (*see* Reference committees)
reports of, 185–189
agreement on, 186–187
amendability of, 187
consideration of, 187–189
dangers of adoption, 188
disposal of, 188
form of, 185–186
minority, 189
in order of business, 119
presentation of, 187
recommendations of, 185–186, 190–191
record of, 189
special (*ad hoc*), 176–177
standing, 176
sub-, 180
of the whole, 184–185
working materials for, 180–181
Common law as source of parliamentary law, 3, 5
Congress, distinctive rules, 4
Consideration, informal, 128–129
Constitution and bylaws, 203
Consultants, 228–232
Conventions, 191–197
committees of, 192–197
reference (*see* Reference committees)

Conventions (*Cont.*):
definition of, 109, 191
delegates to, 191
credentials of, 193
instruction of, 192
notice of, 107
structure of, 191
Corresponding secretary, duties of, 167
Councils, governmental, 235–242
Credentials committee, 193

Debate, 121–129
on amendments, 53–54
bringing question to vote, 127
closing by motion to vote immediately, 67–70
cutting off, 127
dilatory tactics in, 124–125
informal consideration, 128–129
members' conduct in, 125
on motions, extent of, 26–27, 121–122
motion to limit or extend, 64–66
obtaining floor for, 122
open for, 37–38
presiding officer's duties in, 126
recognition of members, 122–123
more than once, 123
relevancy in, 124
right of, 121
time limits on, 126
what is not, 123–124
Debatability of motions, 26–27, 30–31
Delegates, convention, 191–193
Delegation of authority, 169–171, 179

INDEX

Discretionary powers and duties, 171
Dissolution, when adjournment has effect of, 81–82
Division of assembly, request for, 103–105
  effect of, 105
  form of, 104
  purpose of, 103
  rules governing, 105
  timing of, 104
Division of question, request for, 100–103
  alternative proposals, 103
  effect of, 103
  form of, 101
  motions that presiding officer can or cannot divide, 101–102
  purpose of, 100
  rules governing, 103
  when proposed, 102–103

Elections, 147–160
  ballots:
    casting by secretary, 157–158
    counting, 154–155
    determining legality of, 155–156
  bylaw provisions on, 147
  of candidates not nominated (write-in votes), 149
  challenging, 159–160
    of vote, 159
  committee (or tellers) on, 154–157
    report of, 156–157
  effective date of, 159
  of groups, computing majority, 137–138
  importance of, 147

Elections (*Cont.*):
  motion to make unanimous, 158–159
  slates, single and multiple, 153–154
  vote necessary in, 157
  (*See also* Nominations; Vote)
Emergency situations, 16
Executive board (*see* Board of directors)
Executive secretary (or director), 228
Ex officio members of committees, 178–179, 183
Expunge, motion to, 44
Extend debate, motion to, 64–66

Finances, 214–217
  reports, 188–189
    of auditor, 215–216
    of treasurer, 214
  safeguards, 216–217
  setting up records, 214
Floor:
  nominations from, 148
  obtaining:
    for debate, 122
    for presentation of motion, 11

General order, postponing as, 62
Governing board (*see* Board of directors)
Governmental boards, councils, commissions, and committees, 235–242
  attending, 242
  minutes, 238
  no seconds required, 239–240

INDEX

Governmental boards (*Cont.*):
  notice of meetings, hearings, and matters requiring notice, 236–237
  organization of, 236
  and parliamentary law, 235–236
  powers and duties of members, 239
  presiding officer, 239
  quorum, 237–238
  removal of members, 241–242
  vacancies in, 241
  voting in, 240–241

Hearings:
  committee, 182
  by reference committee, 196–197
Honorary officers, 169
Hostile amendments, 52

Incidental motions:
  definition and list of, 16–17
  discussion of types of, 84–105
  form of, 19, 21
  rules governing, 30–31
Incorporated organizations, 219–220
Informal consideration, 128–129
Installation of officers, 159
Interruption of speaker, 25–26

Labor organizations, special provisions concerning, 242–250
Law:
  common, as source of parliamentary law, 3, 5

Law (*Cont.*):
  parliamentary (*see* Parliamentary law)
Lay on the table (*see* Postpone temporarily, motion to)
Legislative duties and powers, defined, 170
Liability of officers, 169
Limit debate, motion to, 64–66
  effect of, 66
    on pending motions, 65–66
  form of, 64–65
  purpose of, 64
  rules governing, 66
  termination of, 66
  types of limitations, 65

Mail, voting by, 143–145
Main motion, the, 35–39
  defined, 36
  discussion on, 37–38
  disposal of, 38
  effect of, 38
  form of, 35
  phrasing of, 36–37
  purpose of, 15, 35
  in resolution form, 37
  rules governing, 38–39
  (*See also* Main motions)
Main motions, 35–47
  already voted on, procedures applying to, 32–34
  classification of, 15, 30–31
  the main motion (*see* Main motion, the)
  precedence of, 21
  specific, 15, 39–47
Majority vote, 129–134
  bylaws should define, 131–132
  different meanings of, 132–133
  general principle of, 157

Majority vote (*Cont.*):
  of legal votes cast, 133–134
  as principle of parliamentary law, 9, 129
  requirement of less than, 131
  requirement of more than, 130–131
  significance of, 129–130
  (*See also* Vote)

Meetings, 105–112
  adjourned, 81, 108, 111–112
  annual, 107
  committee, 108, 181–182
  conventions (*see* Conventions)
  defined, 109
  failure to call, 112
  fairness and good faith at, 10
  to form organization, 217–218
  minutes of (*see* Minutes)
  notice of (*see* Notice, of meetings)
  quorum (*see* Quorum)
  regular, 107–110
  right of members to call, 112
  special, 110–111
    notice of, 107–108

Members:
  during debate:
    conduct in, 125
    recognition of, 12, 122–123
  discipline and expulsion of, 225–226
  notice of meeting protects, 106
  personal privileges, 75
  relationship to organization, 221
  resignations of, 226–227
  rights of, 222–223
    associational, 222
    equality of, 8
    to inquire, 96

Members (*Cont.*):
  rights of (*Cont.*):
    to know meaning of motion, 10
    parliamentary, list of, 222–223
    parliamentary law regarding, 8–10
    property, 222
    relationship to organizational rights, 224–225
    to request privilege, 74
    to vote, 140
  when they cannot vote, 139–140

Ministerial powers and duties, 170–171

Minutes, 197–202
  accuracy of, 197–198
  approval of, 200
  correction of, 118, 199–200
  importance of, 197–198
  minute book, 202
  model, 246–248
  preparing, 198
  reading of:
    and correction of, 118, 199–200
    in order of business, 118
    postponed, 118
  responsibility of secretary for, 198
  should contain, 200–201
  should not contain, 201–202
  standing committee on, 118, 199–200

Motions:
  addressing presiding officer, 11
  adhering, 46, 72
  amendability of, 27–28
  applications to other motions, 28, 30–31

Motions (*Cont.*):
  classification of, 15–21
    changes in, 18–21
  debatability of, 26–27
  defined, 11
  incidental (*see* Incidental motions)
  informal consideration of, 128–129
  interruption of speaker for, 25–26
  main (*see* Main motion, the; Main motions)
  other motions applied to, 29–31
  precedence of, 21–24, 30–31
    basic rules of, 22
    example of, 22–24
    order of, 21–22
  presentation of, 11–14
    example of, 14–15
    steps in, 11
  privileged (*see* Privileged motions)
  proposal of, 12–13
  purpose of, 20
  recognition by presiding officer, 12
  renewal of, 29, 32
  ruled out by presiding officer, 91
  rules governing, list of, 24–33, 30–31
  seconding, 13
    rules on, 26
  statement by presiding officer of, 13–14
  subsidiary (*see* Subsidiary motions)
  unlisted, classification of, 17–18
  vote required, 28, 30–31
  written, 13, 37

Motions (*Cont.*):
  (*See also* individual motions under specific names)

New business, 120
Nominating committee, 149–152
  duties of, 150–151
  importance of, 149
  members as candidates, 152
  selecting, 149–150
Nominations, 147–152
  bylaw provisions on, 147
  committee on (*see* Nominating committee)
  from the floor, 148–149
  importance of, 147
  to more than one office, 152
  seconding speeches, 148
  slates, single and multiple, 153–154
  (*See also* Elections)
Nominees, 151–152
  to more than one office, 152
  nominating committee members as, 152
  qualifications of, 151–152
Nonprofit organizations, 220
  consultant to, 229–230
Notice:
  of amendments to bylaws, 207
  of meetings, 105–109
    annual meetings, 107
    conventions, 107
    importance of, 105–106
    as protection for members, 106
    regular meetings, 107
    special meetings, 107–108
    waiver of, 109
  of proposed actions, 105–106, 108–109
    importance of, 105–106

Object to consideration, motion
    to, 89–91
  effect of, 91
  form of, 89
  limited to main motions, 90
  purpose of, 89
  rules governing, 91
  unsuitable motions ruled out
    by presiding officer, 91
  voting on, 90–91
  when in order, 89–90
Obtaining the floor:
  for debate, 122
  for presentation of motion, 11
Officers, 160–174
  corresponding secretary, 167
  delegation of authority by,
    169–171, 179
  honorary, 169
  installation of, 159
  member parliamentarian, 168
  powers and liabilities of, 169
  president (see President)
  presiding (see Presiding officer)
  as referred to by law, 183
  removal of, 173–174
  reports of, in order of business, 119
  resignations of, 227
  secretary (see Secretary)
  sergeant at arms, 168
  temporary chairman, 217
  term of office, 171–172
  treasurer, 167–168, 214
  vacancies (see Vacancies)
  vice president, 165
Order of business, 115–120
  adjournment, 120–121
  agenda, 117
  announcements, 120
  call to order, 117
  defined, 115–116

Order of business (*Cont.*):
  flexibility in, 116–117
  list of, 116
  new business, 120
  reading of minutes, 118
  reports:
    of committees, 119
    of officers, 119
  unfinished business, 119–120
Orders, general or special, 62–63
Organizations:
  bylaws of (see Bylaws)
  importance of leaders to, 147
  incorporated and unincorporated, 219–220
  meeting to form, 217–218
  members of (see Members)
  nonprofit, 220, 229–230
  and parliamentary law, 4–5
  relationship to member, 221
  rights of, 223
  staff of, 228–232
  temporary and permanent,
    218–219

Parliamentarian, 230–232
  member, 168
  professional, 168, 230–232
    duties of, 230–232
    importance of, 231–232
Parliamentary authority:
  and bylaws, 210–211
  requirements for, 7
  as source of parliamentary
    rules, 6
Parliamentary inquiry, request
  for, 95–98
  addressed to presiding officer,
    97
  effect of, 97–98
  form of, 95–96
  interruption of speaker for,
    96–97

Parliamentary inquiry (*Cont.*):
  members' rights regarding, 25, 96
  purpose of, 95
  rules governing, 98
Parliamentary law, 1–11
  defined, 3
  organizations that must observe, 4
  principles of, 7–11
  as safeguard of rights, 1–2
  sources of, 5–6
  when organizations must observe, 4–5
Parliamentary strategy, 10
Pending motions, 24
  and motion to limit debate, 65–66
  and motion to vote immediately, 68–69
Personal privilege (*see* Question of privilege)
Plurality vote, 134–135
Point of order, request for, 92–95
  effect of, 94
  form of, 92
  how raised, 92–93
  purpose of, 92
  rules governing, 94–95
  ruling on by presiding officer, 93–95
  when raised, 93
Policies, 212–214
  bylaw provisions for, 213
  examples of, 213–214
  importance to organization, 212
Postpone definitely, motion to, 60–64
  compared to other motions to postpone, 61–62

Postpone definitely (*Cont.*)
  consideration of postponed motions, 63
  effect of, 64
  form of, 61
  as general or special order, 62–63
  limitations on, 62
  purpose of, 60
  rules governing, 64
  types, 63
Postpone indefinitely, motion to, 47–49
  compared to other motions to postpone, 61–62
  effect of, 48
    on main motion, 48, 61–62
  form of, 47
  opens main motion for debate, 48
  purpose of, 47
  rules governing, 48–49
  suppression of main motion by, 48
Postpone temporarily, motion to (lay on the table), 70–73
  compared to other motions to postpone, 61–62
  effect of, 72
    on adhering motions, 72
  form of, 70–71
  purpose of, 70
  reasons for, 71
  rules governing, 72–73
  termination of effect of, 71–72
Postponed motions, consideration of, 63
Precedence of motions, 21–24
  basic rules of, 22
  example of, 22–24
  order of, 21–22, 25, 30–31
Presentation of motions, 11–14

President, 160–164
  as administrator, duties of, 161
  -elect, 164–165
  as leader, 160–161
  as presiding officer, 162–164
  (*See also* Presiding officer)
Presiding officer, 162–164
  addressing, 11
  adjournment, responsibility for, 81–83
  answering parliamentary inquiries, 97
  appealing decisions of (*see* Appeal, motion to)
  committees:
    appointing, 58–59, 178
    instructing, 58–59
  deciding renewability of motions, 32
  determining quorum, 113–115
  dividing motions on request, 101–102
  duties during debate, 126
  enforcing rules, 92–93
  ideal, definition of, 163
  as leader, 160–161
    in meetings, 162
  motions ruled out by, 91
  recognition of speaker by:
    during debate, 122–123
    in presentation of motion, 12
  responsibilities of, 162–163
    for adjournment, 81–83
    during discussions, 162
    to explain, 163
    to protect rights, 163
  ruling:
    on points of order, 93–94
    on questions of privilege, 74–76

Presiding officer (*Cont.*):
  statement of motion by, 13–14
  temporary, 217–218
  vote, announcing and verifying, 104, 146
  voting privileges of, 136–137
Previous question (*see* Vote immediately, motion to)
Principles, parliamentary, 7–11
Privilege:
  of assembly, 75
  personal (*see* Question of privilege)
Privileged motions:
  definition and list of, 16
  discussion of types of, 73–83
  form of, 19
  in order of precedence, 21
  rules governing, 30–31
Proposals, notice of, 105–106, 108–109
Proxy voting, 145

"Question!", 69
Question of privilege, request or motion for, 73–77
  of assembly, 75
  effect of, 76
  form of, 73–74
  interruption of speaker for, 75
  member's rights regarding, 74
  motions as, 76
  personal, 75
  purpose of, 73
  rules governing, 76–77
Quorum, 113–115
  computing, 114
  defined, 113
  determining, 115
  necessity for, 113
  presumption of, 115

Quorum (*Cont.*):
    question on, 114–115
    requirements, 113–114

Recess, motion to, 77–79
    compared to motion to adjourn, 77–78
    effect of, 78
    form of, 77
    limitations and restrictions on, 78
    purpose of, 77
    rules governing, 78–79
Recognition of members, 12, 122–123
Reconsider, motion to, 39–42
    debate on, 42
    effect of, 42
    form of, 39
    proposal of, 40
    purpose of, 39
    right of any member to propose, 41–42
    rules governing, 42
    what motions can be reconsidered, 39–40
Refer to committee, motion to, 57–60
    effect of, 60
    form of, 58
    instructions to committee on, 59–60
    provisions included in, 58–59
    purpose of, 57–58
    restrictions on amendments and debate, 59
    rules governing, 60
    what may be referred, 58
Reference committees, 194–197
    duties of, 195–196
    hearings of, 196–197

Reference committees (*Cont.*):
    reports of, 197
    recommendations of, 197
    uses of, 194–195
Regular meetings, 107, 110
Relevancy in debate, 124
Removal of officers, 173–174
    invalid causes for, 174
    valid causes for, 173–174
Renewal of motions, 29, 32
Reports:
    of auditor, 215–216
    of committees (*see* Committees and boards, reports of)
    of treasurer, 214
Request:
    for division of assembly (*see* Division of assembly, request for)
    for division of question (*see* Division of question, request for)
    for parliamentary inquiry (*see* Parliamentary inquiry, request for)
    for point of order (*see* Point of order, request for)
    to withdraw a motion (*see* Withdraw a motion, request to)
Rescind, motion to, 43–45
    and motion to expunge, 44
    effect of, 44
    form of, 43
    purpose of, 43
    rules governing, 44–45
    vote required, 43–45
    what motions can be rescinded, 43
Resignations, 226–227
    of members, 226–227
    of officers, 227

Resolution, main motion in form of, 37
Restricted debate, 27
Resume consideration, motion to (take from table), 45–47
  and adhering motions, 46
  effect of, 46
  form of, 45
  limitations on, 45–46
  precedence over other main motions, 46
  purpose of, 45
  rules governing, 47
Rights:
  of members (*see* Members, rights of)
  of organizations, 223–224
Rising vote, 141–142
Roll call vote, 142
Rules, 210–214
  and adopted policies, 212–214
  and adopted procedures, 211
  interpreting, 210
  and parliamentary authority, 210–211
  special, 210
  standing, 210
  supplementing by motion, 211–212
Rules committee, 193

Seconding a motion, 13
  rules on, 26, 30–31
  when not required, 237–238
Secretary, 165–167
  casting of ballot by, 157–158
  corresponding, 167
  duties of, 165–167
  minutes:
    correction of, 199
    preparation by, 198

Secretary (*Cont.*):
  minutes (*Cont.*):
    reading of, 199
  service to committees, 180–181
Sergeant at arms, duties of, 168
Session, definition of, 109
Slates, single and multiple, 153–154
  (*See also* Elections; Nominations)
Speaker, interruption of, 25–26, 30–31
Special (*ad hoc*) committees, 176–177
Special meetings, 107–108, 110–111
Special order, postponing as, 62–63
Staff of organizations, 228–232
Standing committee, 176
Statutory law, 3
Strategy, parliamentary, 10
Subsidiary motions:
  definition and list of, 16
  discussion of types of, 47–73
  form of, 19
  in order of precedence, 21
  rules governing, 30–31
Suspend rules, motion to, 86–89
  effect of, 88
  form of, 87
  purpose of, 86
  restrictions and time limits on, 88
  rules governing, 88–89
  rules that can be suspended, 87
  rules that cannot be suspended, 87–88

Take from table (*see* Resume consideration, motion to)

Term of office, 171–172
Tie vote, 136
Time limit on debate, 126
Treasurer:
    duties of, 167–168
    report of, 214

Unanimous consent, vote by, 143
Unanimous vote, 135–136
    decision by minority of one, 130, 135
    motion to make, 158–159
Unfinished business, 119–120
    effect of adjournment on, 83
    postponed motions as, 63
    at time of adjournment, 80–81
Unincorporated associations, 219

Vacancies, 172–173
    bylaw provisions on, 172
    declaring, 172
    maneuvering to fill, 173
Vice president, duties of, 165
Voice vote, 141
Vote, 129–146
    on amendments, 55–56
        to bylaws, 209
    announcing result of, 146
    binding during meeting, 146
    bringing question to, 127
    on bylaw amendments, 209
    challenging, 159
    changing, 145–146
    computing:
        for separate offices or questions, 137
        when electing a group, 137–138
    deciding method of, 140

Vote (*Cont.*):
    for equal positions, 139
    as fundamental right, 140
    in governmental bodies, 238
    for a group of equal offices, 137
    ineligibility of member, 139–140
    majority (*see* Majority vote)
    method of, 140–146
        ballot vote, 142–143
        by mail, 143–145
        in meetings, list of, 140
        by proxy, 145
        rising vote, 141–142
        roll call vote, 142
        test vote, 146
        by unanimous consent, 143
        voice vote, 141
    necessary to elect, 157
    plurality, 134–135
    of presiding officer, 136–137
    required:
        on amendments, 56
        to bylaws, 209
        to elect, 157
        importance of defining, 131–132
        on motions, 28, 30–31
    for separate offices, 137
    tie, 136
    two-thirds, 130
    unanimous, 135–136
        decision by minority of one, 130, 135
        motion to make, 158–159
    verification of:
        by division of assembly (*see* Division of assembly, request for)
        by presiding officer, 104
Vote immediately, motion to (previous question), 67–70

Vote immediately (*Cont.*):
  confusion caused by former name, 67–68
  effect of, 70
  form of, 67
  duration of effect, 69
  proposal of, 68
  purpose of, 67
  "question" as improper form of, 69
  rules governing, 70
  termination of effect, 69

Withdraw a motion, request to, 98–100
  effect of, 100
  form of, 98–99
  permission of assembly required for, 99
  purpose of, 98
  recording, 100
  rules governing, 100
  when proposer has right, 99

Written motions, 13, 37

ABOUT THE AUTHOR

The author is widely recognized as the foremost parliamentarian and the leading authority on the actual workings of organizations. As practicing parliamentarian and organizational consultant, the author works with more than 100 large national and international organizations, including professional, scientific, political, educational, fraternal, and trade associations, and business corporations. She has taught at the University of California and Stanford University, and is a frequent speaker at colleges and conventions. She was awarded a Guggenheim Fellowship for a study of larger voluntary organizations. Author: *A Textbook in Parliamentary Law, Learning Parliamentary Procedure,* and *Your Farm Bureau.* Columnist: "Mr. Chairman" in *Christian Science Monitor;* "Questions and Answers" in *County Officer.*